WITHDRAWN
FROM STOCK

Fully Functioning Human (Almost)

Melanie Murphy is an award-winning lifestyle YouTuber and all-round social media person slash 'virtual best friend' from Dublin, Ireland. She has reached almost fifty million people with her videos on self-care, confidence, hobbies and happiness, from the office that is her bedroom. Reaching half a million followers with her YouTube channel, she promotes body positivity and activism while working with brands she loves and travelling the world to meet her subscribers.

YouTube: Melanie Murphy
Twitter: @melaniietweets
Instagram: @melaniiemurphy
Facebook: /melaniiemurphy

FULLY FUNCTIONING HUMAN (Almost)

Living in an Online/Offline World

First published in paperback in 2018

The right of Melanie Murphy to be identified as the Author of
the Work has been asserted by her in accordance with the
Copyright, Designs and Patents Act 1988.

First published in Ireland in 2017 by
HACHETTE BOOKS IRELAND

1

Some of the names and details have been changed within this text

Cataloguing in Publication Data is available from the British Library

ISBN 978 1 4736 3915 7

Typeset in 11 on 16pt Archer Book by Claire Prouvost

Illustrations © Charlie Belle

Printed and bound in Great Britain by
Clays Ltd, St Ives plc

Hachette Books Ireland policy is to use papers that are natural, renewable
and recyclable products and made from wood grown in sustainable forests.
The logging and manufacturing processes are expected to conform to the
environmental regulations of the country of origin.

Hachette Books Ireland
8 Castlecourt Centre
Castleknock
Dublin 15, Ireland

A division of Hachette UK Ltd
Carmelite House, 50 Victoria Embankment, EC4Y 0DZ

www.hachettebooksireland.ie

For dad, my best friend and my strongest pillar
of support in life. Mammy too, for my fiery passion for
reading and writing! For my siblings, stepfather and
ex-partners, who believed in me when I didn't believe in
myself. For Albus Dumbledore, who taught me that words
are a source of magic. For my nana Chrissy, who read up to
five books a week but never got around to publishing one
of her own (this one is mostly for you). And, finally, for my
online followers, without
whom this book wouldn't exist.

Contents

BEAUTY and CONFIDENCE

SEX and SEXUALITY

LOVE and HAPPINESS

A MESSAGE for MY READERS

I want to thank you from the bottom of my heart for choosing to read this book out of all the millions of others available to you! (I just realised ... you're reading the final version. That means I'm finished. Which means there's now a cover. Is it good? I hope I'm not doing that pouty smile I always do when I feel like a spare tit ... smile with your eyes and your teeth, Mel.)

For ages, I had no idea how to begin – I mean, how do you spark off a *whole book* about the absolute fool that is yourself? Especially when it's not-quite-a-memoir-because-I'm-only-twenty-seven and it's also not-quite-an-advice-book-because-again-I'm-only-twenty-seven. What you're about to read is rather a compilation of the experiences and thoughts that have shaped who I am, sprinkled with hindsight and encouragement. It's stuff I feel compelled to share because sharing and connecting with other people is *almost* as important to me as pasta and ... well, because I've wanted to be published since I was old enough to form legible sentences with a pencil.

I've always loved to read and to write fiction and fantasy stories in my free time – escapism is my jam (living on an island will do that to you!) so writing *this*, a book rooted in (my) real life, has been a little like walking on virgin snow for me.

As a YouTuber, my viewers often ask me to make videos on 'how to impress a guy/girl', 'how to get abs' and 'how to cure eating disorders for good' and, *feck*, I don't know! I won't pretend I do, nor will I throw blanket solutions over enormous groups of people like so many do nowadays, making a quick buck with the promise of a quick fix. I'm just a nitwit girl who's sort-of stumbling through life with the bitter taste of its lemons in her mouth and her head *way* up in the clouds, learning that we all have our own roads to walk – that our maps don't all quite align but that it's still valuable, and rather lovely, to hear about other people's journeys.

I like making people feel better when I can, and I've found that I can do that through sharing and by being an open book. Honestly, I'm not so attached to my dignity any more. I've accepted that we humans are silly by nature and sometimes do things that make us look stupid. I try not to hold myself back from challenges in which there's a risk of ending up looking ridiculous, but still – I'm human, so *of course* I feel hyper-vulnerable putting this book out there, just as I do when I overshare on YouTube in ten-minute-long vlogs and on Twitter in 140 characters (but more so now because I get *mega* deep here, and I can't delete a book).

The past few years have been some of the most wonderful yet challenging of my life, and they've taught me *so much* about who I am and how to enjoy this weird and wonderful world in the moment. They were also the driving force behind my decision to write everything you're about to read.

Like most people, I've crawled through several of life's sewage pipes on my hands and knees, but I've emerged with a growth mindset and a sideways smile (that's just kinda how my face goes). I've hurt bad, lived wildly and learned things no schoolbook could ever teach me – like how NOT to deal with a break-up; why body-con does nothing for my figure; that I should unplug from technology for a few hours every day; and *please don't believe everything you read online, Melanie.*

New friends walked into my life where others dived out (or were shoved out, by me). I've honed my self-image. My confidence has flourished. I've learned that a night-time walk followed by honey and salted butter on toast is a cure-all, as are cuddles with my new rescue kitten and deep conversations with my dad. I've accepted that no cream gets rid of stretch marks, that I'll always have acne scars and that high heels turn me into a whiney arsehole but that red lipstick paired with matching undies makes me feel like a boss.

I do *more* to feel good now because I finally understand the preciousness of time, how fleeting moments can be – the good ones and the others (those ones I'd rather forget: drunken falls and family fights and that time my new love went off with my friend). I try to be present in the moment and to really *feel* all of the pain and magic and monotony of living.

How will my future be penned by the universe? NO idea. But I want to continue to be kinder – to myself and to others. To push myself. To love myself. To laugh a lot (even at things you're not supposed to laugh at, like people falling over in the street). I want to keep my focus on the positives and good people and jolly things and to remain thankful that I'm able to think this way in a world where narcissism, negativity, impatience and dissatisfaction walk every street and haunt every online platform and stalk every thought.

Words can be so *nourishing*, especially in this erratically paced, plastic, modern world – this landscape of clickbait advertising and social divide and wanting things to just hurry up and happen *yesterday*. So my (rather colourful) journey to almost-fully-functioning-hood in this online/offline world is splashed across the next few hundred pages and I really hope you'll curl up with this book, enjoy it and take from it some of my hard-won wisdom, a little piece of me, to keep inside you forever. (I mean that in an entirely NON-sexual way, of course. But by all means, put things inside you all you like – I don't care ... just ... OK, I'm done, I'll stop now.)

Mel

A HIGGLEDY–PIGGLEDY INTRODUCTION to YOURS TRULY

ME. EARLY 2016. WHEN I FIRST ATTEMPTED to WRITE this BOOK

I'm wearing odd socks, sat snug on a flight from Dublin to LA while the *Harry Potter* soundtrack blasts my eardrums. I'm off to live with an American comedian whom I fell madly in lust with after we met at Buffer Festival, where we both premiered films we'd made. My cheeks sting like a smacked arse with excitement. I can't believe I'm actually doing this ... me. A jiggly, spotty, formerly anxiety-ridden twenty-something from a working-class family in Ireland. Crossing seas to La La Land, all in the name of love.

This is *such* a Carrie Bradshaw from *Sex and the City* moment!

But *what ifs* didn't hold me back from booking this trip because I'm impulsive and I like to follow my heart over my head. Money didn't stop me either, or the worry of taking time off from my 'job' – I earn a living doing things I enjoy, so it feels disingenuous sometimes to refer to it as *work*. I often feel like a total eejit explaining my job to humans who lack secure internet dwellings – people who don't spend a lot of time online, people who don't already *get it*. I make money from, well, *oversharing* and being a Jack of all trades. I work mostly from home, wearing coffee-stained Disney pyjamas and a messy bun.

I'm proper happy (for the first long stretch of time in my whole life so far, which actually is a very sad sentence to write) and I wish I could bottle this happiness in little purple-painted potion jars to hand out, free of charge.

But I can't. So I decided to write a book instead.

And here we are!

ME. MID—2016. When FINISHING this BOOK seemed NEAR IMPOSSIBLE

A journal entry from 8 April 2016

So, my heart lied this time.

That LA move went outrageously tits-up. I want to whack the Melanie who wrote that first humblebrag introduction attempt across her stupid, smug face. Ugh, I'm an idiot. I felt like a jigsaw piece that some snot-encrusted kid was trying to shove into the wrong jigsaw, and I'm not at the point yet of 'it's just another mistake that I'll learn and grow from, it's fine!' – that seems quite far off right now. Back in Ireland, living with my dad and my cats in our family home in Dublin, post-ex-cheating-on-me-after-convincing-me-to-move-across-the-world-for-him mess, drowning my sorrows with endless cups of tea.

I'm fragile at the moment ... a bit lost, no ... very lost, but thankfully NOT depressed again. Wearing a brave face because I feel like that's what people expect of me. At least ... online. And I've started to really question this faux reality we create on the internet, a fantasy world in which everything is sunshine and lollipops; where food is always perfectly placed and colour enhanced; where people are photo ready 24/7; where nobody ever breaks down and bawls on the floor in a pool of their own saliva and tears. Though I do think a heightened awareness of how others curate their online selves is helping me to get better at being honest about my down days. The shitty days.

And yet right now on Instagram I'm posting pictures of pretty scenery, while in the real world I'm listening to sad eighties music about heartbreak and gobbling my feelings (cake, I'm eating lots of gloopy cake with nice, thick icing).

Also, I just scrapped the entire first draft of this book. I don't even know why I'm writing this right now – I just know that journaling always helps me. I've changed so much in the past few months that reading the chapters back felt like eavesdropping on a stranger's soliloquy. Dirty and embarrassing. It screamed at me, 'Mel, you're trying to teach other people stuff that YOU mostly still HAVEN'T fully figured out yourself! Stop being so preachy!' But that's life, Melanie. Change is inevitable, growth is good, we teach best what we most need to learn, blah blah – I know these things and so ... yeah.

I'm already wishing I hadn't scrapped it.

A year after writing this book I'll have an entirely new perspective on life again and much of what I say going forward may end up strange and dirty and embarrassing to future me, but no less valuable for those reasons, so ... why did I scrap it? Why the dramatic PMS-fuelled purge of mid-healing Melanie's words?

Oh, shut UP, Mel – pizza is here. Lights off, Netflix on.

ME. NOW. *Actually* WRITING the ACTUAL BOOK'S INTRODUCTION

Who I am and what I do

Hi there. I hope my impulsive, ever-evolving nature has made itself known and hasn't scared you off just yet so we can get on with this *who I am and what I do* section.

I'm Melanie, an openly queer food addict from a broken home in Ireland with a penchant for lipstick and pretty dresses and cats and films and baths and candles and wine. Many describe me as the most optimistic person they've ever met. Others as a loudmouth with an uncomfortable level of transparency. Some say I have a dirty mind and a crude sense of humour and I choose *not* to argue with these people – these people are very correct. I think I'm generally a good human being. I mean, I don't steal (anymore ...), I value kindness, I love complimenting people, I don't hog the remote and I've *almost* mastered the art of properly listening to other people when they talk about *their* problems ... Lo and behold, I am NOT the sun that the earth revolves around.

And although I think I'm a 'good' person, I'm also a sloppy work in progress who swears a lot and has meltdowns and loses her shit and is *terribly* disorganised, and it's important that you know that now. I'm *literally* typing this while sitting on the toilet, having a poo.

Remember that 'job' I mentioned in my first failed attempt at an introduction? First, ignore past me's enthusiasm ... I mean, I love it, but it *is* a job! A mostly unglamorous, full-on job – the amazingness and ease of which I like to exaggerate in moments of elation.

I'm qualified to teach, with a 1.1 BSc (hons) degree in Education and Training from Dublin City University. However, as I write this book, many would refer to me as a 'YouTuber'.

I created my own lifestyle-based channel on YouTube (the most popular video-sharing website in the world) in the summer of 2013, while studying at university. Four years later, my channel now attracts up to/over a million views every month (which is very weird – *all* the weird) and I'm the director of my own company! I make new videos every week, exploring everything from beauty, body image and confidence to health, hobbies and sex.

I script, film, feature in, edit and produce all of my content.

It's a bit like having a virtual diary (but one you get paid to make and that lots of people have a nosy in and judge you upon at first glance, every single day).

YouTube allows me to be creative in connecting with people from around the world, on both unifying topics, like acne, and divisive ones, like bisexuality. And I get to throw stuff at walls to see what sticks – to practise all kinds of production roles, to try on lots of hats. I'm still figuring out what suits me most and what I'm best at. The job is a box of chocolates and, sure, there are the gross-tasting coconut ones that I never want to eat (hours of emails, equipment breaking, having to film because it's upload day but I'm on my period or I just got dumped) *but*

I wince through – it's a job, after all. No job is *always* fun and games, even when it's a hobby at the core. As a YouTuber/all-round media person, there's gonna be sixteen-hour work days and back-to-back trips and stress and tears, and even an odd sense of isolation and loneliness because *so few other people really get what it's like.*

After putting together my little videos I upload them to the internet and I never know how they'll be received, but I get a weird butterfly buzz out of that. It's fun! TERRIFYING, but fun. Which is what keeps me going and what holds me back from throwing it all away for the stability of a nine to five. I've bared my acne and my eating-disorder struggles, discussed my anxieties and relationships and even introduced my viewers to my family and friends. In doing so, I've sort-of woven this beautiful tapestry of people and experiences all in one cubbyhole of the internet.

My virtual life has become my bread and butter, but more than that, I'm unexpectedly now part of this exciting, blossoming industry. I mean, just imagine, say, being a semi-popular actress in old Hollywood, around the time movies were first 'a thing' – to be attending YouTube parties at conventions in 2017 feels kinda how I imagine that felt back then!

It still turns my brain to chewed gum every time I realise that I'm *in* this, living and breathing it. Because once upon a time, just four short years ago, I was a fan of YouTubers who I'm now friends with!

'*How* is it your job, though? How do you actually make money?' These are questions I'm asked daily. And I figured, rather than beat around the bush like many others do, I'd just tell you straight – because why not?

1 **I earn money from the advertisements placed on my videos,** in the same way traditional media has worked for centuries.
2 **I'm also lucky enough to work with various brands and charities on campaigns, both on and offline.**
3 **I do some presenting on the side,** with traditional media and various other YouTube channels.
4 **Sometimes I even get paid to simply show up somewhere** and talk about my social media experiences. 'And now we have Melanie Murphy, a person who overshares ... professionally!'

(Trust me, I know how weird it is.) I spent two years working in retail and if you'd told me then that, one day, the likes of Google would be paying me to talk to advertisers and that said advertisers would hang on my every word, I'd have spat hot tea in your face.

'But how did you start?' Fast forward from me working in a shop at nineteen after finishing school, to me at twenty-four in Dublin City University, finishing up my teaching degree having found myself unhappy and unfulfilled in retail work. I wasn't in the best place mentally. Or the worst. Granted, I'd come a long way by then, but I wasn't at all happy. I didn't know what I really wanted to do with my life, what my passions were ...

It was then I started watching a lot of YouTube. It filled this big, gaping hole in my life during that time. The people I watched and followed on social media gave me so much hope that, one day, I too could like myself and travel, attend exciting events and shake off negativity and be fulfilled ... I connected with what they were doing. It wasn't just entertainment for me: it was something I had this strange longing to be part of. THIS IS WHAT I SHOULD BE DOING. I'D BE GOOD AT THIS. I'D ENJOY THIS. I dreamed of becoming part of this ever-growing online community, of sharing my interests and having my voice heard, but I was shy as lightning and I put off starting for years.

Then another Irish girl I followed randomly mentioned in a Q&A video that posting to YouTube gave her a lot more confidence in herself, so I started seeing it as a chance to become less crappy at public speaking (a part of my degree that I struggled with) and to be a bit less socially awkward.

Man, was I socially awkward! When you desperately want other people to like you while you don't even like yourself all that much, it can make you do and say some really, really stupid things.

One cloudy day, my then-boyfriend (who we'll call 'James' in this book and whom I dated for six mostly happy years), believing in me as always, bought me a cheap camera, a microphone, a tripod and a soft box light plus some video editing software. 'Happy birthday, honey,' he'd said, 'you can do this.' And although that relationship ended up being wrong for me in the long run, he wasn't wrong. I could do it. I just had to actually start. In one act of blind faith he shone a torch on a pathway to a bright new future.

I fast became hooked. It wasn't talent: it was obsession. The process of learning about online marketing; coming up with an idea; filming all the scenes and cutaways; importing the clips onto my hard drive; editing them together in whatever way I saw fit; uploading the finished product then sharing it around and interacting with viewers – this cycle engaged my brain on every level. So I began uploading two or three videos a week, and because I'm an idiot, I took this on while writing my thesis! Sometimes, though, terrible ideas are wonderful ideas wearing capes. I excelled in my final exams because my excitement and drive for YouTube pushed me to work harder in class. And the more layers I peeled off myself online, the more confident I found myself becoming and the thicker my skin grew.

There was a solid year during which I slept no more than four hours a night but it was worth the eye bags and coffee bills because, as I've come to learn, success necessitates sacrifice. The special recipe that helped me to make that time period my bitch: a sprinkle of hard work, a dash of self-belief, a pinch of peer support, a vial of visualisation and a shot of luck.

Once I'd submerged myself into the whole YouTube thing ... well, 'snowball effect' would be understatement of the century. My channel gained so much momentum that I couldn't keep up! I just watched it vanish on the horizon. My brain stopped comprehending the number of people who watch every month. It's easier to picture a few faceless individuals and pretend that's who I'm talking to when I hit record on my camera, and this method of perception also helps me avoid the dreaded nervous-poo cramps and that odd feeling of empty-bedroom-stage-fright!

I've recently started being offered really fun, wonderful jobs and opportunities with some of my favourite celebrities and companies, plus magazine work and TV slots and so on. I won a few awards (ha-ha *ha* – I've never been the kind of person to win awards so I still find this bloody hilarious) and, well, now I'm here. In the thick of it. Publishing a book. I make videos and do random-arse jobs and I get to travel the world for events and for 'work', making wonderful new friends along the way and meeting many of the people who made it all possible. The people who watch, subscribe, like and share my online content. The millions of girls (and, *ahem,* 15% guys! Google analytics, baby) who watch me and take comfort in hearing me open up, who find me in some way entertaining or relatable. This book is for you, and anyone who may stumble upon it and think, 'Ooh, it's about a YouTuber, ooh, I need to read it.'

Word-vomit wisdom in book form, let's have you. Here's much of what I know now, from the other side of that dark tunnel of growing up in the digital age. If I can make *one* thing easier for one of you then every misstep I've made so far has been worthwhile.

Section 1

MEDiA
and My
MiND

BALANCING
SOCIAL MEDIA
and REAL LIFE

I'll never forget the first time I created a social networking account, back in 2006. I was sixteen, I'd just moved in with my dad (Mammy wouldn't have me near that 'shite', as she called it) and the website was called MySpace. A prehistoric Facebook. It was clunky and customisable and *completely* addictive.

Foetus-Melanie brain: *Balance? What's that?* I spent hours every evening after school hunched over the keyboard taking selfies (before they were even called selfies), designing my Bebo profile (Bebo was just MySpace but more slick!), stalking the profiles of people that I liked (and plenty that I didn't like, just 'cause I could) and messaging anyone who'd talk back for a bit of reassurance that I was cool enough to talk to.

Our internet speed was brain-meltingly slow and our old, massive computer looked like something you'd see now in a museum, but at the time this new 'social media' thing was *the* most exciting procrastination tool and I lived for it. I'd shove my homework to one side so I could instead find funny YouTube videos to share, judge people's photos from parties I hadn't been invited to and dribble over pictures of my first love.

Social media went on to change my life, many times, in different ways. Some great. Others terrible.

Here's a diary entry of mine from 2010, when I was twenty-one years old:

> *I'm in bed, it's late and dark and the light from the laptop screen is blinding me through my glasses. Dad's in the sitting room watching war documentaries and my brother's playing the Playstation in the bedroom next door. I went online when it was still bright to 'quickly' check Facebook, reply to a couple of messages and then I intended to go help clean the kitchen (after making a massive mess cooking Bolognese for our little family of three) before finishing up an important psychology assignment. Somehow I instead ended up arguing with someone in a nutrition forum, ordering a bunch of dresses from ASOS (that I can't afford and don't need) AND stalking my ex boyfriend's friends on Facebook to find untagged photos of him. I eyeballed a picture of Katy Perry's bikini body at one point tonight for an entire five minutes and I cried about the fact that my body doesn't look exactly like hers. Then I tumbled into some dark, pro-eating disorder areas of the internet and that rabbit hole gobbled me right up. The kitchen is still in a state, I didn't finish my psychology assignment and I'm now going to try and fall asleep in this face full of tear-smudged make-up.* **Takeaway: I think I need to break up with the internet.**

Pre-internet (from childhood right up until my sweet sixteenth), before my life was infiltrated by iPods, Skype and podcasts galore, I was always highly susceptible to media influence – not gonna lie (or NGL as they say these days. What's with that, anyway? What's with LOL and OMG and BRB and TBH ...? *Grasps onto English language, like Rose to Jack at the end of* Titanic). Magazines, music videos and movies lacking in diversity shaped my then-ideas of what constituted beauty, success and happiness. And my parents and teachers never really talked about how or why these things might affect me. By age thirteen I was riddled with self-doubt and insecurities, and then, with the arrival of digital media, I went through what many millennials did, unprepared – *technology slave syndrome*. A mighty serious illness, really.

At dinner with my parents and siblings I'd be texting friends instead of talking to my family. And I hate that. Nothing annoys current me *more* than sitting with someone who's mentally elsewhere ... it's like trying to communicate with a creepy, lifelike doll. My relationships suffered hard because I'd much rather go online than spend (foetus-Melanie brain: *waste*) time with them.

Internet access became all I cared for. Me, in angry or upset mode, wouldn't talk to the people around me – I'd plug in and vent virtually instead. That habit was born when tissue I'd shoved into my bra to make my boobs look bigger started poking out of my school shirt and everyone in my friend group saw it and started tearing me to shreds – rather than turning to an actual human being for connection and comfort, I turned to a device without a pulse.

Baaad lifestyle choice.

I stopped going outside as much as I used to – to cycle through forests and explore abandoned buildings and play around with a football while sharing gossip – so face-to-face interaction quickly became very difficult (almost unbearable) for me. Talking to people via text and text emojis (which we used before emojis existed), using things like MSN (Windows Live Messenger), became easier for me than in-person conversations. And without practice at it I sort of just ... *lost* that mental muscle.

My unrestrained time online affected my mood (door slam), my ability to spell (it's 'arguement', right?), my concept of true friendship (she didn't like my new photo – she hates me) and of love (he replied with no kisses or love hearts – he *must* be cheating). Even my sleep and dietary habits suffered (me and an entire extra-large pizza, together in bed at 4 a.m.).

It's clear to me now that social media in my young, incapable and uneducated hands was like a bomb in my grip.

It could have utterly destroyed me.

I'm surprised I'm only a *little bit* messed up from all this, and not an absolute train wreck of a human. There was pretty much no education about social media or the internet when I was growing up. We were the blind leading the blind. *We were pissing into the wind!*

But luckily, as a young teenager I only had my mobile phone to deal with – the mobile phone I had to *beg* Mammy to buy me 'because everyone else in school has one!' – so I managed to squeeze in a few years of finding joy in the little things, like reading and writing and going exploring with groups of friends, because there was no option but to live life as it unfolded. I actually dread to think how much more difficult it would've been to adjust to the real world if I'd had to deal with social media too during those formative, early 'tween' years of about age nine to fourteen. But the reality for many kids nowadays is they're born and then, BOOM, internet.

I know you love consuming that digital media, though, that delicious digital media – me too, *mmm* it's so good … We just need to be *smarter consumers*, gang.

About a year ago I decided to take control and tidy up my online space. It was becoming more out of control than my unwaxed, post-break-up pubic hair. My Facebook feed-scrolling experience was shockingly bad *before* I deleted and unfollowed a bunch of people and pages but, even now, I take one scroll through my feed and I'll consume images of heavily Photoshopped, almost-naked bodies, junk food, weight loss before-and-after pictures, people looking like they're having *way* more fun than they probably were, articles about war and rape, wedding photos, break-up notifications, people throwing 'shade' (indirect insults) ... It's a lot to absorb.

The ridiculous memes – mostly funny, virally-transmitted, RANDOM images, videos or pieces of text – are all that keep me coming back (ha-ha, I'm joking, I still don't really GET memes even though I like to pretend that I do) and, well, the positive updates – the happy photos, the good news.

And even now, sometimes my five-minute Facebook break with my afternoon coffee becomes a two-hour-shaped hole in my life. This is something I'm still struggling with – it's a habit I need to take more steps to change. But at least I'm aware that it's a problem, and that I'd rather spend more of that Facebook time creating, or reading, or playing with my cats. And you can't buy that self-awareness – you either develop it and work to change things, or you keep the blinkers on.

Don't get me wrong. I adore social media. It's a big part of my job. It's my main creative outlet. It helps me to feel connected to the world at large. But (and that's a big arse *but*), I've learned that *what* I follow, *who* I befriend, *how long* I spend plugged in and *how* I behave online matters a lot in how social media makes me feel. I can come away feeling enriched, or empty and sad.

I remember the day I first realised how much control I have over this stuff. I'd been browsing a black hole of a YouTuber gossip forum regularly that particular month, reading horrible rumours about myself and panicking just from the idea that others might believe the nonsensical things written about me (it's totally bothersome seeing cruel misinformation about yourself being spread around) but *then* I figured, *I gotta start with the 'why'*: why *I'm looking*, why *I care.*

After figuring out that I (weirdly) enjoyed misery, that subjecting myself to gossip websites was a dangerous method of self-harm and avoidance of emotional baggage, *and* that I'd need to dig deep to find a bit of empathy for the people sparking the rumours, I decided to reflect and journal a *lot* and I came to these conclusions.

1 Some people talk shite about other people and that's life. (It's probably because they're unhappy or have nothing better to do.)

2 I'm actively participating in this by reading it, and worrying about it, and talking to my friends and family about how upsetting it is – why not simply stop looking?

I kept reminding myself that I'm not alone in being gossiped about, that gossipers gossip because they're in a bad place, and I *did*, eventually, stop looking at the forum. In some situations, obliviousness really is bliss!

To a certain degree, I now filter what I see and interact with when I'm online by muting, blocking or straight-up ignoring people and pages that make me leave the internet feeling worse and shitty (like, people who only ever post 'woe is me' status updates; people who consistently share posts about horrible things out of my control – I don't know about you but I'd rather *not* witness shootings or child abuse or animals being kicked, thank you very much, people who present unobtainable perfection 'cause perfection don't exist, or anyone and anything that thrives on drama).

Sometimes, I slip up – we all do. We engage with stuff that'll do us no good.

There have been *so many times* where I've had no sense whatsoever and I've made terrible decisions about how to spend my internet time. With the freedom internet access provides comes the ability to crash and burn, and on social media, mistakes rarely go unnoticed (many even go viral) – leaked nude photos, comments made in the heat of the moment on Twitter: it's happening more and more. Our mistakes have become the lowest form of entertainment for other people.

I've posted things that I honestly sometimes wish I hadn't (shady subtweets) and I've said things in videos that came out completely wrong or were politically incorrect. You see, it's difficult to remember that perception is reality. That even when intent is positive, the results of my words and the takeaway from what I've said or my behaviour matters infinitely more, and not just because I have a following. Because the internet at large is always waiting and ready to twist words, and to shatter reputations. Like other mortals, I fuck up. LOTS. The other day I posted a caption underneath a selfie on Instagram expressing my feelings on a terrorist attack, without thinking about how that might come across to others who don't know much about me and just casually follow my posts ... the backlash ('how dare you make this about YOU?') made me want to hide in a bin for all eternity. I defended my intent, but my intent was misunderstood and that's what mattered. I'm the first to admit that sometimes, when I mess up, it can take me a while to admit to my mistake(s) and to apologise.

The ability to make mistakes on our journey to fitting the internet around our lives (and not our lives around the internet) and to *learn* from these mistakes is an amazing thing, though. I think of it as free education and character-building, even when embarrassment stings my cheeks like nettles.

The next time you write something nasty about someone and it gets screenshotted and shared into a group chat (yeah, *cough*, this example HAS been lifted from the shameful script that is my life), use it as a chance to clear the air with the person. Throw up your hands. Talk it out. Laugh about your stupidity. Maybe (like me) you'll make a new best friend – one who gives 10/10 scalp massages and *the best* dating advice. At the end of the day, everything we see shapes who we'll be. My goal with media is simply this: become *expert* at sniffing out the stuff that'll make me a better human and help me discover myself, while surfing the negative ripples flowing out from all the other crap. And don't worry – I don't just sit there staring at a blank screen! I follow lots of comedians, activists and empowering women, among others, while balancing my internet life with a social life in the real, non-virtual world!

A HANDFUL of PEOPLE and PAGES you should FOLLOW if YOU DONT ALREADY

- ♥ **@bodyposipanda** on Instagram, for body positive mantras and feel-good vibes
- ♥ **doddleoddle** on YouTube, for beautiful songs and artistic videos
- ♥ **Humans of New York**, on Facebook for amazing photographs of and captions about inhabitants of New York
- ♥ **J.K. Rowling** on Twitter: the woman's got sass. She stands up for what she believes in, always
- ♥ **The School of Life** on YouTube, for emotional education paired with gorgeous animations
- ♥ **Thomas Sanders**, a Vine star who now posts everywhere and makes millions happy
- ♥ **The Trews** by Russell Brand (YouTube): the only 'news' channel I view as worth my time
- ♥ **Carly Rowena** (YouTube), one of the most positive and lovely fitness bloggers I've met
- ♥ **booksandquills** (YouTube), for all things book-related

There are thousands of people and virtual places worth exploring. You just need to open your eyes. And, maybe more importantly, learn when to close them. Because the time *before* I learned to close mine at the right moments is seared into my memory …

How MEDIA MOULDED ME

One day when I was about thirteen I walked to the shop to buy (far too many) sweets and a magazine. I used to love reading gossip magazines. *Well,* 'reading' – I exaggerate. I bought these magazines – these intensifiers of the modern body-hating phenomenon – to gawk at pictures of celebrities in tight-fitting clothing, at pictures of singers and actresses who'd gained weight, had botched surgery or dimpled thighs or who looked upset after a public break-up, all in an effort to distract myself from my own problems and zone out of my then-cobwebby brain.

I remember one magazine cover in particular *so* vividly. The headline, the font, the image. Britney Spears, on a beach, in a bikini. 'I do 1,000 crunches a day for my washboard abs!' the cover screamed. My teenage brain understood from this headline that I could continue to inhale entire packets of cookies and tubes of Pringles *but* if I did a thousand crunches a day, I'd definitely have abs like Britney and then maybe, just maybe, I'd be as successful and important as her. My teenage brain *didn't* question why any of this mattered to me or why I was measuring my own worth against how much I believed others were valued.

Media, and those around me who were also influenced by it, conditioned me to believe that having a strong marriage, a million quid in the bank, perfect, youthful looks and a taut, flat stomach would

make me somehow far more impactful, attractive and desirable as a human being. And along the road of life, many seeds like these were planted deep inside my mind and were watered (daily) by the media.

So having bought the Britney magazine and eaten all my sweets I tried to do a thousand crunches. After about twenty-five, my abdominals were on fire and I gave up (*and* treated myself to some ice-cream from the freezer, then wallowed in self-loathing with each delicious spoonful because movies always show the sad, fat girl, who nobody wants to be like, in the corner, alone, eating ice-cream).

I'd fixate on actresses who had beautiful skin, and I was so incredibly envious of them. Comparing myself to Emmy Rossum in the *Phantom of the Opera* movie left me wanting to pull my fifteen-year-old acne-drenched face off like a mask to reveal a smooth layer of crystal-clear skin, just like hers. The fact that 80 per cent of people deal with some form of acne in their lifetimes (making it more normal to have blemishes than not) is a stat I often wish I'd known then.

But leading ladies never had acne. My dolls didn't have acne. Models on magazine covers didn't have acne. So, maybe, being told how common it was wouldn't have made me feel any better about it.

The lack of representation at the time of what constitutes 'normal' skin left me isolated in a sea of 'you are disgusting, wear a paper bag on your head forever' thoughts. I would have needed to see it to believe it.

And nowadays it's even worse! Pre-teens and vulnerable young people are being spoon-fed videos by certain YouTubers who use real-life Photoshop filters – filters that literally illuminate and airbrush moving video footage – *yikes*, man.

I even longed for larger, perkier breasts as a teen, perhaps after too many years spent watching boobie close-ups of nearly naked busty backing dancers in music videos. Ever-aware of my bisexual nature, my attraction to female bodies, I knew deep down (even at the peak of my longing-for-massive-breasts phase) that I found *all* kinds of female body shapes attractive, which was the weirdest thing when it came down to my relationship with my own body! On *other people* I loved the look of tiny tits, of big, smushy in-your-face tits – they come in so many lovely shapes and sizes and colours – and yet I spent ages stuffing my bra and looking up prices for surgery.

I sat doodling in school one day, thinking long and hard about how this made absolutely no sense. Horny teenage Melanie, doodling titties in the back of her copybook, decided then that, without variety the world would be an extremely boring place. I concluded that my 'larger, perkier breasts' dream *must* have been built entirely by media, because it was born from that place in my head that's home to millions of carefully curated images I've unintentionally taken in over the years.

The narrow view we're shown has such an effect on our wiring – I mean, I *genuinely* believed for a long time that guys only really found blondes sexually attractive. Thanks for that, nineties rom-coms and top-shelf porn magazines, and cartoons even, for your token hot blonde girls.

For much of my life my self-image was on the floor. Looking back now, I know that was a huge source of unhappiness for me. Some media almost programmed me to worry about and judge myself. But funnily enough, it turned out to be other forms of media (certain types of magazines and certain articles and blogs on the internet, books, documentaries, the good stuff) that taught me all about self-reflection and about honing in on my qualities as a person – ya know, on the *inside*. The bit we all tend to forget about.

Books didn't do me wrong at all. I found loads of positive role models through reading novels, to the point that I'd *look up to* fictional characters! It's a bit mad to think that even make-believe people can imprint on us so deeply.

Throughout my life, reading has hugely shaped both me as a person and how I've been driven to contribute to the world. Take darling Jo from *Little Women* – so much of my love for reading and writing originated with her, a character who adores literature, composing plays for her sisters to perform and writing stories that she publishes. I'd read *Little Women* and walk around the house playing a game where I was just Jo, in my head.

Writing has since become a massive part of my life – I wrote throughout my teens, wanting to emulate her in some way, I guess, and, well ... now we're here! You're reading a thing I was paid to write.

That shit came full circle.

And my desire for a degree in education (which I finally received aged twenty-four) was sparked by the teachers in the *Harry Potter* series – I initially wanted to be a teacher because of them, to connect with others and nurture their talents, to encourage them to be their best selves and to learn and grow. I was also inspired by Miss Honey from the classic novel *Matilda* by Roald Dahl. The soft and gentle Miss Honey was the first person to fully appreciate Matilda's incredible intelligence, even bringing it to the attention of the school's horrible head teacher, Miss Trunchbull, in an attempt to do a good thing for the girl. I absorbed these characters and knew from a young age that aiming to be a Miss

Honey type was a good thing and I should do my utmost not to end up like a Trunchbull. The contrast between these two imagined-by-a-man women really affected me. I wanted to be an advocate for others just like Miss Honey – to be kind and warm and mild-mannered and loved by children! I'm still working on the children bit, and I'm a lot more in-your-face than Miss Honey, as you've likely gathered.

Then there's the lovely Hazel Grace Lancaster from fellow YouTuber John Green's very successful novel *The Fault in Our Stars*. Hazel is a teenage girl with terminal cancer and the story chronicles her relationship with another cancer patient, Augustus Waters. I read it and thought, *I want to be likeable and creative and witty and sarcastic and smart and open to love as well!* I really admire how Hazel doesn't sit around feeling sorry for herself. She's under no illusions. She's just trying to make sense of life and find significance in it – all while facing oblivion. The way she tackled her illness with humour latched onto my bones.

Hermione Granger from *Harry Potter*, too, is one of my favourite characters of all time. I'm a *huge* Potterhead – I read the books as a child and queued up at the midnight book launches. I still get giddy with nostalgia any time I see or hear anything *Harry Potter* universe related. But, yeah, this girl is my fave – throughout the books she demonstrates that it's OK not to be perfect, and she never gives up on her strength or on her beliefs. Hermione made it cool to love studying, and to flaunt intelligence and to ignore hard-work-related bullying – I so badly wanted to be her as a kid! She pushed me a lot in school and even uni, young Granger did. Even the way she stands up for other creatures in the books led me to want to make smarter decisions in life and to get involved with animal charities. I learned so many lessons from her – about compassion, about strength.

And, of course, the classics had their way with me. The lively and playful Lizzie from Jane Austen's *Pride and Prejudice* influenced me in such powerful ways. She knows her own mind, stands up for herself and lives her life by *reason* as well as emotion – this enables her to be brave and stubborn in her wish to marry for love and not just money and convenience, as was expected in the time and environment of the book. Largely thanks to Lizzie, I'll never settle for comfort – I'm waiting for the right person to share my life with. If it hadn't been for characters like Lizzie, perhaps I'd be married and divorced twice over by now. Who knows?

Even *Game of Thrones*, one of my favourite things in the universe, fed me self-reliant, loyal and ruthless role models by the fridgeload.

So, media kind of left me a little bit all over the place. Indeed, it moulded some destructive thoughts about myself but it also stoked a fire in me to become a conglomeration of my idols – real and imaginary – and to be the best version of myself.

Thanks to several evenings of sprawling on my bed after a bath and getting lost in the depths of the web, and in movies on my laptop, and in books, my eyes were pried open: I don't *need* abs like Britney and I don't *need* baby-doll skin and I don't *have* to have a prom king or queen partner to feel good and enjoy the world. And I don't have to hate on others for having things that I don't.

For years I didn't live and enjoy my own life – I beat myself up for not living someone else's apparently perfect life. *How ridiculous is that?*

I began to realise I could pretty much filter out all the online media I *didn't* want and I could focus on media that mattered to me. I could find someone funny and relatable on YouTube to talk at me about Disney movies for a while as I ate my morning bagel; someone to give a funny commentary over a computer game while I bounced around on a lengthy bus journey down Irish country roads; several people to talk to me (with accents – *love-heart-eyes emoji*) about cool new make-up products before my shopping trips to give me some ideas; a ukulele pixie to sing me a song as I shaved my legs.

By constantly typing in 'top ways to look skinnier' or 'how to be more attractive', I would basically force those words and images into my brain and make myself even *more* obsessed with the wrong stuff and less concerned with the things that actually make me smile. Such as Disney cup collections and computer games and new, fluffy make-up brushes and animals jumping into walls and the sounds of nature. I try now to focus on stuff that I *love* and to mostly absorb media that I know will have a positive impact on my mind.

It sounds easy, right? Simple?

Because it is. We have complete control over what we look at online.

At first you might be a bit resistant but then ask yourself, *Am I self-sabotaging? Why?* (Ah, you can *so* tell I took psychology classes in uni!)

Social media gets blamed for a lot of our self-esteem and psychological issues these days, and while I don't argue the fact that imbalanced use of it can contribute to these things, I think it's fiercely important to note that all forms of media impact us. Movies, song lyrics, magazines, billboards, all of it. In good and bad ways. Though I don't believe it's the fault of media that I was impacted by it so much. It all runs much deeper.

How we respond to media 'triggers' is actually mostly to do with how we've been emotionally equipped growing up, how we've been educated (or how we self-educate). Technology is SO fast and ever-changing that schools and teachers aren't yet able to tackle social media management with students head on ... in my opinion, anyway. I realised that I had to develop an understanding of how to consume media in a way that doesn't turn me into a self-hating technology drone. If I spend *way* too long online each day, even I can get sucked into very negative communities and ways of thinking. (Like the other day, *ahem*, when about five hours flew by during which I sat in a bitter puddle of jealousy because I kept comparing my success to other people's success before I slapped myself out of it. So unproductive and pointless!)

And that's something I think about an awful lot. Numbers. Data. Followers. Shares. Retweets. Likes. Friends. Indicators of where we *think* we fit in modern society. It's pretty obvious that social status has long been important to us as a species, and I think it's natural to want to be seen in a positive light by others – but I'm part of the first generation who grew up with the internet, an internet that has exposed me to some uncomfortable truths and bizarre new methods of calculating social status.

It could be argued that the things we actually *do* in the real world no longer carry as much weight as they once did, because now we have this online extension of our inner selves, a digital self-representation to be viewed (and judged) by other people. I'll be honest – I find myself unintentionally comparing my social media profiles to others' sometimes, and then fighting against a voice in my brain that whispers, *More people care about what he's doing; your shit looks unorganised; these stats define you as a person.* But I keep fighting those thoughts because if I allow myself to define *me* based on vanity metrics and the like, I'll completely hinder myself and my life will *suck*. If I chase numbers, I'll never be satisfied because I can always gain more. It's the same thing with chasing wealth – it's like legging it in a hamster wheel.

Life is about quality, not quantity.

One day in college, a good friend said to me, over canteen pizza, that a billion likes on social media would never be enough if I didn't learn to like myself. This was around the time I started my YouTube channel and would get disheartened if there weren't 'enough' likes on the video or if there were 'thumbs downs'. I was in the middle of a phase where I was really trying to be more positive but I kept finding myself focusing on the negative in every single situation.

I'll be forever grateful to the friend who said that to me – it stuck to me like toffee to the teeth. That was the first day I decided, 'You know what? Once I like my next video, that's what matters. If other people like it, great. If they don't, at least I like it.' This tiny shift in my thinking led me to make some of the content that I'm most proud of and freed me of a lot of self-doubt and eagerness to please.

Of course, I still doubt myself sometimes, but now I know how to tell that inside-head-voice to shut up. Not everyone is going to like you, and there are always going to be people who achieve more, and that's perfectly OK. Social status shouldn't be determined by popularity anyway, but by the meaningful relationships you share and by the impact you have on those you're connected to, virtually or otherwise.

MY TiPS for a HEALTHY MiND in a WORLD of MODERN MEDiA

1 Embrace digital media's existence because it isn't going anywhere! We can adapt and grow and learn and utilise or curl up in balls and forgo all the positive experiences the internet can bring.

2 Every Sunday I sit down with my notebook and my chewed-on, unsharpened pencil to schedule time for proper human experiences – or even Skype calls! Seeing and talking to family and friends regularly made my mental health go from about 10 to 80 on a scale of 0 to 100.

3 Diversify your YouTube subscription box and social media feeds. Because anyone can upload anything at any time, there are mountains of great content on all kinds of subjects from all kinds of ordinary human beings – not just from the

human/goddess hybrids that much traditional media pits us up against.

4 Don't be a slave to the numbers. Worry less about how many likes your new sexy-but-also-cute-and-perfectly-cropped profile picture gathers from your 'friends'. Share for the sake of sharing and not for validation. Take back some of that power that you're giving to other people by worrying about whether or not they're interacting with your posts or what they think of you based on your online activity. You are not your social media presence. You'll feel so much better when you give less of a toss!

5 Have a bit of 'cop on', as we say here in Ireland, when it comes to unfollowing and whatnot. It's all just common sense, what's worth our energy and what's not – **if you're involving yourself with media that's making you feel down, then *stop doing it* and do *anything* else**. *Delete, unfollow, mute, report, block* – never forget that these bad boys are options.

If you relate to anything from this chapter in the slightest, *chill*. There's hope. You're *not* doomed. It's all about tapping into the right information and using it in a positive way. Think trying out that delightful avocado toast recipe you saw on Instagram for breakfast over, say, crying about a Facebook unfriending from someone who you rarely ever speak to anymore.

At the end of the day, it's impossible to avoid a good, hard moulding by modern media. You know it. I know it. Between TV, radio, newspapers and the internet, the labyrinth of 'fake news' and unfiltered information that exists has become a second shadow following us around. Media *can* be like that one friend you frequently consider distancing yourself from, phasing out, unfriending on Facebook ...

only to wind up on another mindless phone call for two hours with. I know I'm not the only one with this strong love/hate relationship with media; it can be enriching and educational and can bring us wonderful new relationships and hobbies – but depending on how we interact with it, it can also completely limit our experience of life and lead us to become lazy, self-involved, self-hating, socially awkward little so-and-sos.

Media may have moulded me in the past, but now I mould my media. And that self-awareness is the most important thing when it comes to moving forward – you're in control of the bubble that you live in! So consume wisely and don't forget to look at the sky sometimes. It's ever so *pretty*.

CYBERBULLYING

Y'know, I think I finally understand trolls (internet slang for those people who wander virtual spaces intent on starting arguments, upsetting and provoking others through the use of inflammatory and/or irrelevant comments). But if I had a euro for every time a troll (or, indeed, any species of cyberbully) affected me in the past, I'd at the very least be able to afford an expensive diamond-encrusted designer handbag ...

I had this one troll stalk me for two years straight. This person showed up as soon as my YouTube channel morphed into my full-time job – as soon as I was seen to be doing well online and reaching a lot of people through my videos. Over the course of two years, they impersonated me as well as several of my friends and family members online; started ridiculous rumours about me; leaked my address and somehow discovered my phone number; *and* threatened me with rape and torture. This harassment case ended up with the Irish police and made my anxiety disorder balloon to the point that I was suspecting almost everyone. Even the idea of stepping outside my front door scared the absolute shite out of me.

This troll would go from being super threatening, to offering backhanded compliments, to just perpetuating lies about me (which they started in the first place) by making a ludicrous amount of fake profiles across many online platforms and gossip websites (using similar names and language or misspellings of my name each time, like a creepy signature – their way of saying, 'Hey, it's me again!') and they'd always post during certain windows of time on specific days of the week. They'd make it appear as if several people had reputation-killing information about me (none of which held any truth – that I cheated on my boyfriend, for example, or that I come from a wealthy family who 'bought my success', or even that I troll *myself* and make up accounts to support me).

And the trolling wasn't just directed at me through my social media channels – it spilled onto other people's profiles. I'd receive confused messages from peers within the YouTube community citing messages from the troll, asking, 'Do you really hate me?' or 'Is this true?'

It felt like some masked demon was standing amidst a crowd of confused onlookers, swirling around my shit-stained underwear for giggles.

I can't help but laugh at some of this now, even though it's *super* disturbing that anyone would give me that amount of mental energy, but sometimes you've got to find humour in the pain and difficulty of life. At least, that's what I try to do.

Guys, *bullies thrive online*: a diamond-hard fact about virtual life that tarnishes online experiences for so many people every day. It's like going to McDonald's for a chocolate fudge sundae with a smile on your face then having some wild, scabby hand emerge from the shadows to slap it out of your grip ...

Bullies have always been around. They go above and beyond to suck your comfort away, like leeches, and nowadays bully culture is worse because these people have so many new platforms that enable them to follow you into your own home, into your bedroom – sometimes, nowhere feels safe.

And any one of us can fall prey to technological attacks. It happens to students, teachers, parents, young kids, elderly people – and the attacks can be extremely difficult to deal with because anonymity online seems to bring out the very worst in some people and because growing a skin as thick as one might need can take a while.

It's not normal to be targeted for threats and humiliation, to be tormented daily – these aren't things I was brought up to understand how to deal with. Sure, we'd have anti-bullying week in school, but there were no classes equipping us with the skills to endure such treatment, no lessons on *why* people bully in the first place. Nobody ever sat me down and told me, 'Mel, there'll come a day when someone across the world will be able to mentally abuse you any time, anywhere, and they won't be arrested for doing it or face any consequence other than karma, and you'll just have to get used to it.'

And when we ignore the ghastly existence of trolls and bullies, there's still the problem that, well, technological dialogue is impersonal to the point that it's often impossible to detect another person's tone, so sometimes we can think we're being bullied even when we're not.

I've found myself caught up in disagreements with people I care about, and with people I sort-of know, and the littlest nuances in their text communications can send me spiralling. I'll become withdrawn and down and I'll jump with nerves every time my phone beeps.

Basically, I've felt those 'I'm being bullied right now' feelings in the pit of my stomach during text conversations, even when I'm *not* being bullied whatsoever. You know that feeling I mean – when you open up a message from someone you know and get along with, but for some reason reading their text instantly makes your insides squirm and your heart race and you feel like you've been cornered. You question where you stand with them in that moment because the style and tone of their message has rubbed you up the wrong way. It's often just *much* easier to get a point across in a face-to-face chat.

Other shitty things we millennium babies have to put up with include: being purposefully excluded from online groups (this sucks); online sexual harassment and/or having private or embarrassing photos leaked (yes, this happened to me once ... and, yes, I've stopped sending people nudes, as glorious as my nudes are, *ha-ha*); being publicly pranked; and having comments directed at us that *nobody* would dare say to our faces in the street. (I probably should add an example here, but if I shared some of the things that have been said to me, you'd probably feel an overwhelming urge to douse this book in bleach.)

I'm intensely aware of how I speak to people, both off- *and* online – perhaps even more so when typing out my thoughts. I like to come across positively and to wrap people in kindness and calmness. I aim to diffuse warmth by throwing in emojis and all-caps and exclamation marks and kisses (when talking to people in my personal/non-professional life, at least). Then, when I'm feeling off or being short with someone (hello PMS, my old friend), I'll subtract some of these gestures of affection – one less smiley face, no kisses at the end – as a way of getting across how I'm feeling. Of course, this isn't the only way to do things; the modern human has to establish their own way of communicating virtually. But I think it's super important to, firstly, be nice; secondly, be clear; and thirdly, understand that not everyone is aware of how not-nice and/or unclear their messages may come across.

And although I do understand that, I still have to deal with the *actual* bullies.

My self-esteem has absolutely been squashed to dust by cyberbullying. I mean, yeah, I've rebuilt it, but, man, it would've been a bit bloody lovely to have saved that precious time. Bullies have zoned in on my skin problems, my sexuality, my weight, my personality quirks, my fashion sense (well, to be fair, I'll give them that one), my accent and way of speaking – basically *everything* about me. Different bullies and trolls have picked me apart, little by little, at different times and for different reasons. But *why*?

Psychology was one of my favourite subjects at university. It injected me with this unquenchable thirst for knowledge of the human mind and how it works. Because, let's face it, people are weird. And people are fascinating – bullies included. Understanding their motivation has been invaluable to me!

SOME of the REASONS WHY BULLIES BULLY:

1 Many bullies are actually **victims** themselves. It's a trickle-down phenomenon, passed from generation to generation; they may have learned how to bully by observing their parents, siblings or friends getting their own way by being angry, pushing others around or making others fearful.

2 People who bully are often directing their own frustrations, anger and hurt at their victims – bullying becomes their **coping mechanism** and one way in which they feel in control.

3 Some people are brought up to be **insensitive** to other people's feelings – certain bullies can lack a common level of social intelligence.

4 **Loneliness** and lack of attention in a bully's life (from friends, teachers or parents) may lead them to lash out in order to stand out.

5 A lot of bullies bully because they have **low self-esteem** and feel insecure about something in their own personality or physical appearance. Sometimes bullies are people who don't feel worthy enough and they are drawn to bullying as a means to make themselves feel better by dragging others down. It can be an act of deflection.

6 If someone is **afraid** of the unknown (or threatened by something), it can lead them to discriminate or act out in cruel ways. Also, they may just be part of a 'pack' and following along with the group leader to avoid being bullied themselves.

On that last point ... alright, well, I used to bully people in school myself, in a way. At the time, around age twelve or so, I figured I was just a bystander, as I was only going along with things to impress my friends. But, nope. The more I reflect, the more situations and experiences I recall and the more I want to shrivel up in a cupboard that has the word 'shame' carved into its door.

I joined in. I actively partook in pulling people apart. I laughed along as friends bitched, and I mirrored by bitching with them, about people whom, deep down, I held nothing against.

And I shudder inside when I imagine a version of me, just as sheep-like but born a few years later, with 2017-level social media at my twelve-year-old fingertips ...

It's embarrassing to admit these things. The memories I have of calling people names and slagging them off for their looks or their voices or their personality traits – that's a stain on my spirit that I can't wash away. But because of it, and my psychology classes, I try not to jump to conclusions about bullies anymore, of the cyber- and real-world varieties. I understand that some amount of empathy is needed – *without*, of course, making excuses for their behaviour, 'cause it ain't cool nor okay. But by hanging on to a smidgen of compassion I can at least avoid stooping to their level now, for revenge.

When I was at my lowest while getting trolled a couple of years back, by that ruthless anomaly discussed previously, several things helped me to pull up barriers and materialise a mithril-like mental armour. (*Mithril* is a fictional metal from one of my favourite book series ever, *The Lord of the Rings*. It's described as resembling silver but being stronger and lighter than steel, and I like to pretend I have this wrapped around my mind.)

HOW to DEAL with BULLIES and TROLLS

1 **Seek comfort and support** from people you trust – parents, friends, teachers or counsellors – or even share anonymously in safe forums online. I talked everything out over and over and over again with loved ones and in private Facebook groups to come to terms with what was happening to me. It helps even more to talk to others who've experienced the same thing and to read personal accounts of bullying – it can help you feel less isolated and alone in what you're going through.

2 **Remember that it's not your fault but also *don't play victim.*** It's not about you: it's about the person that's

bullying you. However, perhaps they've identified a weakness in you – maybe you allow people to walk all over you, maybe you *are* a pushover (I know I certainly was). This is something you can fix and, again, this *isn't* a green light for a bully, so it's still completely and utterly on them. But try to figure out how to avoid submitting to their power play and, at the same time, *never* blame yourself for what's happening to you.

3 **Don't respond or show the bully/troll how their behaviour is impacting you.** By all means, confide in people you trust (like I said) but *do not* add fuel to the fire the bully's started. They want to know that their efforts are paying off. They want to see that you've been negatively influenced. If you make them feel like they're barking up the wrong tree and let it all roll off you, they won't be getting the desired response from you and (eventually) they'll get bored and move on. Their efforts to hurt you may even begin to embarrass them, instead of you.

4 **Screenshot/save posts for evidence** if the bullying is happening online. It's so easy now to screenshot everything from our phones and our laptops and to record phone calls – gathering evidence can make it easier to catch bullies and punish them accordingly.

5 **Separate yourself from your bullies.** Use avoidance strategies on social media such as tinkering with your privacy settings and blocking/reporting/muting/unfollowing/unfriending. Also devise escape plans for real-life situations where you might be cornered in school or work.

6 **Never be afraid to speak up.** Your own safety needs to be your main concern, so sometimes it's vital that you

address what's happening directly, either by pointing out their behaviour and/or telling someone who can actually help – like a school principal, a work manager, a human resources department or the authorities.

It's not weak to ask for help. Nobody should have to tolerate a toxic environment – and the environment that my stubborn troll dragged me into was as toxic as an environment can get. But the experience I had with this aggressive cyberbully ended up making me so much stronger, so it was a blessing in disguise!

And, ooh, dat mithril, baby.

DEPRESSION

A MENTAL snapshot

Me, aged nineteen, squished into a tiny plastic chair in some random doctor's office. I'm chewing the insides of my mouth (a weird habit I've had since I was a little kid). The doctor points it out yet I don't get self-conscious like I have all my life when people notice it. I'm rather spacey and out of it, to be honest. I didn't put up a fight when Dad dragged me here to talk to a professional. He is at a loss with me. I've given up washing myself, my bedroom is a literal dumping ground, I'm not opening up or showing interest in any of my once-adored hobbies – even trips to the cinema are failing to get me excited. Dad says I just stare at the screen passively with no real investment in the story, and this is how he twigged that something's up with me. Some days I lie on the couch all day long, staring at a spot in the corner of the room, and then I play a computer game called World of Warcraft *throughout the night, as there's nothing better to do. This game offers me an escape from reality, a reality I can't bear to face right now. 'You appear to be showing signs of clinical depression,' a blurry voice says from across the doctor's office. This doesn't faze me one bit.*

Depression is the worst friend I've ever had. But as a lonely and emotional teenage wreck, I welcomed its presence. I'd danced with situational depression (a short-term form of depression that can occur in the aftermath of traumatic life changes) after my parents' divorce when I was seven, during those bleak evenings after Dad first moved into a damp and cold little flat far away. When I first saw his new 'home' through bloodshot eyes, the reality of the situation hit me and I threw up *everywhere*, all over the mouldy carpets. Dad having this new bed in this horrible new place felt so foreign and unsettling.

Depression came knocking again about a decade later, after the death of my incredible grandmother. She was one of the few constants in my life at the time, a wise old bat who didn't look after herself at all – her face had never seen a lick of moisturiser, it seemed, and wild hairs grew from her moles – but she made me belly laugh every time I visited her. She'd stay awake late into the night with my brother and me, playing Scrabble and watching murder-mystery movies and documentaries about Egypt. I loved this woman dearly, this ancient lady who lived in a fog of cigarette smoke amidst a stack of crossword puzzles and library books. Seeing her become frail with sickness (which turned out to be cancer) really dragged me under.

That sort of depression is something many of us experience after a traumatic event – that feeling of not caring about anything other than surviving the grief and shock.

But having met and fought with a more severe form of depression down the line, the one I touched on in that mental snapshot that sparked off this chapter, which I wrote during a time when life served me despair from every angle – well, let's just say if this illness had its own Facebook page, I'd have it blocked.

It isn't a feeling: it's an anti-feeling – complete and utter apathy. It hung over me like a thick, dark blanket – a barrier to emotion. No light got in, no darkness got out, for almost an entire year of my life: a black hole of a year in which I lost a job (the job I had after school and before university), a job that I really enjoyed, in a shop selling video games;

a year in which I failed to endure the crippling break-up with my first love (let's call him 'Freddie'), with whom I also suffered a miscarriage; a year during which I was caught up in conflict with those closest to me *and* was still mourning the loss of my grandmother.

Constant online connections – texting, social media and so on – exacerbated my harsh focus on my looks too, and on other judgements from peers. This is something that *so many of us* experience today, so if you're there right now – I feel you!

I remember lying down on my never-made bed feeling like I'd been beaten to within an inch of my life and like I couldn't get the right words out, ever, and like talking was pointless anyway. *Nobody will understand*, I'd tell myself. It was the most unpleasant thing that I've ever experienced, that absence of the ability to even *imagine* my future self being happy. There was no hope – no sadness, even. Just nothingness and emptiness. I stopped caring whether I'd wake up or not every time I went to sleep.

Sure, being sad is painful, but sadness is a healthy emotion to experience, and I remember just *wishing* I could even feel sadness! Just so I wouldn't feel so ... absent from the world. Sadness serves a purpose, setting off important alarm bells that something's wrong or has changed; it helps a person to cope and to grow. But depression? That's just a complete loss of interest in everything and anything in life.

I was so cold and mentally smashed – I wouldn't wish that feeling on anyone, ever. And some people fight this feeling for their *entire life*.

My favourite metaphor for depression has always been the Dementors in *Harry Potter and the Prisoner of Azkaban*, which I've re-read several times throughout my life. J.K. Rowling describes Dementors as foul, faceless, soulless creatures that feed off happy thoughts and memories until a person is left with nothing but the most terrible experiences of their life. Dementors can't be killed, just warded off or temporarily driven away, much like depression, which is something that can absolutely be managed and controlled but can't easily be beaten.

It's a common problem yet there's so much unnecessary shame attached to it, that word: depression. Why do we find it so difficult to open up about it? Why do so many of us settle on fighting it in silence? On pretending we're okay when we're most definitely not? If a person has diabetes, they see a doctor. But for some reason, when it comes to mental health problems we take the 'insert head into sand' approach as a society. Our brain is a muscle that also needs exercise, and a depressed brain needs as much TLC as a broken bone does.

If I hadn't talked about it with my dad (admittedly after he pretty much *pried* it out of me – thanks, Dad, you gemstone) I don't know how I'd have found my way through the fog of it, eventually agreeing to counselling. Allow me to be your gemstone: if you're depressed, *please talk to somebody*.

How we learn to respond to difficult life events is key to becoming a mostly happy adult that positively contributes to the world, and we can't learn how to become stronger if we stay silent and hold the D word prisoner inside us. *We've* got to be the ones to turn the key and set it free. Psychotherapy has our backs. Great speakers and thinkers and teachers have our backs. Healthy food and fresh air and warm beds have our backs. And medication can be there for us, too.

We're never as alone as depression would like us to feel.

My family's support was the concrete foundation upon which my recovery was built. I found sharing how I was feeling with them and my counsellor, along with major mindset and lifestyle changes, to be far more helpful than medication (in the long run).

Antidepressants *do* reduce symptoms – I relied on them *heavily* for a time and, yes, it bugs me that there's such a stigma around it – but they couldn't cure or address the actual *cause* of my depression. One doctor said to me, 'You can't just remove the batteries from a smoke detector instead of looking for the fire so you can actually put it out,' and that's stayed with me through all these years! I always knew I had to get off antidepressants eventually and learn to be happy by myself again, because depressed was *not* my normal state of being and my doctor knew this. He knew it was the result of a bunch of things that had happened to me – of life events and thoughts that I didn't yet know how to cope with. And for many people who struggle with it, depression is just something that kind of *happens* after a bunch of big, scary changes. Not to mention all the side-effects of the drugs – I mean, *yikes*. I was constantly nauseous and constipated and I couldn't sleep and my mouth was all dry – just, no thanks.

Determined to be drug-free, I reasoned that treating the symptoms instead of the disease was never a long-term option for me, so I read and I read until my eyes stung, seeking non-medicating ways to feel better and address my imbalanced brain chemicals. And here are the results of all that reading, summarised, in case any of it helps you as much as it helped me. Everything's worth a try, right? Because happiness is worth fighting tooth and nail for!

THiNGS That HELPED me to TRANSITION OUT of DEPRESSION

♥ **I kept a mood journal**, noting how I felt day to day, all the while trying to identify why I felt that way. The simple act of writing things down was extremely therapeutic.

♥ **Lots of laughter** – I'd call friends, watch funny movies and YouTubers and observe my cats being ... cats! In the thick of it, I didn't find many things very funny but building humour into my environment really did help over time.

♥ **Daily meditation** – this one was tough for me but eventually I stopped feeling like a spare tit and got the hang of it and actually came to love focusing my mind and relaxing.

♥ **Better/more balanced nutrition** – I focused on incorporating natural, unprocessed foods more than on cutting out junk. This made the whole process easier and, with time, I discovered that the more healthy things I ate, the less junk I craved! Foods containing niacin, such as cashews and chicken, are thought by professionals to help lots, so I ate them often!

♥ **I bought a sun lamp** for my room and got outside more often for natural sunlight which, apparently, is super important for people who are feeling depressed.

♥ **Daily walks** (sometimes alone with my headphones and music, sometimes with my family): this is still one of my favourite things to do to instantly boost my mood.

♥ **I established a daily routine** and adjusted it as needed. Having structure to my life helped immensely with developing a feeling of purpose.

- ♥ **I set weekly goals** for myself every Sunday in a diary and made to-do lists.
- ♥ **Sleep** – going to bed at a sensible hour and not wasting the morning in bed was crucial. To do this, I'd zone out of social media for an hour before bed and if I needed entertaining I'd opt for a show or a book instead. I'd also have clean PJs, a bubble bath and a hot water bottle on standby for restless evenings!
- ♥ **I challenged negative thoughts** by watching and re-watching uplifting documentaries or reading about positivity and the law of attraction. This really helped with my outlook on life and my stress levels.
- ♥ **Every week I'd do something new** to change up my environment – something as simple as going to a new cafe or museum worked wonders.
- ♥ **I removed fake/toxic friends** from my life by slowly fading out of the 'friendships' and focusing on positive people. Misery loves company – choose good people to be around!
- ♥ **Social support** – I leaned on family and friends, I volunteered so I could meet new people and sometimes I called helplines for people with depression. Building stronger social networks made me feel far less isolated and meant I could talk things out or feel distracted when I really needed to crawl out of the hole in my mind.
- ♥ **Pets** – it was the best excuse ever for me to finally give in and become a crazy cat lady! Animals provide us with uncomplicated, unconditional love, responsibility (which is a positive focus to have), physical touch and companionship, and they flood our brains with feel-good chemicals.

The year-ish that I was depressed is shades of grey in my memory, a colourless, joyless existence I once lived and one which I hope I never have to return to. I'm keeping depression blocked on Facebook, people. I'm not afraid of depression anymore because now I understand it – and, boy, is it worth trying really hard to learn about and to fight off. Life without it can be oh-so-blissful. Having happy days, just-fine days, even sad days, when you can really enjoy a good cry because you know how terrible it is not to feel anything at all, well, that's a bloody wonderful thing, in my book. (Hehe ... 'in my book'.)

ANXiETY

'Generation anxiety' they call us (*they* being most people born before, say, 1980). Our modern world is ever-changing but expectations of us are not. So I totally get it when I hear them say things like: *their lifestyles lack routine; they marry later and spend longer in education and too long living with their families; they're more uncertain about their futures than we were; too much technology, not enough sleep, political correctness gone batshit and politics are just as mad; they can't afford houses; too many opportunities; they eat garbage food ...*

STOP!

Deep breath in through your nose, allowing your belly to rise up, and breathe out through your mouth. Breathe out all those worries and all of your fears in this moment.

You're not lazy, you're not 'broken' and your anxiety isn't your fault. You were just born during a storm – like the wild one that whipped Dorothy's house up into the sky in *The Wizard of Oz*. You're scared; I understand. *But storms always pass.*

Anxiety is crucial to survival because it prepares us to cope with stress and with danger. When we feel danger, our bodies release hormones that cause mental, emotional and physical changes – our thinking becomes more focused; we can feel short-tempered or even *numb* when we're anxious; sometimes our muscles will tense up and we'll breathe more, we'll sweat and our digestion and blood pressure may be (temporarily!) affected: it's that 'fight or flight' sensation. It ripples through us, priming us for action. And then it all passes, and our bodies return to a calmer state.

No matter where you feel a panic attack coming on – perhaps you're on public transport, or out for dinner, or watching a movie in the cinema, or simply tidying up your bedroom; maybe you have generalised anxiety disorder and suffer panic attacks all the time (I experienced this for a couple of years, aged nineteen to twenty-one); or maybe you've just been feeling anxious (like *everyone* does sometimes, like I still do now on occasion, particularly in new social situations); maybe you've only had to deal with this panic a couple of times in life so far – either way, **you can stop a panic attack in its tracks**.

I want you to do these three things each and every time you feel one coming on, OK? This is how I conquered my panic disorder in my early twenties and how I manage panic attacks now, to this day (they do still strike on occasion, but much more rarely):

1 While breathing deeply, slowly, in and out, **remind yourself of all the panic attacks you've had in the past.** This might seem like a weird thing to do *but*, as bad as they were, *you survived them all.* Yes, they were terrifying, but *they didn't harm you.* You didn't die. You were, and are, fine. Remember that a panic attack is simply an age-old protection mechanism built into your brain and wired to your body. It's natural. It's not designed to cause you harm.

2 **Don't try to stay calm.** Instead, face the panic attack head on, knowing it's going to pass soon, and get excited by it! Say, 'This is exciting!' over and over, as if you're on a rollercoaster in a theme park. Fear and excitement are very similar states for the body and mind to be in, so flip your fear into excitement. Panic grows when you fight it, so just bring it on and pop the bubble of fear. It will feel scary and exciting at the same time, but the wave of adrenaline you're experiencing will pass any minute now.

3 **Shake it off!** Do a Taylor Swift and literally shake your entire body. Flick and kick all of the stress hormones out of you, right now. Tense up your muscles, then stretch them out. Do it. It doesn't matter how silly you think you look. This is more important!

Listen to me. You can go *anywhere*, you can do everything you need to do to make it through your day, because panic *cannot* stop you once you understand what it is and why it's happening. Take baby steps to push outside of your comfort zone, little by little. I started going to new places more often and socialising again as soon as I learned what was actually going on when I was having these fits of feeling unable to breathe – of doing weird things like yawning, over and over again (about five times a minute), of crying and screaming and being unable to move.

Don't let anxiety steal your entire life away. *Manage it*. Don't throw your hands up and accept that you're part of 'generation anxiety' because *fuck that* – amiright? Knowledge is power.

THiNGS I'VE LEARNED about my ANXiETY

♥ It's actually very common and it takes many forms.
♥ It has evolutionary roots, so it's not entirely pointless and random!
♥ It's a liar (example: an interviewer isn't a predator who's trying to kill me – chill, Melanie).
♥ Eating well, exercising and meditating do actually help it.
♥ It doesn't like when people get all up in its space, so it leaves me alone when I'm at home.
♥ I have separation anxiety from my dad, so I feel safe when he's around.
♥ It affects new relationships and makes me careful about who I get close to.
♥ Panic strikes me randomly, often for no good reason.
♥ It demands patience from others.
♥ There's no switch – I can't immediately turn it off when it comes about.
♥ Patronisation from others makes it grow – it craves understanding.

USING 'THE FORCE' to TURN DREAMS INTO REALITY

The first *proper* story I ever wrote (aged eight) was a total rip-off of a novel by R.L. Stine. The first time I stood up to present in front of a group of people at college brought on a severely fizzy panic attack. My first pay cheque from YouTube was for about a hundred dollars, which didn't even slightly cover the cost of the camera I was using to record the videos. And my first 'brand deal' was about enough to wipe my arse with. The first hundred or so videos I created were so terribly planned out, so badly lit and edited, that watching them now makes me want to break stuff. But my whole point here is this: *I'm not a quitter*.

But I used to be. I've been working toward getting to where I am for years, and I'm constantly working to achieve more and more through perseverance and determination. I swim in the pool of thought that says you're a success if you have a goal and are constantly moving toward it. And here is where I share with you *how*: how I became a doer, how to move toward your goal, how I've turned my dreams – of making a living from creating and performing and all of the rest – into reality.

This bit is important, gang. I mean it! I really, *really* want you to read this section with zero distractions, OK? Take off the headphones, ignore the TV or the screaming children in the background, stop eating and read it, then re-read it another day (and read *all* of it, so you understand that I'm *not* trying to say I smiled my way out of depression or some other silly nonsense).

When I was in the depths of despair during my very own dark ages, the 'depression and anxiety years', I became so disgusted by my situation that I developed an overwhelming desire to feel better and to improve as a person. I don't know where this desire came from, but one day I just decided I was going to get through all of this *mud*. And then something I'd later discover to be very important happened – three times over.

My mammy and two of my aunties all gave me the same book, on different days, within weeks of one another. So random and unexpected.

I've always been a bookworm – they knew that, but they also knew I'd stopped reading as I wasn't finding joy in ... well ... anything ... So I was like, *eh, what?*

It was a seemingly cheesy, admittedly flawed self-help book called *The Secret*, which explores the age-old 'law of attraction' – the power of positive thought and feelings – in a very straightforward and accessible way. It's an easy read that hammers home the value of *intention* in life: that important shift in thinking that makes you feel like you're going to do that thing you *really want* to do, even if you don't know yet *how* you're going to do it. It actually reminded me of the concept of 'the Force' in *Star Wars*, and as a huge fan of that series, my interest was piqued!

I'd heard a lot of people make fun of this book and other books like it. And I honestly think if only one of these women had given me the book I'd have been like, 'Cool, thanks, yeah, I'll read it,' with no intention of *actually* doing so (blame my innate Irish over-politeness and what-would-the-neighbours-say syndrome). If *two* of them had given it to me I'd have thought it a bizarre coincidence, but

I reckon both copies would've gathered dust under my bed along with unopened exercise DVDs and my diary collection. But three copies of the same book? In the end, I read it with a scrunched-up face that screamed, 'OK, OK, *fine* then.'

And although I was embarrassed and didn't want to be seen reading it (based on what I'd heard the many denigrators say), it ended up being one of the most enlightening reads of my life.

I didn't finish the book believing, 'OK, so I just need to think happy thoughts and I'll get everything I've ever dreamed of' – I never discounted the importance of *action* – but I acknowledged, for the first time, that actions are created *by* thoughts. And that through controlling my thoughts I could essentially 'manifest' desired outcomes and situations, because as humans we put our energy where we put our thoughts. I hadn't known or even considered that I can control how I feel, even while things are going bad in my life. I can control how I react to external influences. I can be the director of my own life. And so can you!

The Secret spurred me on to read many more books on the subject of the law of attraction (I began by diving into the work of Abraham-Hicks, and took it from there), to watch TED Talks online and documentaries, to simply broaden my mind. Physics, theology – you name it, I was reading about it. Which is exactly why I ignore all the piss-taking people throw my way when I bring these things up now.

Get this: those people don't *need* to understand the impact that this little book had on me, and *you* don't need to understand either.

Other people understanding or failing to get why something has a positive impact on someone else doesn't in any way undo or increase the impact of that thing. I can't stand football, for example, and I don't for the life of me understand how so many people get *so much* from watching a match, but how I feel about football doesn't matter to football fans (nor should it) – they still love it! I'm glad they get so excited over a little ball on a green television screen – good for them!

Still, though, I'm compelled to summarise here, somehow, just *how much* my mindset and life experiences changed after reading *The Secret*, in case I can spark a new mindset in even one new person. I came away from that book with a big smiley head, feeling more motivated than ever to be *glass half-full* about life after learning how many great things I could attract to me by doing so. I discovered a thirst for knowledge about visualisation and positivity and the origins of quotes by history's great thinkers – bearing in mind, at the time I filled my brain exclusively with soap opera storylines and what so-and-so had said about so-and-so (a load of distracting shite, basically).

Having 'used the Force' by practising visualisation and the law of attraction for years now, I truly believe that how we think, and therefore *feel*, largely determines our future and surroundings.

The toughest pill to swallow in all this for me is that *we get what we think about whether we want it or not*. So I really try to stay on top of the thoughts I focus on. I'm big on *protecting my energy* – I don't want illness and drama and pain but it takes resilience to keep the mind from dwelling on such things (especially if and when they do happen, because life is peaks and dips and there are always going to be circumstances out of our control). It's admittedly much harder when I've fallen into a dip to keep my mind in check, but that's why I believe I succeed at things: because I push through. I always know that I can, because I've endured traumatic events in the past and none of them killed me. When things out of my control strike and turn my life upside down, I just follow the steps on the following pages, then I adjust my thoughts. I paint a new picture of how I want my life to go – I remember I'm not *helpless*.

I still struggle with this from time to time, but, hey, I'm still a twenty-something baby-child. Here are a few ways that I stay positive in the face of illness and death and global destruction and all of the horrible things out of my control …

1 **I dig deep.** I remind myself daily that, firstly, I'm like a grain of sand on a never-ending stretch of beach, and secondly, a beach wouldn't be a beach at all without *every single grain of sand* on it. What I'm getting at here (me and my stupidly elaborate analogies!) is that I don't control everything that happens in the world, or even in the little bit of world enveloping me. The universe is massive, and it's happening around me, but I'm part of it nevertheless.

People get sick and die, rainforests fall, animals are killed, I won't always be here. I breathe deep and then I exhale my fears related to such things. Carrying around anxieties and worries won't stop these things from happening but it *will* stop me from living my best life.

2 **I live in the moment and keep myself grounded.** Even in the shitty moments, I allow feelings to run through me. I don't hang on to the past. I don't fret about things that haven't happened yet. When something bad happens, I feel it. I cry. I scream. I talk it out. Because those sad, hurt and angry feelings *always pass*. When I'm in the throes of a truly happy moment, I'll sometimes remind myself of a dark time in my life, just for a split second (like me trembling and crying with grief on my old bathroom floor – naked in the night, empty and alone) and I'll smile wider with the realisation that *I survived that*. That's what we humans do. Life goes on. **Some little exercises I do to ground myself:** touch and stare at a textured object in a quiet room; lie with a sleepy animal like a cat or dog, in silence, and look into their eyes; walk at night time with classical music playing in my headphones and gaze at the stars.

3 **I remember that it could be worse.** It could *always* be worse. I count my blessings (literally: I scribble out lists of all the things I'm lucky to have, the things I should be grateful for) and I drench my world in the things I love. Any time I lose someone to illness or when something terrible is happening, I escape into books and music and TV shows and long conversations with friends on walks through fields.

4 **I give myself time to go through the motions after a shock or an upset.** I let myself be sad. I grieve. I be angry. *I don't repress feelings: that only leads to wallowing in them.*

It takes real effort to keep our brains swimming in warm, happy thoughts, and in the modern world we live in, it's more important than ever to take control of what media we consume, and who we get close to, and so on. I don't mean to only surround yourself with yes-people who'll tell you you're the best – not at all. Constructive criticism needs to be distinguished from negativity. It's important, it builds you, it makes you tough against bad energy and it conditions you for it, enabling you to deal with it.

I've let go of trying to be perfect all the time, of expecting everyone to be nice to me. If I'm editing a YouTube video of me with fake tan streaks all over or a big pimple on my top lip, or one in which I say something that I know not everyone will agree with, I'll still upload it even though I know people will slag me off or attack me in the comments. I anticipate bad energy. It's always going to come. But I welcome it, and I let that bad energy wash over me as though I'm standing under a heavy flow of water. I want to continue conditioning myself against that forever. Because I'm going to find myself in negativity bubbles regularly due to, well, THE WORLD.

But we're looking at the bigger picture here. I'm talking about the difference between being mostly-in-a-good-place and being mostly-miserable. When I shifted my focus from worries and 'what if' scenarios to things that I *did* want to happen in my life, my thoughts became so soaked in positivity that it definitely rubbed off on me and put me in the right state of mind to get creative and make shit happen. This attitude also made me much better at coping with life's curveballs and not allowing them to knock me back ten steps (rather, just one or two steps).

My new positive thoughts generated new positive actions. Like, I cringed so hard when I considered making an actual vision board, after reading about the benefits of it in some tattered library book. So I compromised and instead created a new folder on my desktop that I called my 'vision folder' – quick and private, I'd encourage anyone to do this!

Into the folder, twenty-year-old Melanie saved lots of images from the internet that made her feel happy and that represented her *then* life goals: smiling faces at dinner parties; fluffy pets; a home near the seaside; healthy food; aeroplanes and holidays; books (as I always wanted to be published and, well, hello?); people holding hands; and also more superficial things such as models who looked like me with slender figures and fancy clothes, money and so on.

I glanced at this folder every day, just for a moment, and I started just ... expecting things to go well, *without doubt*.

We're almost taught to doubt that our lives will go well. 'You'll never make any money from publishing books, so why bother?' 'Everyone cheats and most marriages end in divorce so don't expect your happily ever after ...' I mean, just shake this shit *off*. How can you experience anything if you go at life with such a defeatist attitude? How will you make memories and try and then fail and then try again only to improve or succeed?

It took a while to learn to think this positive way and for my attitude and body language to change – I *still* have to practise this new mindset all the time, but it's a lot easier for me now because so many things I've asked 'the universe' for (some might pray to God – we all have our own way of making sense of this world) have come to be.

I've 'manifested' the most random little things as well as bigger life goals – my online following; my peaceful state of being; my friends; the location of my home and various experiences which I'd dreamed about in the most *minute* detail. (I'd share some of these stories but many of them involve sexy times and, well, we're not in the right chapter for that!) Oftentimes, I find the reality is much better than the dreams, too – the manifestations always kick the arse of the thoughts and feelings that created them!

During times of doubt and worry, and in my down-day uniform of pyjamas, I reignite my passion for positivity by watching or reading interviews with famous personalities who also incorporate this positive way of thinking into their life, such as Irish MMA fighter Conor McGregor, actors like Will Smith and Jim Carrey, even the glorious Oprah Winfrey herself! Humans can have up to sixty thousand thoughts a day, but research suggests that up to 80 per cent of those thoughts are negative. It takes effort and will to override worries and fears, as they come to us so naturally.

My favourite time to practise the law of attraction is when I lie down in bed at night – during those last twenty minutes before I fall asleep. As we're drifting off into deeper levels of brainwave activity, we have a stronger ability to influence our subconscious minds, and our subconscious mind speaks in the language of *feeling and emotion*. I love to lie there and really use my mind's eye to generate the feelings from within, about things I wish to experience. Playing soundtracks I love helps me to get in the right frame of mind for this! See, we can communicate with our own subconscious through this medium of feeling and emotion, but the thing is, we don't attract what we *want*, we attract *who we are*. So if we learn and train ourselves to *feel the feelings we desire more of*, if we see things in our minds and embody the related emotions, those thoughts becomes part of who we are.

And I mean, you can't just visualise stuff and then go eat a doughnut and expect stuff to materialise. *Duh.* This book you're reading right now is actually a great example of this point: I actually designed a mock cover (seriously – don't laugh!), printed it out and stuck it on another book just so I could feel the feeling of holding a book I'd written and published in my hands! Obviously that wasn't enough – I'm having to sit down and put pen to paper, over and over again, for months and months. But simply seeing the mock-up book every day by my bedside somehow drives me to just get this done. And it was key in pushing me through those tough months during 2016 when finishing this felt impossible, after a very messy and public break-up.

I know that keeping positive images in my mind and visualising things that make me happy, like great conversations with friends, getting to date certain people or meeting my idols or winning awards, and even random things that don't really matter but that *do* make my heart sing – things like me wearing a fancy swishy dress, walking a red carpet, feeling accomplished and smiling – I just *know* that picturing these things and *feeling* how they would feel, as if I'd already experienced them, makes it more likely that I will take action to make it all happen and to attract more of these things into my world. It was easy to adopt this mindset during tough times, too, as I kicked off this new life approach while depressed, so if you're struggling, start taking baby steps and making little changes right now. I would have done it all sooner if only I'd known.

The alternative to choosing this mindset of abundance, even in times of struggle, is, pretty much, to potter along and assume that you're doomed to feel so-so, forever and always, to always want what you don't have, rather than being grateful for what you *do* have so that you *feel* abundant and therefore *become* more abundant.

I feel like a total arse talking about this because I used to roll my eyes *so hard* when people said things like this to me, but I'm being real with you here.

At first I absolutely questioned all of this and would think things like, 'Surely if everyone can have what they want then the world wouldn't work?' but as I discovered, through talking to people and reading various studies, most people – when seeking from the heart – want *completely different things*. Each of us has our own life experiences that mould our desires and we all find pleasure in different things – and as I've learned, *there's plenty to go round*. Sure, you might have to spend a while working somewhere you don't enjoy before you begin to push yourself to follow the career path you want. I did – heck, all of us do! And we sometimes forget that some people enjoy doing jobs that others don't. My ex-boyfriend's mother, for example, would always say how much she adored her job, cleaning a school kitchen and heating up lunches for teachers. She *loved it*. See, we're all wired differently ... this job wouldn't be for *me*, for example, in the same way that my job wouldn't be for her.

Sometimes, too, we don't know what we want until we've tried a variety of different things. Sometimes, we need to focus on the *feeling* that an activity or idea gives us, and we can use that feeling to guide our own way into a job or situation that'll make us happy.

It might end up being packaged differently – take what I'm doing currently, for example! People call me a YouTuber, or an influencer, or an 'online content creator' – I never set out to do this. *But* it brings together so many of my favourite things and I adore it. I always loved the feeling of performing to a camera on my own (Dad had a big clunky camera when we were young teenagers that I'd film vlogs on before they were called vlogs), I always enjoyed editing videos (I used to combine photographs and video clips and songs and upload them to social media before I even knew what YouTube was) and I always liked to help people, and the idea of informing, of entertaining, of connecting. So the situation I'm now in is a perfect example of how my focusing on these *feelings*, and the impact I wanted to have, brought me into the right situation.

When it comes to relationships, sometimes we think we're in love with a person who doesn't want us back. *Raises hand.* But actually, we're missing how we *felt* with that person. So focus on the feelings you felt with them – the comfort, the safety, the cuddles, the laughter, the companionship – focus on that stuff, and not on their face (stop stalking their social media: *stop it now*) and you'll attract another person into your world. I'm feeling indecisive right now on this one, as I'm loving singledom, and also I don't know if I want a husband or a wife (damn bisexuality, clouding up my law of attraction buzz!) but I know precisely how I'll go about this when the time comes.

My point is, not everyone wants the same partner, or the same wardrobe, or likes the same food or has the same hobbies. This law of attraction applies to everyone, everywhere.

Don't be swayed by what you think you want or by what everyone else wants: learn what you want, and then focus your energy on that. Hold it in your mind. All the time.

Human nature means that *not everyone* is going to think this way. Not everyone will trust it or care to look into it or practise it. There are always dreamers and doers, and there are always people who roll their eyes at dreamers and doers.

I've been both.

One of the main things that pushed me over the line, to change how I live, was an observation experienced through social media – through watching videos and following public profiles of a specific breed of people. I noticed that many of the happiest, most successful people I followed appeared to immerse themselves in good things – they'd share positive, happy posts; they'd celebrate their successes and the successes of others; their pages were always filled with optimism and colour and jokes and powerful quotes. These people seemed to avoid adding fuel to the fire that is negativity. I'd rarely, if ever, see posts on their profiles complaining about things or status updates reflecting negative emotions. Instead of talking about war, they'd talk about *peace*. Instead of sharing articles about terrible things, they supported marvellous things through uplifting campaigns.

As you'll have noticed, though, there are indeed a lot of people in the world who are drawn to negativity, who seemingly have *no intention* of changing their situation. People who like to drag others down for simply trying to ascend. I encourage you to do everything in your power to *not* be one of these people.

I wanted to emulate the happy, positive, successful people who brought me fuzzy feelings through their online posts. So I do! And now I'm pretty happy, doing things I never thought I'd do, with people I never thought I'd know, in a job I never knew I'd have, with money I never thought I'd earn, and things just keep improving all the time – even when horrors come knocking that are out of my control, I'm more capable of coping.

I've become resilient. *Elastic.* I know how to bounce back now. And that's because I stopped planning against catastrophe and thinking about things I didn't want to happen and my experience of life became so much easier. There are less thorns in the forest and they don't cut as deep as they once did when I walk through it. I released repressed emotions. And I don't focus on eliminating problems now when I'm faced with them – instead I try to focus on creating something new.

I used to think things like, 'I want to get rid of my acne' or 'I want to lose weight', but, as I experienced through trial and error, by putting out there thoughts of 'I want', thoughts of 'acne', thoughts of 'weight', I kept attracting more of the same. I had to instead picture what I *actually* wanted over and over again, all the time: 'clear skin, clear skin, clear skin', 'health, health, health, health' and so on, and these thoughts would spur me into action.

When I think about myself a few years ago – lonely, sad, unhealthy, bitter, resentful, selfish – I don't even recognise that person. I'm constantly becoming the person I ultimately want to be: a person who is mostly happy, kind, surrounded by love; a person who is healthy and optimistic and giving. Some people might think I'm tooting my own horn here but guess what?

I like myself.

And I'm so *over* following the crowd and *not* liking who I am just because it's the 'normal' way to feel. That mentality is a disease that'll keep on spreading unless we act.

Please 'try' all this out for the next month, but, see, with this approach to life there is no try: there is only *do* or *do not*. In 'trying', a person isn't really expecting it to work out, in which case it likely won't because the right actions won't be taken.

So, actually, just do it, OK?

Simply replace the language of your thoughts. And visualise more often (or 'daydream' as my dad calls it every time he spots me doing it!) – do it while you go for walks or take baths, whenever suits you, and make a vision folder on your computer (it helps!). Remind yourself daily about how grateful you are for the things you *do* have. And that the glass *isn't* half-empty. You're the boss of your own brain. Perhaps you're currently cowering on a closet floor in that head of yours because you've been overwhelmed? Well it's time to stand up and take control. Get things in order. Think the right thoughts and turn them into ALL THE LOVELY THINGS.

Like attracts like, so get attracting some bloody marvellous stuff, please. And enjoy the shite out of it all.

Section 2

FOOD
and
BODY

FROM 'the WRONG TYPE OF SKINNY' TO OVERWEIGHT and UNHEALTHY

Fat. Those three letters combined in that order had the impact of an atomic bomb on younger me's self-esteem. I was a skinny kid who loved to run around and play sports, though I ate copious amounts of shite food. I was a proper bottomless pit when it came to gooey chocolate bars and sweets, cheese and onion flavoured crisps, pasta with little hot dogs from a tin and greasy pepperoni pizzas – my first true loves! And no, I had no idea what I was putting into my body. There was no conscious decision made to 'live off shite' – it just sort of happened that way.

I comfort ate from a very young age, mostly behind my parents' backs, starting around the time they divorced and Dad moved out (when I was about seven). *Dad's gone but, hey, there's loads of food in the cupboard to fill the gaping void!* I ate when I was happy, when I was sad, when I was angry – food became my main source of contentment.

And not just any food. Not apples, not lentils, not foods that are impossible to mindlessly munch on 'coz *nutrients* ... (foods from nature that actually fill us up and make us feel satisfied). Rather, the 'food' that many parents feed themselves and their families nowadays because it's convenient and cheap and tastes great – 'food' from brightly coloured packets, combining saturated fats with lashings of sugar and processed carbs. 'Food' that's addictively dribble-worthy and *never* leaves us feeling satiated.

I'd clean out the junk food in our house (which was supposed to be reserved for weekends and special occasions), and I'd steal junk food from shops, and I'd ask for extra sweets and cakes when staying in friends' houses for sleepovers.

Thanks to a fiery young metabolism, there was never a pick on me as a young 'un but I was often very unwell and wasn't getting the nutrition I needed – I'd throw out the fruit Mammy put in our lunchboxes for school, and I'd kick up a fuss if Dad asked me to eat veggies with my dinner. In hindsight, my health should have mattered a whole lot more to me – I was *always* sick, with colds, constipation and digestive problems. But kids aren't taught to value their health very much ... during cartoon binges the TV advertisements would scream BUY THIS CEREAL, EAT THIS CANDY!

The original purple Calpol Pain & Fever Relief for 3 Months + was a staple in our household. I weirdly looked forward to bi-weekly doses of it, that purple goo and all its delicious chemicals. And I vividly recall stints in hospital during which I'd be given laxatives because my diet contained little to zero fibre – I even ended up shitting all over my mammy's lap one time after she insisted on staying by my side overnight in the hospital.

Good times, good times!

When I was about twelve years old, I noticed Mammy doing little workouts the odd time – she had this special pink mat she'd pull out onto the living-room floor – and eating 'weird healthy-person food', to feel healthier and look her best. I also observed that 'fat' kids in school

were the butt of everyone's jokes on a daily basis at lunch break and that bigger people were always, *always* cast in movies as comic relief.

Everything around me was communicating that pretty much nobody wanted to be called *the F word*.

I grew taller quicker than I grew outward so when I hit fourteen I was scrawny as a winter branch and longed for bigger boobs and a bum. Yep, I actually craved *more* body fat, BUT only in certain places. Girls in school told me I looked 'like a boy', as I was one width the whole way up, like a lamppost. My millennial brain then decided, *tits + ass = girl*.

Yet when I turned sixteen and my body went berserk and decided to answer my yearnings for womanly curves by planting thirty pounds worth of wider hips and lumps and bumps on me (in places where I didn't expect to *ever* have lumps and bumps) I started to really struggle with my body image. *What is this? What is that? Why is that there?* I'd think, grabbing at my belly and thighs and arms in front of my bedroom mirror. I wasn't big by anyone's standards (and I *was* still eating a terrible diet) but one girl in school said I was shaped 'like an apple rather than an hourglass' and that she'd 'hate to be my shape'.

These physical changes of puberty struck me like a brick to the head.

While getting ready for my debs (the Irish prom) aged eighteen, I recall being forcefully pinned against the bathroom wall by my ex and his mother as they tackled the job of pulling my dress zipper up my back; my boobs had doubled in size in the weeks since buying the dress and were seen to be spilling out of it in every single debs photo taken! You'd think I'd have been over the moon about the extra tit going on but no. Because my waistline had expanded along with my bra size.

And I felt genuinely confused by the attention my bulging breasts received on the night of my debs, because I didn't know whether to feel annoyed or embarrassed or delighted that I was being ogled. The intention had been for the dress to fit correctly, but because it didn't, people conversed with my chest and not with *me*. Part of me enjoyed this, another part felt objectified and those conflicting thoughts clouded the entire experience. All this amazing stuff was happening around me, memories were being made, while my thoughts remained fixated on two glands hanging from my chest.

I mean, imagine being down the town on your lunch break surrounded by teen boys practically dribbling over your curvier, *fatter* body while, at the same time, the girls from your own school are hating on their own thinner bodies. Pinching at their imaginary muffin tops mid-scoff of a chicken roll and calling themselves *fat* and *ugly* when they looked completely beautiful to me. Overly hormonal and self-judgemental teenage me would look down at my own body and notice how my thighs touched, how my tummy poked out further than these other girls'. 'Are they calling *me* fat? Are boys lying when they compliment me and just chancing their arm at a notch on their bedpost?

We all thought we needed to look thin but be curvy in all the right places too – to be the 'right type of skinny' – and I have no idea when exactly I woke up with that mentality.

It all happened so fast, my body changed so fast – the bewilderment I felt sent me spiralling into comfort eating again, just like I had as a child going through big life changes. It didn't help that my on-off boyfriend at the time ('Freddie') liked me with more meat on my bones. He genuinely seemed so much more into my bigger body, which made me more complacent about my plummeting health. It's like I somehow figured, 'Well, if he likes me better like this then it's OK because that's what matters, right, what *he* wants?'

Dad had a lousy lifestyle back then too and, living with him during my late teens, I picked that up. We become a product of our environment – it affects our habits *so* much unless we become aware of it and consciously change it. And that's *not* to say I blame anyone other than myself, but, sweet baby Moses, it would've been easier to avoid becoming unhealthy if I was surrounded by salad-munching sports fanatics! To be fair, my mammy and stepdad worked out lots and ate well ... but I didn't live with them anymore, and anyway, the idea of gym-type workouts made me actually retch.

Fast forward a year and a half to me, aged nineteen and a half, and I couldn't even cross my own legs. My dad pointed out in the car one day that I no longer had knees. *No knees.*

Yeah.

I'd 'gotten fat'.

During my depressive episode, and not necessarily skinny to start with, I comfort ate so much that I blew up like a tampon dipped in a glass of wine (hey, I'm not the only one who's done that – don't you judge me). I stepped on a scales in the doctor's office and at five-foot-five and weighing 180lbs I was skimming the 'obese' BMI (body mass index) category. My doctor also told me that I was on a road to developing diabetes and, with the health issues running in my family on both sides, this was very bad news indeed.

I felt worthless. Subhuman.

I called my friends and wailed down the phone. Because society ridicules and loathes fatness and this doctor was telling me that *I* was overweight. And because I could've done long-term damage to my insides. And, well, also because I hadn't really even *noticed* myself gaining so much weight – at the time, I was coming out of my severe depression. I'd been living in a bubble, avoiding mirrors. It was shocking, really, that I hadn't realised. I mean, how do you *not* notice something like that? Especially after spending so many years previously so conscious of my size! Now, post-depression and with my weight defined by a number, the fact that my body was covered in angry purple stretchmarks (not to mention the bi-monthly upsizing of my jeans) made more sense, but my measurable loss of control *crippled* me.

I was suddenly hyperaware of my previously unnoticed waddling as I left the doctor's office. I caught my reflection in the side of a bus and started crying in horror. I got home, ran myself a bath and noticed that I'd plugged up the middle of the bath with the sides of my body, preventing the water from filling up the entire tub. Cue more wild tears. Now add some snot to that image. (I hope you're laughing – even though it was very, very traumatic at the time!)

So, yeah, I sat there for a bit to think objectively about my bad habits, crying and naked, stuck in the middle of the bath like a human-sized water dam as memories from my depression stabbed my brain like pinpricks: me absentmindedly polishing off entire family-shar-ing-sized chocolate bars myself; me eating whole packets of biscuits and tubes of Pringles while playing video games; me always asking for seconds of Dad's Bolognese and having up to three daily lunches along with copious amounts of fizzy drinks. I genuinely don't think I ate a piece of fruit or a single vegetable or drank a glass of straight-up *water*, aka human fuel, for about a year and a half.

I'd become so disconnected from my body that I hadn't been in tune with my sluggishness, my general overall feeling of unwellness.

To best illustrate then-me's diet, here's a section from a blog post I wrote on a collaborative blog in 2013 (when I'd regained my health):

> *An average day, at my worst, when I was working in a computer game store and was starting to get super down and super dependent on food, would be: a large fry-up with a pint of orange juice plus a scone with fresh cream and jam for breakfast, mid-morning snacks galore of Coke and Doritos and pastries and chocolate bars, lunch of a man-size lasagne with chips, untouched salad and garlic bread (washed down with yet more Coke), similar afternoon snacks to my mid-morning ones with perhaps some chewy sweets and hot chocolate with marshmallows, then a giant Chinese takeaway after work with yet more Coke and more crisps. I was killing myself.*

Reading that blog reminds me of a story from my weight-gain phase I'll never forget. One night I was lying in bed watching my *Sex and the City* box set after I'd eaten a titanic Chinese takeaway, washed down with two litres of fizzy lemonade. I wanted more food, for no reason other than it temporarily made me feel better – even though I knew I was disgustingly full and that I'd had plenty of meals that day. Guilt-ridden, I ordered an extra-large pizza and some deep-fried cookies. It was late at night and my dad was fast asleep, so I tip-toed out to the front door when I heard the delivery guy's car pull up. I wanted to open it before he rang the doorbell – I couldn't handle the thought of Dad knowing that I was ordering in more food. He'd always throw me this kind of shocked-and-disappointed expression when he'd catch me overeating, because I was spending so much money that I really couldn't afford and because he clearly saw something in me that, at the time, I couldn't see myself – he must have known there was something up. I tip-toed back into my room, arms full of warm calories, and demolished the lot of it. I couldn't even roll over in bed. It was proper agony, and I ended up throwing up into a plastic bag. I woke up the next morning with a food hangover, the puke bag next to my head and garlic dip smeared all over my pillow.

I also remember a trip I took to Switzerland to stay with my cousin Anna, even before all of this weight gain. She'd sit there eating bowls full of leaves and avocado and croutons and cherry tomatoes dressed in olive oil, lemon juice and balsamic vinegar while I retched and moaned, 'Can we *please* go and find a McDonald's?' I couldn't fathom the idea of eating a single thing prepared for me by Anna's mother – I kept making up excuses about why I wasn't eating anything. 'I'm really not hungry, honestly!' *Stomach audibly growling.* Anna grew up with completely different habits to me, so for her eating salad and overnight oats in the mornings and whatnot *wasn't* weird. I think that's when I realised that my habits weren't standard across the board, that healthy people who enjoyed healthy food did, actually, exist. But, because I hadn't yet hit rock bottom, I had no desire to change my ways.

A good 90 per cent of the food I ate during my weight gain was addictive, empty calories in shades of beige, yellow and orange – fried foods, refined carbohydrates, foods that don't resemble anything a human would eat in the wild. Delicious, fatty, sugar-laden foods such as chips, crisps, doughnuts, cookies, white bread, frozen chicken nuggets, waffles, pies, pastries and beer-battered takeaway foods. I feel stodgy just *thinking* about this stuff now, and the vast quantities of it I used to shovel in without a second thought.

A little bit of what you fancy is good for the brain but not ALL OF THE THINGS, ALL OF THE TIME. My blood sugar levels were all over the place and my body was in a constant state of stress and imbalance. I was literally *starving*. These foods I was stuffing in didn't provide my cells with the nutrients they needed: I was *always* hungry.

And while depressed, this glorious combination of saturated fat and processed sugar with refined carbohydrate in a constant stream from hand to mouth to stomach made me feel *less alone*; distracted me from repressed pain I'd bottled up inside; gave me whacks of dopamine and other feel-good hormones. I became reliant on the convenience of it and the pleasure I felt while pigging out. My life was so very *out* of control in every other area at the time – family members were dying, personal relationships were falling apart and I lost my job in the game store – the only thing I *could* control was what went in and out of my mouth. So, yes, I was feeding my face with all the cheap, brightly packaged junk I could get my hands on, oblivious to what it was doing to my body and my brain.

On a date rather recently, whilst tucking into a big, delicious bowl of tomato and basil pasta, the conversation turned to weight gain. The girl who'd asked me out looked so shocked when I told her I'd been overweight in the past – I mean, literally, her face was like a smacked arse. I anticipated her asking if the stretch marks were noticeable or if I have loose skin after the weight loss dangling around under my pretty dress, but instead she asked me something that I'd never answered out loud before. 'In what ways did being overweight impact your day-to-day life? Did your life change much?'

I then poured memories and feelings like a waterfall for roughly the amount of time it takes to order and eat dessert *and* polish off a bottle of merlot.

I told her the whole truth. That being the F-word was really tough for me. That upon realising I'd gained so much weight and then being faced with the weight-loss mountain, which intimidated me for months, I felt trapped inside my own body, as if someone had wrapped a big, thick duvet around me that had somehow become one with my skin.

The extra weight didn't feel like it was part of me. I slowly noticed just how uncomfortable I'd become, how I couldn't get cosy in bed at night anymore with ease. And apart from experiencing less energy (no matter how many cups of coffee I knocked back), a dip in my usually sky-high sex drive (even porn didn't help!) and the horrible feeling of no longer being able to walk long distances with my family, I also had to learn how to endure one of the few remaining acceptable forms of discrimination. The eyes of strangers and friends of the family would sting me and their assumptions of stupidity and laziness were laser beams burning away my self-worth.

Overweight Melanie didn't resemble her former self – all the giddiness was gone, all the sparkle, all the will to live it up every weekend.

I'm glad that I woke up one day deciding that I felt *wrong*. Otherwise I'd never have made things right again. I was trying to rebuild my life after overcoming depression, so eating all day and sitting still and having to donate all my old clothes because they no longer fit me – these things were no longer options. Walking by mirrors, catching glimpses of myself and thinking, *Who was that?* I didn't want to experience that anymore. The extra weight came between me and the sports I loved to play throughout my teens. Between me and my (previously rather colourful) sex life. Between me and new adventures. Because I was too self-conscious and I was always tired and I *didn't* want to just learn how to be happy in this new, alien body.

But, as all my reading of inspirational stories and positive thinking taught me during my depression, I'd never get to where I wanted to be unless I first appreciated where I was. I acknowledged my feelings about my new UK 16–18 dress size and my low energy and my general all-round feeling of unwellness and I told myself, 'OK – how I look and feel right now is the result of the choices I've made right up to this point, so how I look and feel in the future will be the result of the choices I make going forward.' Which made it all a whole lot easier to deal with. 'I accept that this is where I'm at, and I'm not gonna harbour self-hatred: I'm gonna slowly change things up.'

And so began an epic quest to feel *right* again, inside and out.

LOSING WEIGHT — the EASY PART?

So, you know all those magazines with 'Lose TEN pounds in TEN days!' on the cover in bold, neon yellow lettering? Yeah, they're all full of bullshit. There is no yellow-brick road to Slimsville – where do you think you're off to with those ruby slippers, past Melanie? Get up outta that!

Okay, losing weight *is* easy (not as easy as the headlines suggest, but doable) – but *keeping it off* and getting *healthy* is another story.

In my mammy's house one weekend I was standing by the kitchen counter eating handfuls of chocolate cereal from its box, reading one of those obnoxious women's magazines – the kind that publish long-lens photos of celebs on the beach and close-ups of their 'rolls' next to pink subtitles like 'oink oink!' Mam came home from work all flustered and as her heels clicked across the kitchen floor I said, 'Mam, do you think if I go on a diet I'll be skinny in a month?' She stopped in her tracks. I'd never seen the woman laugh so hard in my life.

And I didn't get the joke.

I went through a phase of trying every stupid, borderline *dangerous* diet under the sun. I'd try to live off soup, or protein bars, or jello. I tried no carbs, all carbs, fat free, ice-pops till 4 p.m. They were all ridiculous and impossible to stick to because none of them were balanced. I'd always find myself dipping into the bread bin for 2 a.m. toast sessions.

Most people don't know that it's *so* much easier to stay slim and healthy if you've always been that way. Research suggests that it can be more difficult to reverse damage and *keep it from un-reversing* simply because the body and mind have had that trauma happen. Once a fat cell is created in the body it never goes away. When a person loses a lot of weight, the fat cells shrink in volume but hold steady in number, which is *so annoying* because apparently, according to studies, these cells can rapidly fill up, which is why it can feel like an uphill battle to keep pounds off. So it makes me a little sick every time I see false promises highlighted in the media – to me, the word 'diet' carries more negative connotations than the word 'cunt'. (You'll catch me saying the latter, but you'll never find me professing to be *on* one of the former ever again.)

It became pretty obvious to me that fad diets didn't work, so I did what any education-lacking spawn of the digital age would do. I turned to the dangerous game of googling.

I soon learned how to tell the difference between water weight and actual body fat, the difference between the fat I could *see* on my body and *visceral* fat (the deeper, dangerous type of fat that wraps around your organs). I found out how to distinguish a carb, a fat and a protein. I even typed in 'What is a calorie?'

After a bit of digging, Google didn't really disappoint. Now bear in mind, this was *years* ago, before the internet was flooded with misinformation and purists and pro-starvation forums. There was a handful of YouTubers documenting their weight loss and there were some studies available to read; some guides to the best books on health to read; some lists of natural fibre and nutrient-rich foods that I printed off and found super helpful when meal planning. There were posts about eating intuitively and how to tell real hunger from phantom hunger. It was much easier to navigate back then before every Tom, Dick and Harry with internet access decided to play doctor.

But a week or so of research wasn't enough: I still needed professional advice. My doctor gave me a diagram of a food pyramid (eat lots of wholegrains and vegetables, don't eat many sweets, *duh*) and sent me off. Luckily, though, I knew a couple of nutritionists who I could relay information to and take suggestions from. I wish I could wrap these people in red bows and post one out to each and every one of you. It's so helpful having professional friends who you don't have to pay ... *hee-hee* – #cheapskate.

And it turns out the magic formula is a lot more straightforward than many would have you believe. **Eat better, eat enough, move more – consistently.** Sorted. Better quality of life, fewer medical bills, more energy, boom. Endless list of benefits.

I was a volcano of motivation *and* I had a strong support network at the time, consisting of, aside from my nutritionist friends, my family and my then-boyfriend (not 'Freddie', mind – this guy, 'James' and I ended up dating for six years, and he didn't give a crap how I looked as long as I was looking after myself).

I lived with my dad and my brother at the time and they'd try out new healthy recipes with me from Jamie Oliver cookbooks, go on walks and jogs with me – my brother and I even joined a gym! (All right, all right, we went for a whole month before getting *really* bored of the same shitty dance music and of having to keep rewashing our only gym clothes.)

Once I got the ball rolling, it was a slow-and-steady-wins-the-race kind of job.

I kept a food journal for the first few months to learn how to recognise patterns and figure out what was/wasn't enough food for me. For one thing, these journals proved to me that I ate a lot of the time out of boredom or stress: instead of turning to another person, I'd turn to food. *I've nobody to talk to - come here to me, M&Ms! My life isn't going how I wanted it to - maybe I'll feel better after these four chocolate croissants.* And I only realised how much I was actually eating to begin with through writing it all down! I calculated the calories of my first journal entry, and while calories aren't everything, a general awareness of them is a good starting point because too many of them (from the *wrong* foods, lacking in nutritional value) can cause problems. On a random Wednesday, I noticed that my calorie total for that one day was 3,200 (of straight-up junk food). This was a day when I'd done nothing but sit on my arse, so my body didn't need that much *at all*.

There are lots of calorie calculators online that tell you how much you're apparently supposed to eat based on your body mass index and how quickly you want to lose weight, but a friend of mine with a master's in food science *begged* me not to ever dip too low in calories or to follow these generalised suggestions. He advised me to stick to 1,400 to 1,800 calories a day *minimum* for weight loss, with a 'treat day' once a week where I didn't track calories at all (to keep me sane and to 'jog' my metabolism, so win-win). He also suggested that I eat more on days involving heavy exercise, which he encouraged me to do a couple of times a week to build lean muscle – he assured me this would mean I could eat more food overall, because the body naturally burns more calories to maintain a pound of muscle than it does to maintain a pound of fat.

Where healthy food was concerned, I first had to undo years of automatic gag-reflex face. It came so naturally to me to look at dried fruit or packets of pulses and legumes and roll my eyes – that stuff *wasn't* food to me. Like, if you'd have asked me then to choose an emoji to represent raisins, I'd have selected the crying face. To me, 'real food' was anything that was so sweet and fatty and more-ish that it had to be eaten in enormous quantities; anything that left me so stuffed that I'd need to open the top button of my jeans after eating; anything *dripping* in sauce!

I had to train myself to realise what fullness actually felt like. And I had to try out lots of different foods and methods of preparing them to find meals I could actually get on board with and feel excited about. There's nothing more tragic than the thought of sitting there munching on a boring salad full of unripe, limp things that you don't want. I never settled for unsatisfactory meals and I think that's why I really stuck to my goals to eat better food. I ate better food that I *liked*. Things like sweet potato 'fries'; black-bean brownies; wholegrain rice fried with an egg and a little chopped spring onion; whole Greek yogurt with dark chocolate; coconut oil and peanut butter cooked into oats with almond milk and brown sugar; green beans fried with red onion and rapeseed oil; mashed avocado on sourdough toast with a sprinkling of salt and paprika – a million and one foods and food combinations that I'd totally ignored before were open to me now!

I made a habit of popping into the local library with a notepad to jot down recipes from cookbooks that, at the time, I couldn't afford because I was a poor student. Also, y'know, Google!

And fitness, *Christ*. The first time I went for a jog with my brother I had to stop after two minutes to keel over by a bush and spit everywhere, and it was so windy that the spit blew back and hit me in the face while my brother cackled like a witch. Don't ask me why so much saliva accumulated in my mouth but it did, and it was horrible. Pain burned like fire through my lungs and blood pumped faster and through lost caverns of my body – it felt so strange to be standing there, a young person in these weird new workout clothes, *so* super unfit! But I was determined and I kept it up, walking more often every week, sometimes alone with my headphones and some good music (never underestimate the power of banging tunes to get you into the zone), sometimes with my family or my ex. On 'runs', at first I would in fact jog for as long as possible, then I'd walk, and this, over time, turned into me jogging for thirty to sixty minutes straight.

When I'd improved my cardiovascular system to the point that I felt like an actual human being again, and one who wasn't in the process of dying (this only took a few weeks!), I started incorporating workouts with little weights in my bedroom and I'd do things like drop into squats or push-ups while the kettle was on. *Bursting* with energy, I was. I felt like I could float sometimes and I had such a new bundle of feelings: strength, endurance, stamina.

Feeding yourself right and moving will do that to you, and when you're not used to looking after yourself it can sort of feel like how you'd imagine drugs to feel! I'd get really hyper, and my eyes would feel so much wider – like I could almost see more things in more detail – and my brother and I would talk about that superhuman feeling when we were both on track for a few days in a row with our health. I was so happy that he was on this journey to health with me – he had no weight to lose, but he'd grown up consuming awful food just like me – and his support meant the world to me. During our uni days when we'd be eating well and working out, we'd dance around the house laughing and singing Disney songs – we had so much *energy*. The whole health thing felt wonderful.

I lost about one or two pounds each week (if not, I'd stay the same, which is never a bad thing). It doesn't sound like much when you're used to seeing weight-loss TV shows where people have water-weight losses of 8lbs a week after putting themselves through roaring hell. I'll admit, the first time I stood on a set of scales, having felt like I'd worked *so hard* that week changing my usual routine, I did expect a massive loss. When I saw how little the number had dropped I felt this tight knot of disappointment in my stomach.

My dietician friend then hammered into my head that 2lbs is actually a *lot* for a human body to lose in a single week, in a matter of *days*, so I accepted that the road to healthy, slimmer Mel would be a lot longer than anticipated. A small drop, or even a maintenance, each week would need to be enough to keep me on track eating proper portions for my needs and choosing more nutritious food options.

I kept reminding myself of my newfound energy and how that alone was reason enough to feel motivated every morning to make that porridge mishmash with nuts and berries or that big green smoothie, instead of buying a greasy breakfast roll.

For those who are curious, here's a typical day from my diet and fitness routine *during* my health/weight loss journey. It was really balanced and I included all food groups (and of course, I changed things up day to day).

♥ **Upon rising:** a pint of water, plus a multivitamin and fish oil supplement.

♥ **All day:** water and green tea (because sometimes when we think we're hungry we're really just thirsty), often with slices of lemon in it for flavour.

♥ **Morning workout:** I'd usually do about ten minutes of yoga stretches before breakfast, then after breakfast I'd walk to the bus for college.

♥ **Breakfast, after getting ready:** a big bowl of porridge cooked in a pot with a milk alternative, topped with fresh sliced strawberries, chopped banana, manuka honey and cinnamon! Sometimes I'd stir in some coconut oil or peanut butter. I'd have a Starbucks soy cappuccino then in uni sometimes, with a sachet of stevia – a plant-based

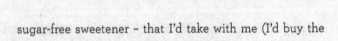

sugar-free sweetener – that I'd take with me (I'd buy the sachets in bulk from a health-food store).

♥ **Mid-morning snack:** a Pink Lady apple, some dark-choc-olate-coated almonds and some organic Greek yogurt (sometimes I'd chop up the apple and mix this all in a bowl).

♥ **Lunch:** a long, thick slice of sourdough bread toasted, topped with basil pesto, ripe cherry tomatoes, sliced avocado, chicken and baby spinach! (Alternatively, I'd prepare this in a wholemeal pitta for on the go.) Also, a bowl of soup and some fruit for afters, like fresh mango.

♥ **Evening workout:** I loved working out before my final meal of the day so I'd be able to refuel! A DVD called the *30 Day Shred*, by Jillian Michaels, made up of simple but tough workout movements, was *so* helpful in fitting in a twenty-minute workout from the comfort of my own home, as I despised going to the gym.

♥ **Dinner:** a baked potato, sliced open with a little bit of tomato relish and some grass-fed butter mashed in; a fillet of sea bass fried skin-side down in a little olive oil, topped with salt and pepper (then flipped until cooked through); and a side 'salad' of leftover wholemeal pasta with olives, tomato sauce, sugar snap peas and bell peppers.

♥ **Dessert:** a cocoa-orange-flavoured fruit and nut bar, warmed up slightly so that it tasted like a brownie, and sometimes a little bag of popcorn and a calorie-free fizzy drink (while I weaned off the sugary stuff).

♥ **Meditation in bed or in a bath:** I always kind of counted this as a workout but more of a mental one. It would help me to focus on my breathing and to relax, reducing stress hormones in my body that led to weight gain. There are some brilliant guided meditation videos/audio tracks you can listen to with headphones.

Because I worked on changing my attitude to and my relationship with food and exercise, my health and weight took care of themselves. I never deprived myself during this first attempt at weight loss – I never ate too few calories in a day and didn't cut out any food groups. I ate little and often and I *always* balanced my meals (protein, fat, carbohydrates and veggies or fruit) so I never felt hungry. I built 'moving more' into my daily routine so it became a habit – I kept it up because I just felt so much better every time I did it! And yes, it took quite a while to lose all the weight I'd put on – I'd say a couple of years, to be honest.

It went so well that I actually lost a little *too much* weight this first time and then needed to work on building more lean muscle, but my weight eventually levelled out (now) at the size I was at eighteen years old, before the weight gain, about ten or eleven stone. I'm a foodie, and I like bigger portions than I probably need sometimes. There. I said it! *I love massive bowls of pasta twice a week, smothered in cheese.*

Some actresses, singers and porn stars who are my height weigh as little as 110lbs (yes, I looked this up, and, yes, this figure initially made me feel like a lump of shite) but I bounce between 135lbs and 150lbs and I feel fine! I'm healthy. I'm 'average'. And average is OK, people. I'd go as far as to say average is bloody fantastic. I'll never be tall and stick thin but I *will* remain fit and healthy, always.

I live by my own standards now.

And I'm *so glad* I stopped waiting around for a magical pill or a celebrity to share some new crash diet secret – instead, I focused on the basics (that are, for the most part, universally agreed upon). It would be silly for me to give you a list of *rules* because, of course, there is no one way to do things and I'm *no* expert, but here's some of the best advice for weight loss, health and vitality I could possibly give, based on my own research and experiences.

LOVE YOURSELF

First and foremost, learn to love who you are *as a person*, and don't view yourself as a mere shape or a size.

CHANGE FOR THE RIGHT REASONS

Don't change yourself for some shitstick of a fella who makes you feel 'less than' because you're not in the best health or shape – *do it for a better quality of life!* Do it so you become confident in yourself (maybe enough to get away from that shitstick ...).

DON'T FIXATE ON YOUR WEIGHT

There's no need to obsess over numbers on a scale. Everybody is unique and everybody carries weight in different areas, stores water weight and builds muscle at different rates – therefore, weight doesn't account for body composition and how you look naked. Go by how you feel health-wise and by how your clothes fit. Never weigh yourself more than once a week, as the number can become an obsession. I decided that my original goal weight wasn't realistic for me and my lifestyle after reaching it, so I settled on a higher goal weight range – this might be something you learn through the process!

FIND WHAT WORKS FOR YOU

Get inspired and excited about changing your life and trying new things. You need to ease into the change slowly by doing your own research, tasting new healthy foods and experimenting with different forms of exercise. I found out that I love walking, jogging, circuit training and yoga.

POSITIVE VISUALISATION

Visualise yourself looking how you want to look and feeling how you want to feel. Assume that you'll look that way in a year or two, and you'll more than likely do things to make that transformation possible.

STOP DIETING

Eat more *real* food and don't follow fad diets – if you are going *on* a diet, it is likely you will eventually come *off* the diet, and you will regain every single pound you lost and then some. Form new habits that you can stick to for life – little things like having breakfast every day make a big difference.

MAKE FRIENDS WITH FATS

Please, please, don't be afraid of fat. I believe that the low-fat craze contributed massively to the obesity epidemic, as people started to eat less essential fats while trying to avoid the bad ones (trans fats and saturated fats) and thus increased their sugar intake dramatically. Most 'low-fat' diet foods are packed out with sugar and chemicals that cause all kinds of health problems. Including olive oil, raw nuts and seeds, avocado and oily fish like salmon in my diet transformed my health entirely. These foods have been shown to aid in weight loss and they promote good health overall.

EAT WHOLEGRAINS

Quinoa, brown rice, oats and so on are *so* satisfying! Avoid overindulging in highly processed grains (white bread, cakes, etc.) *when you can.* It isn't necessary to cut out processed food entirely – I still indulge in my vice items in moderation. I think this is a healthy and balanced approach, as it grants me freedom from the 'diet trap' and I can still maintain a normal social life, enjoying foods that I love and grew up with. Apples are good for my body, but Pringles are good for my mind. (Sometimes – hello, PMS!)

EAT MORE FRUIT AND VEG

Fruit and veggies are the perfect food and fuel for the human body. Eat them and never limit them. Try *all* of them, find out which ones are your favourites and eat them by the bucket load. Vitamins, fibre – they're incredible for you!

INCLUDE PROTEIN WITH EVERY MEAL

There is much debate on the role of protein between paleo followers and vegans, between this guy and that guy, so I won't get into it here, as I'm by no means a professional! I tried vegetarianism for two years and ultimately decided that it wasn't for me at that point in my life. However, this may change. All I'll say is that I find protein-rich foods like eggs, chicken and salmon to be incredibly satiating and I suffer less after a good workout if I include protein at every mealtime. Look out for plant-based protein sources, which are also excellent, like beans, nuts and tofu!

DRINK MORE WATER

Chug, chug, chug! Seriously, do it. Two litres a day – as much as you can, drink it. It will change your life if you're currently a fizzy-drink junkie, and its importance for the human body to function properly is often overlooked.

EXERCISE DAILY

Even if it is just walking for thirty to sixty minutes, do *some* exercise every single day. You'll feel better, you'll look better and you'll live longer. This is all scientifically proven, baby. Sure, you can lose weight through diet alone – but wouldn't you rather eat more and move more than eat less and move less? Moving your body gives you even more energy and revitalises your entire system. It tones your muscles and gives you a better shape. After I did the *30 Day Shred* DVD (oh, it's so, *so* hard at first!), I didn't weigh much less but, boy, did I look entirely different!

Strength training is imperative, along with cardio, for a healthy body. I started with crunches, squats, push-ups and so on – you can find a million videos with routines on YouTube. Do these consistently and you'll see a big difference. *PS: Get a mini-trampoline and a kick-ass playlist. Oh, the fun times I had during uni – can you tell I was a wild student? Ha-ha!*

GET PLENTY OF SLEEP

If you don't get enough sleep you're more likely to be unwell, lethargic, irritable and craving sugary, fatty foods. Plug out of technology a couple of hours before bed if you're struggling and read instead or chat to a friend on the phone or listen to music. Aim for seven to nine hours a night. Also, no late-night snacking! You'll digest your food more efficiently if you stop eating two to three hours before bedtime and you'll sleep better because your body won't be so focused on digesting a big pile of random food. If you can't fathom no snacks at night, keep them light, like a spoon of all-natural nut butter, some air-popped popcorn or a small piece of fruit.

TREAT YOURSELF

A treat day/high-calorie day is non-negotiable in my book! I needed some major feasting during weight loss, often, or I'd have gone crazy. There is also evidence to suggest that this boosts the metabolism. So one day a week go out with your family or friends to a restaurant, or get a takeaway, and eat whatever you've been craving – don't keep track in your food journal (if you decide to keep one initially).

I know you're smart enough to know that this is what worked for *me* and that you *don't* need to follow my advice whatsoever. Ultimately, you need to find what works for you – be it logging your food using a weight-loss app and counting calories, or reducing carbs to control blood sugar spikes and kill intense cravings, or following a set plan.

Whatever the case may be, we're all different and what works for one person may not work for another.

What I do know *for sure* is that it takes time to figure out what'll work for you long-term, because maintenance is more difficult than weight loss. That's something they definitely *don't* tell you on magazine covers – 'Lose 10lbs in 10 days but gain back 12lbs as soon as you go back to normal habits! BUY ME!'

Every time I fall off the health wagon I just give myself a little time and then I climb right back on. I've lost and gained the same couple of stone (28lbs) a few times throughout my twenties, pushing through different eating disorders at different times for different reasons (which I'll explore later) but *now*, I figure, what's the alternative to getting back to good habits each time I find that my favourite Topshop jeans won't close, such as after too many mince pies over Christmas? *Continue gaining and gaining?*

If I didn't stick with this stuff, I'd more than likely be morbidly obese by now. So *now* if I gain a little padding, I get right back to doing what I *know* works: eating right and exercising. There are no two ways about it.

I felt a huge amount of satisfaction and an alien sense of accomplishment when I finished my first 10k race for charity, which was actually an attempt to 'get back on the wagon' after a period of indulgence and laziness. (I'd fallen out with a close friend and was feeling really frustrated with my then-boyfriend 'James' – I was questioning my choice to stay in that relationship and felt a little trapped, so I started pigging out more often and slacking on my walks.) See, food was *always* my fallback, always there for me, since childhood. But when I started to feel unwell again and uncomfortable in my clothes, I decided, nope, screw this, signed up for a race, found some running buddies and got back in the game.

And soon again I was bouncing out of bed in the morning instead of being dragged out by my dad. Pounding headaches vanished, and after just a few short weeks I was back to wearing cute little dresses, string tops – clothes I'd only dreamed of wearing (and feeling good in) when I began my weight-loss journey. *Of course* I wish I'd felt good in them regardless of my body, but at the time, I didn't – I've got to be real. That was my truth. I didn't want to fight the world, its judgements, its standards, and I *did* want to be healthy, and with health comes a huge appreciation of self.

For me, it made more sense to improve my health than to stand my ground in a body that never felt like mine to begin with.

If you're reading this book and you feel how I felt, know that you have access to every tool you need to start changing your life and overhauling your health right now – you have internet access to research what works and what doesn't work, to find exercise videos, recipes, role models: *everything* you need!

Intrinsic motivation will always lead to more rewards than extrinsic motivation – that's something I had drilled into my head during university. When a desire for change arises inside us, we're far more likely to make change happen than if other people or external forces drive the desire. Like, if I want to text a sexy DJ that I met on a night out, if my heart is pushing me toward him, while all my friends are like, 'Nooo, chat up the bartender – she was way better, she's clearly into you and she'll be able to get you free drinks!' I'm sure as heck going to text the person I feel the stronger connection with. Get me? Basically, you'll know what's best for you because you'll feel it. If you're genuinely happy the way you are in this moment and you *don't* want to change anything or get back to a state in which you did feel happy and comfortable, *you won't*, and you shouldn't! I just followed my gut when it started niggling at me to change and I'm so glad that I did because it started me off on a long (admittedly bumpy) road to feeling good in body and mind.

Let's address the bumps then, shall we?

'JUST EATING CLEAN'

Imagine for a second being afraid of a sandwich.

Not of war, or heights, or even death – just, *bread* (and, no, I'm not coeliac).

Imagine getting anxious about the mere thought of eating a non-organic apple bought in plastic packaging or fearing gluten and oil *so much* that even the sight of a cake on television makes you physically uncomfortable and fills you with dread. Picture yourself breaking down in tears because you know you have to meet your friend at her favourite Italian restaurant for her birthday meal and you can't find *anything* on the online menu (two weeks in advance) that'll be 'safe' to eat.

During university, the positive changes I'd made in my life to form healthier habits morphed into a terror-ridden obsession with purity in relation to food. This struggle crept up on me when my life was a bit all over the place during 2010–11. My dad had moved away for a year to work in Prague and I was dealing with extreme separation anxiety – I hated not having him around, and I was worried about him constantly, thinking he'd just keel over and die. (One thing you've got to know about me is that my dad is my bestie for life.) My long-term partner 'James' moved in with my brother and me around this time, too, which was a big adjustment – y'know that point in a relationship when you're comfortable taking a dump while they brush their teeth? Yep. We were there. So I was freaking out about how to bring the romance back into our twenty-something lives. And then, of course, I had all my university exams and assignments to deal with on top of having nothing in my bank account.

When you have no savings and have to stretch your 'back to education' allowance of €188 a week to cover transport, food, rent, bills and a social life, you tend to lose your mind just a little bit.

But, I was fit, healthy, running often and eating well.

Then things took a turn. Not a sharp turn – the more gradual kind that winds up no less scary when you realise you're *completely lost*.

I'd started reading more and more into how to improve my diet *further* (when I really didn't need to) after joining a running team in uni. I subconsciously chose to ignore all of my other problems and focus on the goal of perfect health. It became my singular purpose. My undoing. And, honestly, it could've been anything, but this was the easiest thing to latch onto.

It all started when I signed up to a calorie-counting website recommended to me on Facebook after a two-week-long Christmas pig-out. (I always went hog wild over the Christmas period because my family do the typical 'buy enough food to last a year and feed an army'-type shopping trip for the holidays.) I was hoping to lose the 5lbs I'd gained with a little motivation from other members on the site. I looked forward to having a little fun losing the weight this time round, but I tumbled down a rabbit hole in the forums and all I lost in the end was my mind.

The stuff I read online included lots of unfounded, confusing 'advice': Don't eat food from cans because it's dangerous; dairy is toxic, **unless** you buy it from a local organic farmer; fats are bad; no, sugar is the devil – yes, even the sugar in fruit and you can't **even** have cake at birthday parties; we don't need protein at all – it's not important; zero carbs after breakfast is the best approach; non-organic fruit and vegetables are void of nutrition and will interfere with your body's natural systems; farmed fish will give you all these diseases [insert list the length of an arm]; and if you consume meat you should start looking for a plot of land and a coffin ... **The forum on this website was unfiltered, damaging CHAOS.**

All foods perceived to be harmful or unwholesome were demonised by hordes of health nuts. And the forums were full of links to external websites and YouTube videos and books to purchase online that apparently explained exactly *why* this thing and that thing and the other thing will absolutely, without a doubt, be the death of you.

I was quickly sucked into the vacuum of orthorexia nervosa.

And I didn't even know it. I'd never *heard* of orthorexia, and I wouldn't have for one moment considered that my approach to living a healthier life could have transformed into a full-on illness (seemingly overnight). Each person with orthorexia will have their own 'path' for safeness and health, but the disorder is generally marked by a crippling fear of 'unclean, imperfect' foods.

At that time, I just wanted to be as healthy as possible and make the right choices. I'd thought I was doing enough but all this new information made me question everything I'd come to know and accept about health and moderation. Even the word 'moderation' would make me visibly angry – *There's no such thing*, my orthorexic brain would yell.

The simple act of eating was suddenly black and white for me: good food, bad food; clean food, dirty food. It progressed *so* quickly.

Did I *really* feel energetic after eating eggs on toast, or was it in fact hard on my digestion and rotting my insides? Do I *actually* enjoy penne pasta with tomato sauce or have I somehow tricked myself into eating impure, cooked food for years, with the addition of salt and sugar? Could I *actually* just be extremely misinformed and at risk of dying in my forties? My thoughts became extreme and replayed, on loop, over and over again from dawn till dusk – as I bathed, as I walked, as I worked, as I tried to sleep.

It's proper haunting, orthorexia is. You don't know what's happening to you deep down but on the surface you project this superiority: barking at your family for using ketchup or the odd teaspoon of table sugar in a cup of tea; looking down your nose at people going about their day, munching on nutrient-absent foods drenched in pesticides. *The idiots!* You start to diagnose other people's illnesses and give them advice that you're in no way qualified to give. 'Dad, just give up meat and dairy and gluten [so that's *all* wheat, yes], *and* processed foods and soy and, oh, peanuts, definitely stay away from them because they're genetically modified and, *actually*, this means no takeaways but it's OK – we can make sure to get lovely organic veggies every couple of days from the farmers' market and I'll buy you a new juicer for your birthday so you can do this with me and then you'll feel SO much better! *No, of course you can't eat potatoes – are you mad?* They're starch-based, they just turn to pure sugar. *Well, do what you want then – if you want to get fat and have health problems, be my guest. Whatever.*'

Before all this I'd just been focusing on unprocessed foods and I never worried about eating, well, *anything*. I'd get excited to go out to eat or if someone prepared a meal for me using unknown ingredients. That had actually been my favourite thing, trying to guess how a chef created a certain flavour. I lived for it! I was just going about my life, enjoying my new healthier body and mind. And of course, like most health-conscious people, I'd go through periods where my balanced food routine would be turned completely upside down (like when I was in hangover recovery mode, or on holidays, or heartbroken, where I'd once again comfort eat and literally wake up in piles of empty packets of nachos, torn open and licked from the inside out), but as I said before, I'd always get back on top of things and return to habits that made me feel good.

Now, I was convincing myself that all those good habits, *in fact*, had never made me feel good to begin with, that everything I thought I knew was completely wrong and that I was disgusting for even *looking* at an ice-cream-cookie sandwich that way, with those big, desire-filled eyes.

I decided to try out the paleo diet (the apparent diet of early humans, excluding grains and dairy and all processed foods), then I was like, *nah*, this isn't enough, so I went pescatarian (no meat anymore, just fish), then full vegetarian, then vegan/plant-based (no animal products whatsoever), and after playing around with the vegetarian and vegan diets in various ways (because, well, my period mysteriously vanished and I felt incredibly tired and lacking, so I figured I must still be doing *something* wrong) I decided to go all out and become a 'raw food until 4 p.m.' kind of vegan. *Not good enough, Melanie*, my inside voice whispered (just imagine Alan Rickman's Snape voice), *cooked foods, even if just for dinner, aren't good for the cells in your body, you're* literally *going to die.* So then I tried to eat completely raw – meaning no cooked foods and meaning I'd need to be really organised, planning meals and shopping trips well in advance to ensure I had enough fruit and veggies in the house. See, raw foodists encourage people to eat to their heart's content to ensure enough calories are being consumed (because raw foods break down differently in the body). But, *boy*.

My life soon came to *revolve* around finding places that sold huge piles of (organic) spotty bananas and fresh dates and mangos (all tropical foods that no native Irish person like me would *ever* eat in the wild, so it still went against some of my orthorexic brain) and then preparing such fruit into massive, toilet-sized smoothies mixed with fistfuls of spinach that would bloat me terribly and make me gag.

Farewell, limited finances. Farewell, social life. Hello, constantly pregnant-looking stomach and non-stop shitting and gas and funny looks of concern from loved ones.

And even months later, when I thought I was completely over it all after talking to an eating-disorder specialist (if you're struggling, bloody well go find one), orthorexic thoughts would randomly rear their nasty heads. I'd have these odd moments of frustration with myself, often in public bathroom cubicles, where I'd hunch myself up into a ball on the floor and sob while digging my nails into my arms to hurt myself.

Like during *Vikings*.

I worked as an extra on various TV shows but the most notable one is *Vikings*, which was filmed in County Wicklow in Ireland. One summer – the summer when I first started my YouTube channel – I was an extra in the show up to three days a week. It was 7 a.m. call times and dirty olden-day make-up and costumes. I adored the atmosphere, the people; it was a dream summer job.

But.

BUT in capitals.

The food was provided by caterers. *Dom dom dom* ...

Even though I thought I'd beaten orthorexia, the act of just eating a bloody *sandwich* made by a stranger, containing all sorts of stuff I'd have previously forbidden entry to the temple of my body, was suddenly challenging again, and I couldn't pinpoint exactly why.

I made several lovely friends on the show, other extras, one of whom we'll call 'Kylie'. Part of me worried that 'Kylie' was suffering through the same mental battle as me. The kind of battle that doesn't leave dead bodies lying around; the kind that'll only bruise and pierce and shatter from within.

'Cake o'clock' we called it. Mid-afternoon, after lunch, the *Vikings* team would bring out trays full of fresh brownies and muffins and slabs of gooey rocky road. Everyone on set in the pretend village of Kattegat would go grab a treat – *one* palm-sized treat – to sit with by the beautiful glassy lake. Young women, old men and every age, shape and size in between seemed to enjoy their homemade treats – they'd sit and eat and laugh, they'd exclaim how amazing the new apple pie tasted and then they'd get back to work. Their worlds didn't implode. They'd just added a happy new memory to their mental hard drives, so it seemed. But it was never so easy for 'Kylie' and me.

We'd only allow ourselves to have the cakes on certain days, and on other days we'd be 'good' and we'd take a piece of fruit from the lunch tables instead; or we'd bring in little bags of raw mixed nuts and keep them tucked into our costume shoes for during cake o'clock. Remember now that I *wasn't* trying to lose weight at this time – I *was* eating well most of the time and in the past, before orthorexia, I'd often allow myself little indulgences to keep me on track, so it wasn't coming naturally to me to just *not want* a bloody delicious cake.

'Kylie' and I would compare how many squats we could do as everyone ate their cakes, or we'd point out flaws in ourselves and tell one another that the other was being very silly – and we'd agonise over the treats, practically drooling, and then praise ourselves for avoiding temptation. They always looked and smelled *so good* but we were exercising strong control – to remain 'pure', to feel like we were on higher ground. *Those cakes are so dirty. Those people eating them are mindless morons. It's like putting water into a petrol tank and expecting it to run. I'll live longer. I'm really winning here. I wonder if there's cinnamon in the apple-crumble cakes ...*

Sometimes, one of us would cave and have a cake while the other munched on almonds. The tension on those days (that I felt, anyway) could've been sliced in half with a knife. It temporarily divided us in the strange food-affected universe we'd manifested on set, which occupied no souls but ours.

Most people hear 'eating disorder' and they immediately conjure images of a teenager throwing up into a toilet, or someone who's all bones and grey skin and sad eyes. But disordered eating takes many forms, and the perfectionist inside me happened to fall prey to this one. It was an awfully dark time to be inhabiting my brain. Orthorexic tendencies, as I learned from my eating-disorder specialist, correlate strongly with perfectionism. When you're a person who refuses to accept anything less than perfection in other areas of your life (and although this can be perceived as a positive trait in specific cases, such as with school or university work, it can also hold people back and cause them stress when they fall short), a lifestyle in which you only eat foods that *you* consider to be healthy, and nothing else, well, that's very inviting – having rules, limits, a level of perfection to strive for. But it's a lifestyle lived out in shadow. There's no joy in anything other than the feeling of going to bed 'clean' on the inside.

Without darkness, we can't really appreciate light. I know that *now*. But it didn't even stop there.

I did get through this disorder down the line, day by day – through an inward journey, baby steps, lots of honesty, tears and support, therapy, family, my ex and recovered food bloggers online. I had to crush the part of me that felt like a failure for taking 'backward steps' to a 'more comfortable' way of living; I had to rewire my head entirely and the language I was using internally. My psychology classes at uni did help (I was lucky to have access to a lot of material that helped me to question things and to think more critically) but *shite*, man, it was difficult to nip this thing in the bud.

Beginning YouTube and involving myself with the food vlogger community around that time had been helping me to feel comfortable around food, while also speaking to a specialist during uni, and to my family and my then-boyfriend, any time I felt myself sinking. I loved to see what other people were eating online – the variety of their meals, the way they balanced things. Especially vloggers from around Europe and Asia who didn't seem too keen on the standard American diet of burger and chips, but who also didn't restrict carbs or food groups like the vloggers I followed while orthorexia was kicking my ass (people who lived off steak and asparagus spears, or thirty bananas a day).

However, while I was working on *Vikings* for a second summer, I was in full swing of filming a new 'health challenge' series of vlogs (using my first ever crappy little camera), in which I tracked my progress to get 'hot for Halloween' and lose a bit of weight I'd regained. Looking back, I can't help but wonder, even though I was recovered in the sense that I was eating foods that I'd deemed to be 'off limits' during my orthorexia battle, *was* I still suffering from some kind of EDNOS (eating disorder not otherwise specified)? I was so slim – far slimmer than I am now. I didn't need to lose anything. I *was* hot. I was holding myself to a ridiculous standard, even then. I'm not all that sure my relationship with food and health was yet 100 per cent – which hammers home the importance of talking to professionals.

Ya girl shouldn't have been posting videos about food and body image when she was still dipping her toes in the eating disorder pool. But, well, *now* I'm not afraid of sandwiches. Now I'm bloody well fine! [*2017 Melanie rams chicken-and-brie toasted sandwich with relish and lamb's lettuce into face hole.*]

There was a time, though, after orthorexia and in the late stages of recovery, during which I became a little too acquainted with the sandwich – with eating ten sandwiches in a sitting instead of just the one.

Binge EATING

One evening in 2012 while at home with my dad, brother and then-boyfriend 'James', in my pyjamas, after watching an episode of *Game of Thrones*, I had my first ten thousand calorie (plus) food binge.

I sat on my bedroom floor (door shut) and emptied two plastic bags full of my chosen 'binge foods' into my lap. My family and then-boyfriend called in to me a few times telling me to hurry up (they were waiting for me to come back in to play the next episode) but I begged for five minutes more – over and over again, for about an hour.

I blamed 'period cramps'.

Sour cream and onion Pringles, peanut M&Ms and jammy custard-filled pastries (some of the foods I'd most commonly binge on) surrounded me, and I got to work. Cramming in as much as possible – barely even chewing or enjoying the flavours and textures – I went into autopilot mode. Like a robot, my hands scooped up food and crammed it into my mouth, while I texted or flicked through Facebook.

This was *after* dinner, mind – Dad had cooked us a huge pot of Irish stew, and it was delicious as always, but my brain was *screaming* at me to eat as much dense, garbage food as possible. It craved the feeling of being stuffed to the gills, having experienced the diet rollercoaster of weight gain, then weight loss, then maintenance, then orthorexia.

My animal brain was sending out the signal: *Just eat. Eat everything. Right now.* And the part of my brain that I control obeyed. Because this overpowering urge, to feel that 'good' *stuffed* feeling, overrode everything I knew and felt to be true about how I wanted to treat my body.

I'd clearly become accustomed to finding some form of pleasure in pain, to the point that I was now weakly and willingly eating more food than my body could physically take in.

It was *so* painful, that first big binge. I felt disgusting, despicable, worthless, and I cried into the blanket at the edge of my bed. I propped my head against it – it was thumping – and I thought, *What's wrong with me?* I roared FUCK and threw things at my bedroom walls, bawling over what I'd just done.

Then-boyfriend burst into the room to check what was going on, and I couldn't even move or stand up. *What kind of person does this to themselves? How greedy am I? I'm human garbage.* I couldn't meet his eyes, and I couldn't explain to him what was wrong. I didn't want to even try. He caught sight of all the wrappers and boxes surrounding me, leaned down by my side and silently rubbed my back. He was fantastic – didn't press me, didn't judge me. He then said softly that he'd listen if I wanted to talk, but I just couldn't ... I could hardly breathe.

It's difficult to describe how it feels to have too much food inside you. And I don't just mean the sickly feeling we all experience after a-bit-too-much popcorn and a-few-too-many gummy bears in the cinema – I'm talking food that I'd swallowed that had absolutely *nowhere* to go. Imagine somehow hoovering up a football. Imagine a football-shaped mass in the shaft of your hoover that ain't getting any further up. I was essentially *drowning* in what I'd eaten. It felt as if all my bodily systems were freezing up.

That night, I slept for fourteen hours as my body attempted to digest the whole disastrous mess of what I'd done to it.

You'd think I'd have learned my lesson after that. But because I restricted my food for days after that binge in an attempt to somehow undo it (and going against the advice of my lovely dietician friend), the urges came back like a smack in the face – stronger than the first time – urges to gather up as many calories as possible and to swallow them all.

I didn't know it then but I'd recovered from one eating disorder only to walk straight into another. I was shaking its hand, getting to know it, oblivious to the danger ahead. I became stuck in this cycle of self-abuse for well over a year of my life during university, when I should have been off having fun and gaining the 'freshman fifteen' (an expression commonly used to refer to the weight typically gained during a student's first year at college or university) without a worry in the world. The act of binge eating and then restricting *completely consumed me.*

I'd walk to the store every few days specifically to buy a ton of junk food to scoff in secret. I'd try to make up for these binges by eating better food and less of it in the days following, and I'd work out extra hard, for longer. But doing this always led to *more* binges, even on days when I hadn't planned to do it. I'd just be sitting there eating a bowl of cereal as an evening snack and, before I'd know it, the whole box would be gone, along with half a carton of almond milk. So I'd decide to move on to rounds of toast smeared with Nutella. Then, when the bread eventually ran out (because it was all *inside of me*), I'd rummage through the food cupboards on my hands and knees, desperate to find the next thing (simply because the shops would be closed – otherwise I'd just have ordered a taxi to take me to and from my binge-food shopping destination of choice, Tesco).

I'd often be standing in the kitchen at 1 a.m. cooking gone-off packets of chicken noodles, accompanied by a rounded belly, a racing heart and a veil of self-hatred.

Binge eating like this felt nothing like the overeating I did during my depression or when I'd pig out while watching cartoons as a child. It was *very* different. Because a binge was never really a mindless act. I knew what I was doing – I always somehow decided, 'Well, I've messed up now so I might as well keep going,' eating more than I knew I could handle. And I hate to admit this but it for sure worsened after I realised that I could 'get away with' these binges, that doing this for weeks on end hadn't led to any substantial weight gain (due to the later 'purging' of calories through exercise and deprivation). I'd jot down BINGE in big letters across a whole day (or two days, or even three days) in my journal at the time, as though nothing else of note happened in these windows of time. *It was just a binge, that day – a total write-off.*

I shuddered just typing that sentence.

It was that same black-and-white thinking that I'd experienced during orthorexia. This time, instead of good foods and bad foods, it was good *days* and bad *days*.

I hit rock bottom after admitting myself to hospital for, *gasp*, eating too much. How ridiculous I felt, pitying myself in a building full of sick and injured people. Now I can look back and see that I was being too hard on myself, that all problems are relative and that I shouldn't have been trying to invalidate my pain and sadness. But at the time I felt lower than fleas on rats.

The A&E doctor encouraged me to have yet another psychological evaluation, from which I found out that I had somehow developed *another* eating disorder. I turned *every* direction looking for help. This was unmanageable and debilitating and embarrassing and it was ruining my life. My friendships were suffering because my friends came to associate me with five-hour-long phone conversations filled with non-stop food and self-judgement talk, and my grades at uni slid for the first time. I felt *so* guilty and ashamed and I just wished I could stroll into a parallel world where I could be normal around food. (I'm in that parallel world now. It's pretty sweet. Just had nachos and then went for a walk.)

People around me offered advice they thought would help, and various recovery blogs suggested I do this thing and that thing – that I picture my cat pissing all over a plate full of Pringles to 'interrupt the habit' of wanting to inhale full tubes of them, that I never attend shops unaccompanied and that I inform everyone close to me to 'keep me from' buying binge foods … None of this stuff helped. I knew that a Pringle was a Pringle and that nobody else was responsible for my actions. Nobody but me.

Then I found some YouTubers who really got it, people who described the same behaviours and feelings that I was experiencing and voiced things that I didn't know *how* to voice. There's something inexplicably uplifting about hearing another person say, unashamedly, *out loud*, to the world, your EXACT feelings. Just that alone – no longer feeling isolated in a weird fog of mental illness – was enough to spark my decision to figure out the next step. And then the next. And the next.

Having talked to a therapist a lot about orthorexia, I was able to re-tap into a lot of the work I'd done months before to address my thinking and my actions around food. And it's weird. For a while, I kept thinking, *It didn't work, the therapy,* but this binge-eating disorder, although perhaps a result of (or even part of my recovery from) the orthorexia, was an entirely different beast.

TEN THINGS I LEARNED about EATING DISORDERS from my THERAPIST:

1 The eating disorder chose me and not the other way around. **It wasn't my fault**. Nobody chooses mental illness – it just sort of happens. But we can choose to want to get better and to take steps toward full recovery.

2 **Recovery isn't linear**. You'll hurt sometimes, and on other days you'll be all bouncy and motivated. But that's normal.

3 **Foods are not 'good' and 'bad'**. Foods that aren't the healthiest for the body might be healthy for the mind. Don't think in black and white about food.

4 I needed to drink less alcohol. Surprisingly, I found myself drinking two or more drinks most evenings when I started recovery from orthorexia (the first time I was in therapy for food issues), which basically meant I was replacing one bad habit with another. **Be wary of switching to a new coping mechanism.**

5 **Weighing yourself daily, or even weekly, is stupid.** I'm almost 10lbs heavier before my period, muscle weighs more than fat and *I am not a number.* Checking weight or inches once a month to keep on track with health is OK, but otherwise, I learned that daily weighing is a slippery slope.

6 When your mind is in eating-disorder mode, **counting calories and macronutrients is a dangerous business**. I learned to keep track of my food without doing these things

and I shifted the focus to including a variety of colours and natural foods in my diet while also having a bit of what I fancy most days.

7 **Exercise isn't just for burning calories**. It's something our bodies need to feel good – it's great for our mental health, too. It tones our muscles. It keeps everything functioning properly. And it can be *so* much fun (*cough*, mini-trampoline + music, *cough*).

8 **There is no hierarchy of eating disorders**. They're all bad news. No one is worse than another.

9 Personifying an eating disorder in your mind can be helpful to call bullshit on disordered thinking. **Separating *me* from the disorder helped me to find *me* again** – I was in there hiding behind a wall of lies.

10 An eating disorder doesn't have 'a look'. I didn't look like I had an eating disorder. **Your weight and shape don't reflect your mental health.** I had to stop using the fact that my weight was in the 'healthy BMI range' as defence.

The therapist I'd seen during my orthorexia had helped me to come to terms with trauma from my past that I'd buried deep down. Witnessing family fights, my family breaking apart, my grandmother passing away, my first love cheating on me – I'd gone through so many things (things most of us experience, let's be real). However, my poor way of managing these difficulties involved seeking dietary control. In order to address that, we had to get to the core of what was hurting me inside, and I knew I had to build alternative, healthy coping strategies. However, I didn't really do that the first time round, but we had had a great rapport and I could be *so* open with her.

So, when I realised my bingeing had become a problem, I began visiting her again. And I'll be frank: the embarrassment levels were high. I didn't want her to think she'd failed me. But she greeted me with a smile and listened to me as I cried and offloaded everything.

I reflected on myself a *lot* then, over a period of weeks, while my diary remained based around binge days and non-binge days, as I kept shrugging my shoulders and convincing myself it was *a difficult habit to break*, therefore permitting myself to repeatedly binge. Through talking to my therapist and practising some self-help strategies she recommended – homework-type exercises and tasks that, at the time, I grumbled through because I was so sick to death of feeling broken – I began to realise that I was eating this way for two main reasons.

The first was that I was looking to suppress uncomfortable feelings I'd been having about my body, about my relationship, about my life situation at large. Feelings I'd have to own up to and let go of. Feelings that wouldn't be fixed by binges, but rather were fuelled by them.

The second was that my body was just doing its job. I accepted that my entirely human brain (yeah, sometimes I like to pretend I belong at Hogwarts but, nope, I'm *all* Muggle) has core fundamental needs and it'll take over at times to ensure that I survive. By going on so many diets and putting myself through *so* much change – what with the eating terribly, then the weight loss, then the orthorexia – I set off something in my brain that made me want to binge, because I was basically starving myself by not giving myself what I need: a consistent, balanced, abundant diet. *I control every movement I make*, I reminded myself. *I need to disassociate the urges to binge from the binges themselves. I can prevent the binges from happening. It's just a pattern that I've got to break.*

And I couldn't just jump from one coping mechanism to another. I didn't want to turn to alcohol again, or smoking (not after witnessing both my parents struggle to flush their death sticks down the toilet for God knows how many years), or some other awful thing to replace food. I needed something empowering. I could walk or read a book, sure, but I wanted something new and challenging, something that would really take me into a state of flow, something that would completely engage me.

And that's actually where YouTube stepped in for me. The first time I considered learning how to edit videos was during my binge-eating nightmare. The idea that if I hadn't gone through this grossness then maybe I'd never have landed my dream job actually keeps me going, even now, anytime something bad happens. Because wondrous things can be born from turmoil.

Most of the first videos I ever recorded never made it online, but that became the thing I'd do instead of binge-eating. So when you go back and watch my earliest videos, recorded in the summer of 2013, when I was inconceivably shy and awkward (and, let's be honest, just bad with cameras and editing all-round), you're looking at a girl who's just gripped onto the reins of recovery and is riding cautiously, carefully.

I needed to *stop dieting*. Completely. Forever and ever. And YouTube helped me with that. I started to make food videos in the first place to actually hold myself accountable – to really look at what I was eating, to put myself in the shoes of somebody else on the outside looking in. *Is that enough? Will that keep me full so I don't get these urges? Will that nourish me? But am I also allowing myself to eat the things I once deemed 'bad' regularly enough to keep me from ever wanting to over-indulge in them?* It was an amazing form of self-therapy for me.

I recovered from binge eating (fully) during my time on YouTube, before the eyes of my viewers.

I opened up about it.

And I was free.

I'm so proud to say I haven't binged in three years. (Apart from this one time that I like to pretend didn't happen, *ha-ha* ... I'll never eat another Ritz cracker again!)

I've gone through periods of eating more food during times of high stress since all this, but the emotional disease is dead. I haven't mindlessly scoffed. I haven't restricted in order to 'undo' a 'bad day'.

Though, there was something else going on throughout all these ups and downs with food, something a lot more deep-rooted. I'm a little nervous to move forward and write about this but this book is all about ditching filters and getting real.

So here we go ...

BODY DYSMORPHIA and HOW it CAN BE HELPED

A diary entry of mine from 2012, when I was twenty-two years old:

I'm fed up of this. I wish I could buy a new face and a new figure. I'd do anything to look different and to like myself. I just feel disgusting today – I'm not even going to college. I'll likely miss my assignment deadline on Friday but I don't care. All I can think about right now is how much I want to slice off my love handles and how vile my skin must look to other people and how jealous I am of everyone who doesn't have to deal with this nasty, cruel inside-head voice. My best friend Amy commented on my weight today while we were in the New Look changing rooms shopping for dresses for a night out. She said I've become very thin, too thin … I've downsized my wardrobe four times and I look totally different from when I was overweight but when I look in the mirror my tummy still looks horrible. Why do I care? I don't know. I feel undesirable. My plummeting weight and efforts to be skinny aren't changing

that and it's pissing me off and getting me down. And my FACE, ugh. Don't get me wrong: my eyes are nice and I do quite like some of my features but my skin is so off-putting and horrible. I don't understand how 'James' thinks I'm beautiful. These thoughts are starting to consume me. I can't stop checking how my belly looks in the mirror, how it pokes out over my jeans and bends and folds when I sit down, how obvious my spots and scars are … The logical side of my brain is telling me I'm being silly, that I need to learn why I feel like this and change it. But I don't think I'll ever feel differently. There has to be something I can do to change how I look and feel. I'm crying now just because I can feel a roll at the bottom of my tummy and I've been doing ab workouts every day for two months … Why won't it go away? And I got two new spots today. Nothing is working and I feel like shit.

This passage accurately depicts the mental state I was in just a handful of years ago and I actually still tear up reading back over diary entries like this. I was first diagnosed with body dysmorphic disorder (BDD) in 2011, the same year that I was confirmed orthorexic. It's an increasingly common anxiety disorder related to body image, correlating with the modern pressures faced by young people to look a certain way along with the lack of education focused on 'self-love in the digital age' in schools, often still teaching curriculums that are *decades* old.

If you experience any one or two of the following, it doesn't mean you definitely have BDD, so don't panic. However, it's important to be aware of some common signs of body dysmorphic disorder, which include, but aren't limited to:

♥ frequent weighing
♥ skin picking
♥ excessive use of tanning products
♥ brushing and styling hair obsessively
♥ working out obsessively (especially when the focus is on one particular area)
♥ using very heavy make-up to try to hide something of concern
♥ checking your appearance in mirrors very often or avoiding them entirely
♥ frequent body checking with your hands (for example, feeling areas that you consider to be too big or too small and concentrating your attention on these areas, like I used to do with the sides of my stomach!)
♥ constantly comparing yourself to celebrities and models in magazines or even people on the street
♥ seeking cosmetic surgery/having other treatments to change the area of concern.

If you find yourself doing any or several of these things *obsessively* – and by that I mean that you struggle to think straight and these things occupy a lot of your brain space – it might be time to reach out to someone supportive whom you trust for a truthful talk.

My eating-disorder therapist told me I had this problem after I communicated my obsessive worries about perceived 'flaws' in how I looked. Others would tell me these flaws didn't exist or that I was massively exaggerating them. Looking back, they were completely right! I just couldn't see it. I've dealt with unhealthy thoughts about my physical self for twelve years now, and even though BDD doesn't rule my life or mind anymore, the voice still, *sometimes*, in weak moments (especially after I face some kind of hardship in life), echoes in the back of my brain. It hasn't completely pissed off just yet and I sometimes wonder if it'll ever do a full disappearing act, but I intend to lock it out completely and that's all that matters. My *intent*.

Most days I'm fine now and I look at my facial scars and tummy rolls (I'm significantly heavier *now* than I was when I first developed this problem) and I just smile and appreciate that I have air in my lungs and that I'm alive. But *sometimes* I'll mope around in heavy jumpers and I'll sporadically look at myself in the mirror and focus on the scars and the belly and think, '*Ew.*' I want these days to become fewer and fewer until they're a distant memory. It doesn't feel like a mountain on my shoulders anymore; now it's like I'm carrying an overstuffed backpack. And that's *much* easier.

I tried to open up to my dad about these feelings when I first found out about it, but he shrugged BDD off and said, 'Mel, people have been on this planet for a long time and everyone goes through these things. I don't agree with putting a name on it – all these labels, what's the point?' and this really hurt. I wanted him to understand that knowing what it was and hearing someone confirm that it was something I could work on changing was important to me: it wasn't a case of me just lacking confidence. I wanted *him* to get it more than anyone because he's always been my best friend.

It's *very* common to have low self-esteem sometimes, because although size diversity has always been a (beautiful!) part of life, now we have one model of beauty presented to us while almost every aspect of our lives is set up so that we're inactive and eating junk that, let's be real, leaves us looking *nothing* like that model we're conditioned to see as the standard.

But low self-esteem isn't the same as what I and many others experience – even though both grow from the same soil.

Dad and I went on to have a great discussion one night after dinner about BDD and the labelling of such disorders, the outcome of which was agreeing that the act of identifying a problem you're experiencing becomes step one in overcoming it and moving past it. My dad still struggles with this and wishes I wouldn't think of it as a disorder at all – I can picture him now as I write this, sucking the life out of his e-cig and doing his blank '*pffft*, whatever, Mel, I'm not even gonna argue because I disagree' expression – but he understands that it's helpful for me to know how to identify my experiences and feelings and to feel able to open up to him (and others) about it.

When I was in the grip of BDD, and before my diagnosis, I'd get up for school or uni, and while pulling on my jeans and slapping on my make-up, the negative thought process would begin: 'every centimetre of your body is ugly, misshapen, grotesque'. And then some days the disorder would sit quietly and I'd feel generally OK. But the emotional distress of hating and obsessing over how I looked much of the time hugely impacted my ability to carry on with my day-to-day life in a productive way and I was down more than I was up. Over the years it intruded so much in my relationships with family, friends and particularly my then-partner, who constantly struggled to make me see myself the way he saw me.

I remember getting ready for an anniversary dinner with this same ex, 'James'. I'd bought a lovely new red dress, figure-hugging in all the right places. I had my hair done and spent ages shaving, doing my make-up, finding the perfect perfume to associate with the night – all that fun stuff. I look back at pictures and think, *Dayum, woman, you lookin' fiine!* But I spent the majority of the evening tearing myself to shreds. Putting myself down. Guilt-tripping myself about having dessert at our chosen restaurant. I had this heightened awareness of my belly expanding a couple of inches under my dress (because food and drinks, past-Melanie, they gotta go somewhere while your body processes them: it's temporary, ya big eejit) and I kept hiding my face with my hands because we were seated under some not-so-flattering, harsh lighting. I didn't want him to notice my acne scars or the too-thick make-up I'd applied to try to mask them.

This guy, who I'd dated for *years*, who I met when I was a few stone heavier and who'd seen me *plenty* of times make-up-free – I was feeling this new and inexplicably uncomfortable level of anxiety about my appearance around him.

And why?

Because I wasn't mentally well.

People with BDD can develop *excessive* worry about anything, from their nose to their chin to asymmetry in their face to their body shape – even their genitals. The worries will be related to perceived disfigurement, to things being 'too big' or 'too small' (as if there's some cookie-cutter way we're all supposed to look).

For me, I always *felt* tremendously out of proportion, and the acne I'd suffered from throughout my teens made me feel like a monster. Especially when a child saw me once without make-up and started crying. That stung me deep and made me want to go hide in a bin somewhere far away.

I didn't value the beauty in my own smile or the magic of individuality. I chose to focus on everything 'wrong' with myself based on society's definition of 'right', as it was easier and almost seemed like the cool thing to do, to be down on yourself. All this did was attract more of this feeling. I became comfortable in disliking myself, and that's a terrible thing to have to reflect on.

Boys and girls of all ages can experience this disorder and the constant negative thoughts cause significant anxiety, leading sufferers to frequently spend several hours each day thinking about their own area (or areas) of concern. This can vary in severity from person to person and from day to day so, for some people, appearance-related obsession can make it difficult to go out and see other people; for others, a 'flaw' might be on their mind an awful lot but may not actually disrupt their routine. Nevertheless, BDD can lead to other mental and physical health problems such as major depression, suicidal thoughts and skin picking, so it's really, really important to recognise it.

What a horrible way to live, I hear you think. Well, yep, pretty much! It sucked/sucks. Big time. But for those of you thinking, *This describes exactly how I feel/how someone I'm close to feels*, there are several things that can help a lot.

Something I've learned is that if someone doesn't want to change and get better, they won't. We need to make recovery our new reality because nobody else can do that for us. If you're experiencing feelings like those described above, try to really *want* recovery – please. Visualise complete self-acceptance and imagine how great that might be. I know I'm being all big-sister mode here but, honestly, it took me years to realise this – I think I just *got used* to being miserable. Happiness and contentedness don't just *randomly* happen. For anyone. Happy and content people just have, let's say, a more favourable starting position. We can't catch up if we wallow in the comfort zone of poor mental health without talking to anyone or seeking proper help.

I want to save you some time so bloody listen to me, OK? OK.

So what did I do to push through BDD?

A key part of it was practising cognitive behavioural therapy (CBT), which is a type of therapy that helps you to manage your problems by changing how you think and behave. You'll work with a therapist (shop around for a nice one and don't settle for Mister Magoo down the road if he makes you feel awkward) and you guys will agree on goals – for example, one of mine was to stop checking my skin up close in the mirror multiple times a day because my urges to do this were hugely interrupting my day-to-day life. I'd slink off from lunch dates with friends and stand facing public bathroom mirrors crying for up to twenty minutes. 'Sorry ... I, I think I'm constipated,' I'd lie.

The therapy also encourages you to face situations where you would normally obsessively focus on your 'flaws' so you gradually learn to better deal with these situations over time. For me, this involved going shopping in the city during the day without several layers of clothing and make-up on. At first I'd be an anxious mess and I had a full-blown panic attack during my first try – I bundled myself into a filthy bathroom cubicle in Burger King and sobbed and called my dad, who had to guide me back to the bus station because my brain emptied into anxiety-land. But eventually, I got there, and now sometimes my viewers run into me as I roam the streets with a goofy smile and a greasy messy head of hair, without a bra on and with not a lick of product on my skin. I do struggle the odd time but now I just think, *meh*, rather than, *I'm actually 100 per cent going to die*.

Self-help materials and group work are also part of this therapy process, which did help me a lot more than I thought they would, because I had that desire to get better. That desire is key. I joined various online forums packed full of other BDD sufferers and I appreciated reading about other people's stories – it's always easier to assess where you're at when you grasp that there are plenty of people out there battling the same enemy.

Also, I began an epic quest to find positive role models in mainstream and digital media and in real life – people who are self-accepting and possess that 'take it or leave it' attitude that I always find myself enamoured with. The list of women I look up to and respect is ever-growing and includes YouTubers such as Hannah Witton and Carrie Hope Fletcher, Carly Rowena, Louise Pentland and Estée Lalonde; plus-size models like Ashley Graham; actresses like Jennifer Lawrence and Lena Dunham – even comedians, such as Amy motherfucking *queen* Schumer!

Finally, I changed my online environment by unfollowing people who shit-talk their own bodies a lot because who needs that in their bubble? I filled my social media feeds with girls who frankly don't give a fuck *what* you think and just strive to be the healthiest, happiest versions of themselves that they can be, mentally and physically.

I mean, I'd much rather see people post about movies they love and products that help them feel great and, I dunno, funny shit – anything other than, *Wah, why don't I have a thigh gap? WAH!*

(If you're posting stuff like that, go talk to someone, and if anyone you know posts stuff like that, encourage them to go talk to someone. But please don't engage with influencers of any sort who are this self-hating on the internet because it's doing nothing productive for your brain at all.)

Changing your real-life environment is important too, but a bit more tricky; backing away from people who constantly criticise you for the way you look can be tough if said people are family members or long-term friends, but I beg you to be brave in facing these people and standing up for yourself. The guy I first had sex with made me *ludicrously* aware of my growing body when I was a teenager because his ex had been a ballet dancer and he kept comparing us. Let's just say that didn't last!

We all deserve respect, end of. We're all imperfectly perfect in our own ways.

So many of us despise our stretch marks and fork over thousands on expensive treatments to try have them wiped away. We try to hide them from lovers, placing our hands here and there to cover them up, turning the lights out ... But at the end of the day, they're our war stripes. They remind us that we're growing, that we're living and that our bodies made room for our curves – our indulgent Christmases and, for some, babies! They remind us that we're fragile and that we're not here forever, so we should enjoy every second of the sweet moment we have on this planet. If you've decided that a stretch mark is ugly, examine why. We've been socialised to be turned off by such human things. It's like being disgusted by elbows. It's *so* stupid.

And our bellies ... our lumps and bumps ... so many of us feel shame because when we sit down, we have a little belly pooch. But our bodies are built to bend and no matter how fit you are it is *completely normal* for your skin to roll up. We're not made of plastic. I've had a pooch at 8 stone in weight and I've had a bigger one at 13 stone, and I spent so long attaching self-hate to the existence of this belly, at every shape and size I've been. But when has self-hate *ever* been the best way to inspire change? Why not just cut yourself some slack while you work on becoming your best self?

I'm grateful for my tiger stripes and for my jiggle because at least I'm not dead! My body gets me from A to B. I don't need to look like anyone other than myself.

I've learned a lot from self-disgust and from my body changing over time. I don't think I'd love my body as much as I do if I hadn't had to walk the gauntlet that so many of us do nowadays – the gauntlet of 'I am hideous and why don't I look like the girls on magazine covers?' It takes time to change your view of yourself, but if you're struggling with negative self-image you've gotta do it. Because the alternative is to keep feeling bad, *if* you're currently feeling low about yourself.

If you do what you've always done, you'll get what you've always gotten - I read that quote somewhere the other day and I was just like, feck, yeah. Thank you, logic.

I've stopped wanting to change my body for others. I just want to strive to be my healthiest, while also forgiving myself during times when I'm not quite making the best health decisions. I like myself, just as I am, and I find that because of this, more people like me for who I am ... so I treat myself better because I like myself, and it's this wonderful loop! It's a wheel I'm happy to be a hamster in.

Ten HEALTHY FOODS I always HAVE in MY KITCHEN

People often ask me which healthy foods I always have on hand. My food shopping varies week to week; however, there are some things that I'll *never* fail to throw into my trolley! Remember, I don't only eat 'healthy' foods, but if I were to write out a list of all the junk food I enjoy we'd be here for a good five years. So instead I thought it would be more useful for me to share the staple items that I always have in the kitchen and some health benefits, then meal ideas, for each one!

OATS

Oats are a filling, nutritious wholegrain food packed full of important vitamins, minerals, antioxidants and fibre! Eating a half cup of oats every day has been shown to control blood sugar and can protect against heart disease.

I've now eaten porridge on and off for years (to tackle, ahem, constipation) and so has my dad, who had a heart attack and wants to prevent a repeat episode. I prefer the jumbo oat variety while my dad prefers his to be steel-cut.

Oats can be cooked into a porridge with one part oats to two parts milk (any kind) or water and then topped with all kinds of deliciousness (fruit, dried fruit, nuts, seeds, jam, honey, heck – Nutella even, cinnamon, the list goes on) but oats are also brilliant to use in cooking. I've made oat breads and oat pancakes; I've used oats to make homemade granola and added them to smoothies for a thicker consistency, and I've even made oat-crusted salmon!

AVOCADOS

Avocados are subtly flavoured fruits high in healthy monounsaturated fats and fibre and are abundant with health benefits, containing over twenty vitamins and minerals! They're touted as a great weight-loss food as they keep you satiated for a long time after eating, slaying cravings and (apparently) burning belly fat.

I didn't start eating avocados right away when getting into health food but they have since become one of my favourite foods, full stop! I love how plain and fresh tasting it is with a little salt and lime juice added. I always make sure an avocado is perfectly ripe before I buy it; it's almost as easy to tell a ripe avocado from an unripe one as it is to tell a spotty, ripe banana from an icky green one. When ripe, the skin of an avocado will be a dark, deep green or brown colour and it won't be hard but rather will yield to firm, gentle pressure, so pick one up and gently press – if it squishes in a bit, you're taking that bad boy home.

Apart from being one of the most Instagrammed foods in history, this smooth, buttery green fruit is absolutely delicious and oh-so versatile! I sometimes just mash half an avocado with salt onto some toasted sourdough bread, or I'll make guacamole with it using a variety of recipes, which I eat with nachos or in burritos or in sandwiches. Sometimes I slice it up and add it to a salad (this is supposed to help you absorb more of the good stuff from the veggies so, yes, please!). Some people include avocado in their smoothies and some eat it with an egg. It has a very special place in my heart, or, well, *er* ... fridge.

WILD ORGANIC SALMON

Obviously, human consumption of meat and fish is a huge point of contention – trust me, I know! When I abandoned vegankind for a multitude of reasons to instead just be a 'reducetarian' – a person who reduces the amount of animal products they consume, for environmental reasons and whatnot – I experienced the vegan wrath online! But I feel wonderful when I include oily fish in my diet (I do my best to opt for fish over meat most of the time) and I'll always choose the wild organic kinds. Salmon is my favourite fish to eat with my dinner because it's yummy, *filling* and is an excellent source of omega-3 fatty acids – brilliant all round. It's full of vitamins and protein, too!

I opt for wild organic salmon because these little fishies are nourished with a diet containing only organic-approved, natural ingredients from sustainable sources and are reared in large pens (which allow them to behave naturally) and I feel a little bit better about that. If you have trouble sleeping at night when it comes to consuming animals but also don't want to or *can't* give them up for physical or mental health reasons, just make the best possible choices when you can. It helps!

A fillet of salmon baked with olive oil, lemon juice, salt and pepper, served with a big helping of egg fried rice with soy sauce and spring onions and a big side salad is a really satisfying dinner option! Salmon is also *gorgeous* smoked with cream cheese on a bagel. *Mmm ...*

APPLES

Apples vary almost as much as people do – there are *so many* delicious kinds! Bramley, Pink Lady, Granny Smith, Honeycrisp, Golden Delicious – and they all contain a powerful blend of nutrients and fibre, resulting in the saying 'an apple a day keeps the doctor away'.

Apples make perfect snacks, especially with a spoonful of nut butter, and it's so easy to whip up a healthy apple-pie porridge with some stewed apple, cinnamon, oats, maple syrup and coconut oil!

GREEN BEANS

These tender, flexible little delights are literally the easiest veggies to eat, ever. They're full of vitamins and fibre (some protein, too) and I can pile my plate high with them – steamed and added to a tomato pasta sauce, chopped up into a bean chilli, heck, even as a green addition to a burger and chips takeaway. They're a great way to knock off two of the oul' five-a-day in one generous, easy-to-swallow serving!

ALMOND BUTTER

While I prefer the taste of peanut butter and will admittedly often opt for that (not only because it's cheaper!), almond butter has a better nutritional profile with more heart-healthy fat, vitamin E and iron than peanut butter. It's still delicious and is full of protein, which is so important for repair and for stable blood sugar – I can't get enough of this stuff! I'll dip bananas into it, I'll dump some into smoothies and porridge, I'll add it to homemade desserts and, of course, I'll eat it my favourite way – right from the spoon!

ORGANIC FREE-RANGE EGGS

When I experimented with various vegan diets, I really tried *not* to love omelettes and scrambled eggs on buttery toast and eggfried rice and proper American pancakes but, alas, I adore eggs, and they fill me up and make me feel great, so I do eat them – often – but only ever from local hens that get to roam freely and that are fed the right stuff.

For one, free-range and organic eggs just taste *far* better – sometimes you'll even see the little feathers in the box, which I think is so cute!

Eggs, while low in calories, are loaded with excellent, 'complete' quality proteins (amino acids that our bodies can't produce themselves, that must come from our diets) and these are super easily absorbed – they also contain vitamins, minerals (like vitamin B12 and vitamin D that so many of us lack) and good fats that have been proven *not* to be fattening or bad for the heart, when consumed as part of an overall healthy diet (of course, anything that's glugged down with junk food all day isn't gonna be the best!).

SOURDOUGH BREAD

Mmm, sourdough! Even just *saying* that word makes me salivate. It has become the only variety of bread I really, *truly* enjoy eating! I won't lie – you'll spot me with pitta bread and wraps and rye toast every now and again, but sourdough is my baby. The bread you'll find in any good cafe or bakery, the really delicious chewy stuff that is *incredible* toasted and topped with mashed avocado and eggs.

And it's actually healthy! Ya see, sourdough is a fermented dough – 'fermenting' is when microorganisms in food convert sugars into 1) cellular energy and 2) this stuff called lactic acid, which makes foods more digestible for us *and* promotes the growth of healthy gut bacteria! And because sourdough bread takes a lot longer to make than other breads, the gluten in it (the part that gives a lot of people who've over-consumed it sensitivities) gets broken down into amino acids, which makes this bread more tolerable for many people who are gluten intolerant. Anecdotally, my auntie was told to completely avoid gluten but she eats sourdough and never has any issues with it! So once you're not coeliac it's well worth a nibble.

RASPBERRIES

I've been known to eat sweet, juicy raspberries by the punnet. It's an expensive habit but, hey, of all the vices to have – right? (Well, they're cheap as chips when you buy them frozen, but then they're only really good for smoothies!)

I think flavonoid-rich, anti-inflammatory, vitamin-C-jammed raspberries – when they're ripe – taste so much better than blueberries and strawberries (not quite the 'ugly stepsisters' – let's go with the 'less sexy siblings' of the raspberry). I mainly eat these because they taste *so insanely good*, but also for the antioxidants, vitamins and fibre!

I'll top my porridge with them, I'll mix some into Greek yogurt with nuts and honey, I'll throw some into a little baggie with dark chocolate chips for a healthy cinema treat. They're easy to add to cheeky desserts such as ice-cream too for added nutrition!

DARK CHOCOLATE (HIGH COCOA CONTENT)

Ahh, dark chocolate – my sole reason for living. I'm sure you know by now that I pretty much drowned myself in poor-quality, sugary milk chocolate as a child/teen. Well, it certainly took me quite a while to get used to the bitter flavour of dark chocolate but now I *far* prefer it and I opt for it more often than not when presented with the option of dark or regular chocolate. It's more satisfying and doesn't spike my blood sugar, so I tend to eat less of it (the higher cocoa percentage, the less I'll usually eat in a sitting – my rule of thumb is anything higher than 70 per cent is daily dessert worthy!). And it's an excellent partner to red wine – which I drink a little glass of each evening after dinner.

Unlike regular milk chocolate, dark chocolate is full of minerals, antioxidants and flavanols, it raises good cholesterol and lowers bad cholesterol *and* has been shown to be great for the skin and, well, the brain! So for me it's a no-brainer. Be it raw chocolate or just super dark chocolate (maybe with a touch of natural flavouring, like mint or orange), I'll eat a couple of squares every single day. I'll melt it into porridge in the morning or have it with yogurt or fruit or my evening wine. It's great to melt over desserts too and even to add to chilli (it really brings out the flavours).

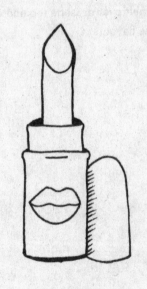

PERCEPTIONS
of BEAUTY

Section 3

BEAUTY
and
CONFIDENCE

PERCEPTIONS
of BEAUTY

My mammy always worked in the beauty and cosmetics industry. As a small child I'd watch her with fascination as she applied her lotions and potions and powders and colours. She's always been a traditionally beautiful woman – exquisite cheekbones and all the rest. A complete head-turner.

And she enjoys looking after herself and making the most of her appearance. Watching her transform with her daily paint job and hairstyle was fascinating to little me, but what *really* got me was how she'd walk out the door to work every morning. Standing tall in her freshly pressed business attire and smelling of Dior perfume, she oozed confidence and purpose. She was a badass, my mam. I never knew if it was expected of her to look a certain way because of her job, or if she did it to feel like she could take on the world, but regardless, there's no doubt that *something* about her morning routines and rituals made others (myself included) perceive her in a certain way, and more importantly, made her perceive *herself* in a positive way.

There were always boxes full of new, unopened beauty products lying around our house because of Mam's job, and I'd often dip into them unnoticed as a young one. I hadn't a clue what was in the products, nor did I know how to use them, but I loved to play with them and I developed this wild obsession with beauty-product play that has lingered all these years! I'd get so excited whenever my mam added to her beauty-product collection – I'd sneak into her room and swatch her eyeshadow palettes on the back of my hand, and try on her foundation, and even steal her fake tan to apply to my hairy twelve-year-old schoolgirl legs (and, *no*, I didn't know about the importance of exfoliation and moisturising so, *yes*, I'd be an orange, streaky mess going off to school!).

One day over breakfast, when I was about fourteen, I asked my mam through a mouthful of Coco Pops if she'd ever go into work without getting all dolled up. Just her, as she woke up – natural hair, bare face. That was the first time we ever had a conversation about how she grew up lacking in self-confidence – like me, she also suffered terribly with acne, and back in the eighties there was no make-up on tap for working-class Ireland. Like many women are, my ma is drawn to glamour. She told me that looking her best made her feel strong as a working woman. And mind you, this was circa 2002 and she was the *only* mother of my entire friend group who had a full-time job. She was a breadwinner, along with my stepdad, ahead of the game, and boy did she win that bread!

It's easy for me to pinpoint *why* flicking through *Vogue* brings me so much pleasure. I'm an art fanatic and, to me, make-up and fashion are, at the core, decorative art forms.

But of course, beauty isn't all about the things we apply to our natural faces and bodies. And aside from these tools we have at our disposal, an undeniable fact of life is that appearances *do* matter – we care about how we look for good reason. Everyone judges us on how we present ourselves. Our looks determine the very first impression we make on others. But appearance is a lottery that some win and some lose, and to deal with the challenge of that it's important to work on becoming a little more, well, wise!

A good-looking person – a tall, glossy supermodel with cheekbones that could slice sandwiches – can't exactly take credit for their genetic make-up. Just as you or I shouldn't *really* get frustrated about our own physical selves because none of us has a say in how we're born. We'll most definitely feel that frustration anyway because we're all morons but we can learn to cope with it. And, sure, we can alter how we look but, regardless, I think it makes sense to make a conscious effort to get better at noticing the less in-your-face sort of beauty that exists in peculiar places.

Our biggest problem when it comes to beauty and self-image as a society is that we *too often* focus on *too narrow* a range of features and qualities in ourselves and in other people.

I think I've always found a lot of beauty in the people I love. Not always the obvious beauty that comes with symmetry and youth and glowing skin, and not only the kind that's created with make-up and flattering outfits and good lighting: the kind that just *is*. Beauty that's inexplicably beautiful in the way that a trusting face or sweet eyes are, or a baby's hands, or a sunset, or a kiss between lovers.

When I connect with another person I look at them and feel soothed by their beauty, which is exactly how I feel when I stare at my cats when they're half-asleep in my lap. *Beautiful fluffy little buggers whose shit I clean out of the litter tray every day!*

I adore people's quirks and all the things that make them *them* – lazy eyes, long noses, big teeth, scars, sideways smiles. I just sort of woke up one day realising that if I feel this way about other people, then surely other people will feel this way about my quirks.

When it comes to dating, I don't think there are unattractive people – there are just people *I'm* not attracted to. And with a population of seven billion, why should I worry about the ones who won't find *me* attractive?

Let me tell you about my friend 'Jane'. We'll have sleepovers, even now as fully grown adults, for a bit of a gossip about our dating lives, a bitch about work, some movie time (OK, OK, Ryan Gosling time), and 'Jane' often admits to feeling terrible about herself while we're lying there fermenting away in our PJs after a mini pig-out. She uses phrases like, 'I'm so ugly,' 'I feel so fat,' 'I look like a hippo,' 'I'm disgusting,' and it upsets me *so* much, every time, because I love her and think she's stunning. I'll be propped on her bed, watching her try on different outfits, each time grabbing at herself in front of a full-length mirror, and pointing out various 'flaws' she perceives, and I'll be thinking, *This woman is astonishing – what's she on about?* I wish she could see herself through *my* eyes sometimes. So she could be blown away by her own sparkly blue eyes and the depth of them. So she could work her sexy, womanly curves and appreciate her smooth, tanned skin. (Her legs look nothing like my pasty, goosebumpy, patchy red Irish legs and – *oh no, look, now* I'M *doing it.*)

Any time I *dare* say anything against myself, she jumps to my defence, showering me with compliments. But she never treats herself with the same compassion.

Maybe you know a 'Jane', or maybe you are a 'Jane'. Regardless, most of us have a little bit of Jane inside us, whispering ugly things. The inner Jane would roll her eyes at the old phrase 'beauty is in the eye of the beholder', but this saying really resonates with me. I'm noticing more and more often, the older I get, that I see *so much beauty* in the things I was taught not to by the world. Well, yeah, in other people, but I'm slowly getting there with myself. My relationship with my own reflection and with my inner Jane is a tumultuous work in progress. But in other people, I can't get enough of wrinkles and laugh lines, and I love looking at raw, unedited images of naked bodies ... I'm going to keep believing that it's just a little more difficult to see in ourselves what other people see in us.

I mean, I'm almost always attracted to the things I've been conditioned to view as undesirable. My friends joke about my weird crushes all the time – how I go for 'unconventionally hot' people and fancy famous people and characters like Seth Rogen (especially when he's chubby), Snape from *Harry Potter* in his sexy black robes with that deep, sexy voice, Sarah Jessica Parker and her adorable squeals and her wild curly hair, and Eamonn Holmes from Sky News (I don't care how old he is – he's got that little somethin' somethin'!). You'll see these guys, and lots of unconventionally attractive men and women, on my 'most definitely would bang' list. When I'm at a party with friends, the nuances of our attractions are fascinating. I'll spot someone and think they're the most beautiful thing in the world while my friend eyeballs their similar-looking friend who I'll have zero interest in. We all perceive beauty so differently.

These perceptions manifest through, *yes*, universal standards of beauty perpetuated by the media but also, perhaps more importantly, through personal experience in our social environments – unique to each and every individual.

One of my first crushes had a long, crooked nose and a lazy eye. Many of my loveliest family members have soft, rounded tummies and brown eyes. And these things definitely inform a lot of my current attractions! I associate women who make an effort with their make-up and clothing with my strong, confident, businesswoman mother so, on a subconscious level, I see put-together women and immediately find myself drawn to this hint of confidence and strength. It's certainly not just random coincidence that I like what I like.

A good friend of mine has this divil of a five-year-old kid called 'Barry'. 'Barry' causes earthquakes in supermarkets and pisses himself at the worst times and recently picked up the phrase 'diabolical prick' from his mother, which comes out of him as 'dye boll kill pik'. Well, when I watch 'Barry' play and run around screaming and eating his crayons, I just see this beautiful blank page – untainted by social expectation, uncoloured by life experiences. 'Barry' couldn't demonstrate a truly judgemental look even if you offered him a golden ticket to Willy Wonka's factory because his likes in life haven't yet been influenced by anything. He just likes things instinctively – he's not yet endured a twenty-year media and opinion bashing.

I genuinely worry about the day when he stops watching cartoons like Disney's *Hunchback of Notre Dame* – movies that teach that appearances say nothing about the heart or nature of a person. He's a little bundle of mischief and joy, this boy, and he'll soon be twisted this way and that by the world. I look at him and think, *What can I possibly do to ensure that he never becomes a bully? Or a Jane?*

None of us is born with the view that wonky features and frizzy hair and cellulite and bumpy skin and baldness and stretch marks are 'ugly'. That's something that we've all gotta scream in the face of our inner Jane until she's sick to death of hearing it.

But just realising that I often fancy people who don't fit with the ideals that've been drilled into my skull, and that children don't discriminate against people based on outer shells, is helping me to accept that other people clearly *must* feel the same way, and that everyone else is *not* bothered by every little detail of me – by my acne scars and gooseflesh and love handles and all the rest.

Maybe, just maybe, they see – I dunno – the stuff that matters? The stuff that makes me *who I am*? My love of make-up and clothes, and the enjoyment I feel when I do a paint job on my face or when I carefully choose a pretty dress for an event. And my smell. And my smile.

Beauty varies as much as earthly languages do around the world at any time, and also through the decades, which I find SO interesting! You could be a tanned size-zero girl with perfect blonde highlights *today*, then somehow step back in time to a banquet in the Renaissance era and you'd be left in the corner ignored while all the handsome men court the fuller-figured, wide-hipped ladies – ladies who today would likely be hiding out at Weight Watchers meetings and counting down the days until they're 'relationship ready'. Then, on to the Victorian era, when corsets and petticoats were all the rage – you might feel like you don't have enough thickness to fill the commonly desired shape.

Man, sometimes I feel like I belong in the 1960s at Woodstock – roaming free and not giving a fuck.

But I'm a kid of the digital age. I'm surrounded by very specific fashions, and make-up looks, and haircuts, and, well, I like a lot of it because I've been exposed to it all my life. By the media, by the people I meet, and it's all grown on me like some weird extra limb – a limb that (annoyingly but nonetheless) helps me better succeed in the business world and makes me feel more confident – a lovely limb that I *can* be without, but it's nice to have that helping hand. The world is the world and I don't fancy fighting it: I much prefer to make the most of my time within it. I think of liquid liner and hair-styling wands and gorgeous strappy sandals as cherries on top of a ginormous cake.

And Photoshop, man. Knowing how to separate a beautiful Photoshopped image – a construction – from reality (bloodshot eyes, morning breath, blackheads, flicky bits of hair that won't sit right) helps me to appreciate such images – like paintings, which also aren't real. Your mind's eye knows what's real and it can also tell what looks particularly beautiful *because* it's been helped along artificially – by lighting, by make-up, by angles and camera positioning. Take away all of that stuff, though, the filters and the photo edits, the dresses and the lippie, and you'd still find yourself comparing yourself to others because, guess what? *It's a natural and stupid thing that we humans do.* But at least it's something we can override.

Perceive beauty in many forms and think of everyone and everything as interconnected in some way: everything that's 'beautiful' now will be 'ugly' one day in the future, or could be hideous to your neighbour; everything that's 'ugly' now was 'beautiful' in the past and will likely stun again.

Be smarter than the masses, gang. Accept that everyone perceives beauty in different ways and just because Jimmy over there doesn't find you beautiful doesn't mean that Joe around the corner won't find you so astonishing that he won't be able to keep his shit together and might even jizz in his pants just a tiny bit. Just because you don't think I'm beautiful doesn't mean that I'm not – my world and your world will overlap but will never coexist as one. But I do think we should make a collective effort to be better at noticing the less in-your-face sort of beauty that exists in peculiar places.

So get ready and style your hair however the feck you want, and strut in that big mustard jumper that you found in a charity shop. Nowadays, cool is what you make it.

Own that beauty that shines so bright it blinds.

HOW I FEEL
about MAKE—UP,
AND BECOMING
'THE ACNE GIRL'

My experience with cystic acne crops up several times in this book – it was so mentally (and, well, physically) scarring I just *can't not* bring it up, over and over again, like your friend who can't shut up about the ex she's still hung up on.

I'm composed of many things, a substantial one of which is the remnants and ramifications of my skin journey.

People often ask me how I'm 'brave' enough to reveal my skin on screen. (The subtext there is *how are you brave enough to show your imperfect skin on screen?*) One word that *nobody* wants to hear in relation to them sharing their naked face is 'brave'. Amy Schumer joked about the same thing happening to her, when a nude photo of herself went viral – people calling her 'brave' for baring her completely-gorgeous-but-just-not-pencil-thin body. I wish I'd had her current level of confidence way back when I first whipped the spots out online! My answer is that getting face-naked doesn't scare me – anymore.

Growing up with a spotty, pus-filled face surrounded by people with silken skin for *me* meant a lot of hiding and spot-squeezing sessions followed by even more hiding and a lot of crying. Throughout my teens I'd hide behind my long hair, I'd lean my face on my hands, I'd stand in the shade, I'd walk around my own home with big, creamy dollops of nappy-rash treatment smeared over my acne so my family didn't see it, but also so that I wouldn't have to look at it every time I glimpsed myself in a mirror. I thought about the pimples and scabs and angry purple marks that plagued my face during every waking minute from age thirteen to seventeen, when the acne was particularly aggressive and when confidence was as elusive to me as gold at the foot of a rainbow.

I didn't want anybody to ever perceive me as 'that girl with the terrible acne' – that was probably my greatest fear and it would keep me up at night during secondary school. I wanted it to melt away. As a teen I would've sooner run through Dublin city naked with a plastic bag wrapped around my head like one of the Rubberbandits than drawn attention to my spots. The harsh treatments recommended to me by family, friends and my mam's magazines never did shit, either. I'd try new face washes that would sting my eyes and dry my skin, and

I'd dot toothpaste all over my face going to bed only to wake up with even more spots. The make-up layer I wore grew thicker over time – I smeared foundation all over my face every morning from age fifteen onwards, rubbing it into my eyebrows and onto my lips – it was a literal mask.

So let me tell you how I became widely known as 'the acne girl' and the impact that label had on my life. After all, few other people have had *over thirty million* see their bare skin mid-breakout.

It all began one morning when I was twenty-three, as I munched on chocolate peanut-butter cups in the university library. I was working on an assignment but I was distracted by the big, painful blemish I'd dubbed 'Mount Doom' that had just come to a head on the edge of my top lip. And if you've ever had a spot there you'll know that those motherfuckers hurt! I sat there staring blankly at my laptop screen, with the peanut butter from the cups stuck to the roof of my mouth, as the day's interactions ran through my mind like a horror movie. I was certain that everyone I'd spoken to had broken eye contact at least once to glance at Mount Doom, and some people just outright stared at it.

What must they think of me? I'm a fucking gargoyle!

I permitted myself a twenty-minute procrastination break, plugged in my headphones and started flicking through YouTube for make-up tutorials dedicated to acne-prone skin and covering up big-ass pimples. Although I was already well-practised at piling on foundation and concealer, after years of not leaving the house without make-up (at this point I viewed make-up as a chore that needed doing every day just so I could blend in), I was still curious as to what products other people with acne used, and I was hoping to find an ocean of videos to boost my confidence. *YouTube has everything – ya just gotta dig.* I was surprised to discover that most of the make-up routines with 'acne' in the title on YouTube at the time, circa 2012, were uploaded by girls with picture-perfect skin – a grand total of two videos popped up from girls with active breakouts.

And those videos were oh-so-comforting to me.

I watched in awe as these beautiful girls bared all on camera to millions of people, confidently and non-professionally applying make-up with instructions and close-ups – and truth be told, although I never took much from these girls in terms of the tips they offered, simply *seeing their skin* was a revelation to me.

Those YouTube videos set off fireworks in my brain. By the time they ended, you'd never look at these girls and think anything other than, *Wow, her make-up is pretty*. They appeared completely transformed, yes, but what really struck me was they'd put it all out there, the 'flaws' – they'd shown the thing they were trying to hide. *So why hide it at all?* I thought. *If they're confident enough to show it in the first place, why are they then covering it up?*

My current view of make-up was born right there, that morning, mid-swallow of a peanut-butter cup in the library.

I'd never been able to understand those women who get ready in front of their boyfriends. *What's the point?* a voice in my brain would whisper. After a house party in my early twenties, about twelve of us woke up hungover in a friend's dank living room and I'll never forget the image of my friend 'Jill' applying her make-up within eyeshot of her boyfriend, 'Tom', in the harsh light of midday. *Surely that defeats the purpose?* my conditioned brain silently screamed. I, on the other hand, used to set an alarm to wake myself up at the crack of dawn to quickly swipe a make-up wipe over my face and reapply my layers of foundation *before my then-boyfriend woke up* – I never wanted him (or anyone) to see my skin, thinking there was something incredibly wrong and disgusting and dirty about it.

Here's the thing. Here's all that I know and believe now, and all that led me to make one of the most significant decisions of my life.

Make-up isn't, or shouldn't be, about *hiding* anything. Rather, it's this wonderful, fun thing that allows us to enhance our features to look more like how we'd like them to, on any given day, for any given situation. It's a form of self-expression and, well, art!

We don't *need* to wear it, like so many of us are led to believe during our formative years – and let's be real: there's a reason we're led down that garden path. That way, with us feeling like we can't live without the stuff, companies sell more product and make more money! Vanity is as old as civilisation itself, and multi-billion-dollar corporations do indeed cash in on that fact. Even the ancient Egyptians were no exception: they *loved* to line their eyes with kohl and stain their lips with red ochre, among other things. Mankind has been gaga for cosmetics for thousands of years. There just happen to be a lot more of us on the planet now, and companies have become genius at developing formulas and marketing them. This is all not to say that the beauty industry is an evil one or anything – it's just supply and demand. It's perfectly OK and normal to *want* to wear it and not to feel like you *have* to.

Because of my experiences as a teen, my urge-to-help-people-rewire-their-brains-to-wear-make-up-for-more-positive-reasons is strong as bricks and mortar.

One person might enjoy a lick of paint on their face in the same way another may love decorating their home and be super into interior design. Some people love to straighten their naturally beautiful curly hair because *they* prefer how it looks and feels when it's straight. They're not wrong, nor is anyone who prefers their hair to be curly. I think make-up should be treated as just another *thing* – another option available to us that some people will find enjoyment in and that others couldn't give a flying sausage about.

Please never think it's necessary that you wear it just because other people do – I mean, some of my friends like watching anime but that *doesn't mean* I should feel that I have to get into it, too! Screw that shit. It's alright to like what you like and I'm good over here with some classic *Simpsons*.

Just like I'm good over here with my make-up bag. I wear make-up sometimes, and I like it, and I really don't care if other people do or do not have a problem with that because it's nobody's business. Nobody should be policing your interests or the harmless things you do that bring you joy!

Each to their own.

People often ask me *why* I wear make-up, saying things like, 'You look pretty without it!' and those people are missing the point. If I had a penny for every time that's been said to me I'd be a very wealthy lady and I'd have bought myself the Hope Diamond.

I view a face of make-up as I do a pretty party dress or a fresh blow-dry from the salon – not for every single day, and entirely *unnecessary*, sure, but nice all the same. I bloody *adore* playing with make-up and presenting myself in different ways for different situations. Dark, sultry eyes for a romantic dinner; an intense red lip when I'm filming; some bronzer on a beach holiday. I enjoy using various shades and textures of product at different times of the year, and from *gorgeous* packaging. (Much more worthy of collecting than stamps, am I right? One glance at my eyeshadow palette collection is orgasmic at the *worst* of times.)

So to answer all the people who question it, I wear make-up because it makes me smile, for one. It's also strangely relaxing to apply, an easy way to fit in some 'me time' during which I can zone out and plan my day or daydream or meditate, only to end up having a reflection looking back at me that resembles the *me* that exists in my mind. Which brings me to my final reason for wearing it. Seeing my own face made up makes me stand taller and feel more like a #girlboss in the same way I feel killer in a pair of black tights with heels, a skirt, a blouse, doused in luxurious perfume. And I don't worry so much about the 'whys' – I focus on the fact of the matter: I'm a peacock who likes her feathers spread.

Though, as much as I love having fun with my appearance, you'll also catch me wandering around shopping centres without a scrap of make-up on, wearing creased clothing and with my freshly washed hair thrown up into a messy bun! *On the regular*. Because why not? I've become comfortable in my natural state, even though it's more fun for me to be dolled up.

I gave up the inch-thick foundation, and the burning terror of going make-up-free dissolved when I started watching those make-up videos on YouTube that morning in the university library.

I stumbled upon girls from all around the world full of passion for make-up artistry, girls who'd always happily get on camera to demonstrate their skincare routines and the process of their make-up application, without a care in the world (by the looks of things, anyway). And other girls who'd squeal with excitement over new product launches, and yet more who'd found confidence in make-up, and even some who collected it in the same way young boys in my school once collected Pokémon cards. I stopped perceiving make-up as a much-hated chore I had to drudge through daily – my perception morphed and it became this much-anticipated and exciting experimental dance with brushes and powders and pencils and pastes galore!

So naturally, when I found myself drawn into the YouTube world during the final year of my teaching degree, aged twenty-four (and not too long after discovering the world of make-up vloggers), I decided to weave make-up and confidence into my channel, which, at the time, consisted of food videos, cat videos, vlogs of my daily life and other random things.

And the response to one of my first make-up videos was, well, staggering! I recorded my first acne make-up video on a super cheap, crappy camera – and it ended up attracting *over eighteen million views*!

The first snippet, shown right at the beginning of the video, was filmed while I was recovering from a mighty and painful acne flare-up brought about by a whey protein powder I'd been taking while briefly attempting to lay some muscle onto my chicken-wing arms, after my 60lb weight loss. Several of my male friends sang whey's praises but, unfortunately, it caused my skin to erupt, turning me into a self-conscious mess and distracting me from my studies. You can be sure I shoved that big €50 barrel of icky chocolate-flavoured powder into the bin, and I moped around like a miserable sod for days. I had actually filmed the snippet of my skin just for myself – 1) to compare the condition of my skin to the girls on YouTube who had acne; 2) for self-reflection after it had gone away; and 3) to show my friend 'Jane' what I looked like without make-up, because she didn't believe me when I told her how bad it was under my foundation.

In the back of my mind, I thought that *maybe* I could use it in a future video – talking about acne in hindsight. But once the worst of the swelling had calmed down, I figured, *Why not just make a video while it's like this, about how I do my make-up to cover it up and feel more comfortable in my skin?* YouTube was majorly lacking in diversity of acne-related videos and I thought, *If those other girls can do it, what's to stop me?* Their videos had a decent number of views, so I knew there was a niche there, but in my mind they were these big, *wildly* successful YouTubers and I was just a drop of water in the ocean – a newbie drop! I had about two hundred subscribers and very limited experience with editing, recording, lighting and on-camera make-up application.

I had so many mental conversations with myself about the idea of recording the video. *To hell with it ... I don't have to upload it but I should film it to see what it looks like. Besides, if I do upload it, even if it helps one person it'll have been worth it! And who knows, maybe it'll hit a thousand views, and maybe some of those people might subscribe to me. But what if my friends see it? What if my ex sees it? They'll think*

it's gross. Nobody will get it – they'll think I'm a weirdo. Or that I just
want attention or reassurance. Well, they already think I'm a weirdo.
And maybe I do want reassurance. It doesn't matter if they don't get it.
I mean, I don't get gardening. Feck it, I'm doing it. The internet needs
shit like this. Girls should know that all kinds of people get acne and
that they're not alone in how emotionally affected they are by it. Plus
I've practised long and hard with concealer and I'm bloody well good
at blending it ... I think. I can do a fun commentary over it – maybe it'll
inspire some people. Ooh, imagine!

I had no idea.

One morning before uni I woke up extra early, dragged a kitchen
chair upstairs to my bedroom and set it up opposite my window,
facing it for natural lighting. I popped my camera onto a cheap tripod
from Argos (at an awfully odd angle, mind you – I hadn't a clue how to
straighten the damn thing) and then I hit the record button. I sat down
in front of my hastily painted blue bedroom wall, heart thumping at
an alarming rate, and, bare-faced, I turned my head far to each side
to show the spots and the hyper-pigmentation – these bits of me I'd
hidden all my life – to the viewers, aka this little camera, this tiny
device that would enable me to kick-start an entire career.

I demonstrated my 'three-step technique', showing all the stages of
my then routine. Looking back now, it was an awful video. I did *so* many
things badly – I used the wrong shades for my skin, I made mistakes
with the edit, it was *entirely imperfect* – and yet, because I swallowed
my pride and latched onto bravery long enough to push this acne
routine onto a stage viewed by the entire world, I realised that people
appreciated that I was a normal girl with no obvious special talents.
I'd still managed to make something with the power to resonate with
millions – people who were likely experiencing the same revelation
from my video as I'd experienced from other girls' acne videos.

All of my two hundred subscribers watched the video within an hour or so, and then more and more people ... I called Dad in hysterics when it hit a thousand views before bedtime (he was away on a business trip). 'That's *amazing*, Mel!' he enthused down the phone. By the time I woke up the following morning, the video had reached over twenty-five thousand views! I remember opening my eyes and grabbing my phone after my stomach flipped, and there were twelve messages from my dad: 'It's at 3,200 views now, Mel!' 'MEL, 5,000 now! Well done!' 'MELANIE, YOU NOW HAVE A VIDEO THAT'S BEEN WATCHED OVER 10,000 TIMES!' and, well, yeah ... gobsmacked would be an understatement.

The first time I tasted 'viral' felt more intensely exciting than that first initial rise on a rollercoaster – you know, before it goes flying. I felt like I was holding my breath for two weeks straight. It's not exactly something ancient man was ever faced with – an action of theirs causing an unanticipated global frenzy. The video still attracts hundreds of thousands of views every month even years later, but nothing compares to my memory of all that happened during the first million hits. It was scary and gobsmackingly amazing all at once, to go from having zero media relevance to having my face plastered over newspapers and massive websites like BuzzFeed.

I was super shy and mid-scurry through my final assessments and exams for my degree when news outlets came knocking, pressing me for interviews about the online explosion of my pimple-speckled potato of a head – a couple of them referred to me as a 'YouTube sensation' and I literally retched! *Sensation*. That tag didn't sit well with me at all – it made me feel all itchy on the inside, like people now had unrealistic expectations of me.

One evening, Dad took my brother and me out for a meal to our favourite Italian restaurant and I sat there picking at my carbonara, unfocused on the conversation. 'What's up?' he asked. The act of gathering my thoughts felt like a difficult level in a computer game. 'I'm just really stressed. I feel like people's eyes are on me, people who don't know me and who shouldn't matter to me but they do, and all I have time to do is study and finish writing my thesis ... I can't live up to all this ... I'm crap at make-up anyway ... I can't delete the video now because other people have stolen it and re-uploaded it ...' And then I bawled into my pasta. Nobody can really prepare you for the emotions that wash over you when your acne-drenched face is plastered all over mainstream media, when you only ever intended it to be seen by *other people with acne* – or at least people who watched YouTube, people who would understand.

I kept thinking it couldn't go any further but it just kept snowballing, and *then* I got an email from Channel 4, a hugely popular TV station in the UK, looking for me to go on their show *Embarrassing Bodies* (which I watched keenly every single week, without fail, after dinner, forever hoping to see footage of other people's acne problems). They wanted me to talk about the success of my video and do a piece on how much I was helping other acne sufferers.

I kinda sorta lost my shit.

In the very best of ways.

I agreed to do it through happy tears and ran laps of my living room screaming and jumping and making a noise that sounded a bit like 'hhhuuuuooooooohmygawwwwd!'

If it's good enough for Channel 4, imma quit feeling ashamed.

All the media attention led to me quickly becoming known as, and referred to as, 'the acne girl' by pretty much *everyone*. I'd be wandering around Dublin city with my brother and a stranger would stop us and ask, 'OMG, are you the acne girl? OMG!' I'd overhear friends engaging in phone calls and saying things like, 'I'm with that girl from YouTube, you know, the one with the acne ...' and on a night out in university, this guy I thought was checking me out was actually trying to figure out if I was 'the acne girl' so he could take a photo with me to send to his little sister who watched my videos.

How has this happened? How have I come to be defined by the very thing I spent years of my life fighting against being defined by? And how come I kind of ... don't mind?

The initial feedback was so warm and encouraging, people would comment things like:

> *I can't tell you how much this means to me! Watching this has relieved me of so much anxiety about my skin problems ... I'm not alone. I've never felt that before. You are beautiful inside and out, thank you so much for daring to bare and for the helpful tips! Much love. PS: are you Irish or Scottish!? Your accent is adorable! Xxx*

> *You wonderful human being! It's so important for young girls to have role models like you, people brave enough to show the world that it's normal to suffer from spots and scars. You are imperfectly perfect and this is one of the most uplifting make-up related vids I've seen yet! I'm subscribing! (Not only because of your pimples, lol, but because of your personality and the light that shines from your eyes and smile). Big hugs from Paris!! <3*

However, with more eyes on the video came more negative comments, more cruelty – more internet trolls:

> *EWWWWWWWW imagine waking up next to that? I'd kick her out of my bed and light her on fire.*

I think I'm about to vomit all over my keyboard – what in God's name is that creature!? You're so ugly. KYS. [I've learned that *KYS* stands for kill yourself – a despicable thing to say to anyone.]

If you dared me to eat dog shit or kiss her I'd get out my knife and fork and salt and I'd eat the bloody dog shit. Grossssssss.

What is with you ugly girls and your make-up tricking us guys to talk to you … I would die if I got home with a girl and she looked like this.

Take a bitch to the pool on the first date.

THAT SHIT'S NASTY YOU MINGER!! Why am I watching this? I need disinfectant for my eyes, ughhh.

It's funny, really, how all this impacted on me.

At first, *yes*, I cried over mean comments. I questioned myself. I wanted to delete and block the people who wrote them. I *almost* deleted the video so I could eventually pretend like it never happened.

'But the thing is, Mel,' Dad started one day as I lay curled up in a ball on the sofa, 'the positivity far outweighs the negativity, and you're the one always telling me to focus on the positive! Well, practise what you preach! Do you think any successful person has made it to where they are now with everybody liking them? With nobody saying a bad thing or starting a rumour or judging them?'

Dad was so right, as always. The video currently has 155,000 thumbs-ups and only 6,000 thumbs-downs and, after re-reading *The Secret*, which I discussed in the first section, I decided to focus on the positive comments and the lovely feedback, on the people the video was *helping* and not on those using it to anonymously vent their disgust or as a vessel to unleash their darker qualities.

'You're just the current target for these losers. Tomorrow, there'll be something else. There are always going to be people like that and you can't let them win!'

Dad helped me to draw on all of the positive messages and emails and articles to fuel my creativity and my drive to keep helping people and to keep pulling back layers of myself online.

Suddenly, as 'the acne girl', I had lots of new people flying into my life like moths, with me as this big torch of emotion and passion and motivation. People who wanted to befriend me, and film videos with me, and get to know me because they trusted me, because I'd trusted them – and everyone – with this delicate insecurity.

In becoming 'the acne girl', I'd shed my facade and cleared a path for people to come closer to me, for the kind of people I'd always longed to have around me to enter my life. I'd also cleared out the cobwebs of the part of my brain that, as a child, played home to *confidence*. Showing my biggest flaw on the internet made me completely accept it, because it meant there was nothing left to hide. And I started believing in my capabilities to do good things – to make things, to share things that would inspire and resonate with others all around the world. Reading through the ten-thousand-odd comments under the video, from fans and bullies, from Asia and from around the corner, it dawned on me that we *all* have scars. Scars are a by-product of life – some are physical, yes, but others are emotional or mental. Some scars are too painful to discuss or even reveal – which is why so many people lash out at others, especially online. They're hurting deep down.

I've come to appreciate the scars on my face in a new light – they're battle scars. I battled low self-esteem and societal judgement for ten years all because I suffered from a skin disorder that affects over 80 per cent of the population! But I won the battle. I know I've won because I wouldn't give up a single one of the valuable lessons I learned from getting these scars in the first place for any judgemental twat in this world. My scars remind me of what I've been through and how resilient I am. They remind me to be careful in the future, to look after my skin (good food, lots of water, lots of sleep, stress management, skincare, yada yada). Each scar on my face helps me to empathise with others who have similar scars or areas of concern – having gone through the whole argh-everyone-thinks-I'm-an-actual-swamp-monster phase, I completely get it when people around me express through either their words or body language that they're uncomfortable, and I do things to make them more comfortable. My subconscious makes me work to distract them from their own insecurities. And my scars prove my body's capacity to *heal* – if there wasn't a huge scar on the top of my right cheek, there'd still be a giant pimple.

I've made it to the other side of the acne tunnel. I was a girl with acne, and then I was 'the acne girl', and to some people I'll always be that – but who cares? Because now I'm a girl who *used to* have acne but who has a whole lot more going on that's infinitely more interesting than a skin condition. I'm that girl who champions body positivity and self-care online, spurring major conversations with enthusiasm and honesty. And it's pretty damn nice to know that I flourished in the face of uncertainty and internet hate. I'm self-assured, I'm thriving, and would I be here if I hadn't first become known for having acne? Probably not.

And for those wondering how I finally got rid of acne for good, here's a condensed version of my clear skin checklist, which I uploaded to YouTube in 2015 and which has since helped *a quarter of a million people*!

CLEAR skin CHECKLIST

1 **Drink plenty of water!** Two to three litres a day (including teas) – jazz it up with mint, lemon or fruit.

2 **Manage stress** through meditation, yoga, walking, deep breathing and journaling.

3 **Test for food intolerance** by tracking intake, then eliminating and reintroducing foods that are commonly linked to acne to see if you notice a difference (dairy, gluten, soy and whey powders are all common culprits). Then learn to manage your diet by finding alternatives and limiting consumption while your skin clears up.

4 **Eat the rainbow!** Consume lots of fresh fruits and vegetables, but also healthy fats and proteins – the skin needs these things, and micronutrients, to look its best. Think of your body as a car: feed it the correct fuel. I take supplements too, just as a precaution, usually an evening primrose oil capsule and a high-quality multivitamin.

5 On this note: **avoid yo-yo dieting** – and dramatically yo-yoing in your exercise routines. Not many people consider this, but the hormone changes in your body when weight is being lost and gained can affect your skin a lot, particularly if you're a teenager and already going through hormonal changes.

6 **Avoid picking!** Squeezing and picking never improves skin and can lead to much worse hyperpigmentation (the marks left over after spots go away), which can stick around for one to two years.

7 **Have good hygiene** – regularly change your pillowcases, and keep your hands clean for any times you may be touching your face.

8 Develop a solid and consistent morning and evening **skincare routine**. Find products that work for you (do your research) and use them consistently for a couple of months, as it can take a while for the skin to adjust. We often think that just because the products are sitting by the sink they're getting used. But nope. *Actually use them!*

9 **Keep active!** Exercise increases blood circulation to your face. It sends oxygen to your skin too and carries waste away. It also cuts stress (which can contribute to breakouts).

10 Get at least seven to nine hours of **sleep** every single night. They don't call it beauty sleep for nothing ...

GiViNG UP ON PERFECtiON *and* #GOALS

I remember this guy I liked when I was a little kid calling another girl in class 'perfect'. The jealousy I felt stung my cheeks and made my guts churn. Her name was 'Sarah' and she had poker-straight, shiny blonde hair, smooth, tanned skin, bright-blue eyes and the cutest pink accessories: a pink schoolbag, hair scrunchies and socks. She was also funny and smart and had the sweetest-sounding voice in the universe. Next to her I felt like Gollum from *Lord of the Rings*.

I focused on every feature and trait of mine that was different from hers and told myself, *You're imperfect, you're disgusting, you're weird and people will never like you the way they like Sarah*. In fact, looking back, I probably just fancied 'Sarah'! (#bisexualrepression, am I right?). But kid-Melanie (who was terrible at maths and had a weird sense of humour that only seemed to make old people laugh) stared at her own reflection, at her naturally frizzy brown hair, her asymmetrical face, her big ears and her birthmark on her neck, wanting to change everything about herself. Because my then-crush had liked the 'perfect' girl, I'd deduced that in order for people to like me I needed to be perfect.

As a teenager, I felt entirely imperfect always. People my own age picked on me when I was about fourteen, pre-curves, tall and lanky, telling me I looked 'like a boy', which, aside from reinforcing gender norms, sparked my self-consciousness. Because other people told me I *looked* wrong, I just ... *felt* wrong. I believed my talents weren't good enough (whatever 'good enough' means anyway), that my physical self was hideous and my personality was embarrassing and annoying. When I spent time with myself or saw photos of myself taken at family events, I just thought, *Ugly, dull weirdo with nothing special to offer the world*. It deeply upset me to feel that way.

And the more I thought of myself as useless, the more useless I became – all I'd do was mope and wallow and complain. I was locking myself in a black misery bubble of my own creation because I didn't know any better.

'You're special,' I was told a lot by family members and teachers growing up. *But in what way?* I'd think. *What does it even mean to be special? Isn't everyone special? Or is nobody special?* My head was all over the place as a teen, so I opted to hide away under big baggy clothes and layers of foundation and curtains of hair, thinking that would be barrier enough between me and everything and everyone else. *Maybe people keep telling me I'm special because I'm not perfect and they just don't want me to feel bad?* Thoughts like this made me desperately want to achieve perfection, feeling like then I'd be happy and accomplished and everything would be glittery and shiny and magical.

I figured that if I dyed my hair to match what was trending and changed my face and style to look more like a cover girl and got a hot boyfriend or girlfriend to show off then I'd be a better person and people would like me more. I was oblivious to (or just didn't care about) two very important facts, though, that many teenagers of the digital age don't seem to understand: 1) your looks, personality and possessions don't define you, *your actions do*; and 2) *perfection doesn't actually exist.* It's subjective, because its definition depends on a person's moral, social, personal and cultural standards and their unique view of the world.

My #goals may be entirely different to your #goals. What I view as perfection now is *im*perfection, but Mary around the corner may disagree with me – she might yell that Victoria's Secret model status is what all of us *should* strive for, then yell that I'm pandering and call me an idiot. And, she'd be entitled to do so, and I'd just smile and get along with my day.

The feeling of not being good enough crippled me and ruled my life for years. Sometimes, now, I just stand bare-arsed in my room smiling at myself in the mirror – at my squidgy love handles and my stretch marks and my asymmetrical boobs, and I think, *How shit would it be if I still felt I had no choice about liking myself?*

Seriously, I wouldn't sing in front of people or allow others to read poems I'd written. I wrote this poem called 'Reflection' that I used to think was the best piece of art ever created by a human. I'd do dramatic readings of it to myself, making the right expressions at the right times, like a proper little actress wannabe, and I so badly wanted to hear what other people thought of it, but I *never* felt like I, nor anything I came up with, deserved anyone's time. I didn't really do anything for the simple joy of doing it; somehow I'd learned that things were only worth doing if other people approved. And rather than reading out my poem *in case* people liked it, I decided, nah – the odds of judgement and rejection are far too vast and terrifying. And rejection and judgement are the worst things ever, right? (Answer: no, past-Melanie, your thinking sucks.)

Me. Sixteen. School holiday, Venice, Italy. I remember so little of this trip, my first time abroad. And that makes me ache with sadness. I was so down on myself the entire time. The plane journey over to Venice is a blur; I refused to try any of the Italian food once we'd landed; I refused to wear loose or revealing clothing to keep cool in the hot climate, so I was a sweaty mess in big black band T-shirts and heavy rocker boots. *Not* Italian-summer appropriate attire. I also remember wishing I didn't have to go in the first place, anticipating days of comparing myself to *them* – my classmates. Specifically, one group of girls who everyone in school wanted to be like. You know the ones – we all relate to *Mean Girls*, right? I just knew I'd end up judging myself harshly for being single while they gossiped about their relationships; glaring at my stomach and my spotty skin in the mirror after jealous stare-athons at their long, lean limbs in their summer shorts, at their glowing make-up-free faces.

My reality of the trip was not *the* reality of the trip. Looking back now at the few photographs taken while we were in Venice, we *all* look great. Like young, healthy teenagers. Nobody looked terrible; nobody looked like a supermodel. But trapped in my sixteen-year-old mind, it was beauties (them) and the beast (me) – they were #goals and I was not, and everything sucked and I couldn't wait to go home. Goodness, I'd give anything to relive that trip as current me!

The first time a guy told me he thought I was perfect just as I was, or the first time a girlfriend complimented me using the word 'perfect' to describe my hair, I shot down the compliments as white lies. I didn't understand or respect that their view might just be different from mine. *No way in the universe could there be people out there who think I'm wonderful and great and fine as I am! Pfft.* I think it was during my mid- to late teens that I first began to grasp the concept of 'walking in another person's shoes', a tough thing to wrap your brain around. It's much easier said than done. To really take a step back and engage your imagination even the tiniest bit to *try* to understand what it must be like to be someone other than you for a moment: that takes practice, a *whole* lot of practice.

I went to Portugal with my first long-term boyfriend 'Freddie' for my eighteenth birthday. The idea of this trip filled me with so much dread that I almost didn't go. We'd been dating for two entire years and he still hadn't seen me without make-up or completely naked in the harsh light of day! The fear of his judgement stood in the way of me enjoying one of the best times of my life. I'd just finished school, I was young, free, healthy, my skin wasn't even doing so badly at the time, yet the thought of being make-up-free in a bikini in front of the guy I was infatuated with made me convulse.

I knew what kinds of celebrities and porn stars he found attractive and I never felt like I measured up.

We had a massive argument one night, in the house we were staying in. I'd locked myself in the bathroom because he'd been having a go at me about taking my make-up off to go to the beach. 'The sun and the sea water will be great for your skin!' he'd said. 'All that foundation will do you no good – nobody else wears make-up to the beach! Come on out, Mel, you look beautiful and I love you, acne or no acne.'

All I heard was, *You have acne and I know it and now I've said that word out loud and acknowledged it.*

I'd also spent two hours getting in and out of my bikini, trying to figure out how to hide my tiny tummy rolls and mask the fact that one of my tits is bigger than the other. When I pointed these issues out to him, standing with a face like a smacked arse in front of the full-length mirror, he didn't deny their existence but simply said, 'Eh, well I love your body.'

Doesn't matter! He's not denying that he can see these imperfections!

Small things like that would send me into a state of existential crisis. I just didn't know how to see things from his point of view. I couldn't understand and didn't even want to try, so I doubted and distrusted instead.

I recently got to exercise my new 'inside someone else's brain' muscle while hosting a YouTuber chat show. (Yep, me, hosting! I'm basically Oprah now.) With my guests, I got to delve into fashion and beauty oddities from around the world that make each culture unique, from WILD fashions in Tokyo to waist-training in New York. In every new episode I was challenged to view beauty and perfection from the perspective of the people featured. The variety in viewpoints and opinions scrambled my brain into a big pile of candy floss.

We talked about this one tribe whose women are known for wearing neck rings, brass coils that are placed around the neck, appearing to lengthen it. The appearance of a long neck is a beauty ideal within this tribe, yet I've never once looked at someone and fancied them or thought differently of them because of *the length of their bloody neck!*

Exploring the many faces of perfection in the beauty industry helped me to really reflect on the word *perfect*. Sure, what we see as perfect or #goals may be influenced by media and by our own culture, but if we don't fit into a narrow definition, we can tweak it and broaden its horizons and create a beautiful new mindset of self-embracement.

I don't know about you, but I don't fancy waiting for the grave feeling useless because I'm not a Victoria's Secret model – what's the point?

When I'm lucky enough to find myself in another country with a bit of time to kill, I go to a local cafe or restaurant or food market, and I people-watch. It's my favourite thing ever to do. The best pastime. I love it even more than bubble baths and lying on the floor with our family cats and eating chocolate cake. There's so much value in stepping out of the inner workings of our own brains sometimes. There are billions of people around us living other realities.

Sixteen-year-old Melanie knew nothing of why the neck-ring-wearing women did what they did to acquire a perfect beauty celebrated by their own tribe. Teenage me would either have used this knowledge as bad-joke material or been so afraid of the information and how it threatened my own reality that I'd have brushed it under a rug as something that didn't matter. The reality I knew and cared about involved fake tanning and diet pills and teeth bleaching and false eyelashes and repressing my personality and being what I thought others wanted me to be.

I still remember my horse-riding friend who lived just down the road and didn't really follow any of the same media as teenage me. She *never* felt the urge to perfect herself to appeal to others – she was happy to wear hand-knitted jumpers and pigtails and to smell of stables. She always had a smile on her face.

I'm taking steps *all the time* to move away from that drive to be identical to others and to have a cookie-cutter life and personality, from existing just to abide by stereotypes and formulas. Life is so mundane when you're trying to live someone else's truth. I figure out who I am when I colour outside the lines – fuck forcing an Instagram aesthetic if it doesn't come naturally. (Mine is literally just pictures of my cats and food and pretty trees and the odd selfie of me in the same-old same-old make-up look.) I'm happier when I'm not trying so hard to fit the mould. It's all I ever used to do, and now it's the last thing I can imagine even *trying* to do ...

It was small realisations like this building up over time that slapped me in the face, waking me up and making me understand that, while there are sought-after ideals, there's *so* much more to life than the constant effort to fit between their narrow borders. Let go of the concept of perfection and #goals. *You* define what is perfect to *you*. We all desire different qualities and characteristics and we all like different things, so we shouldn't feel like *just because* someone else thinks something is #goals that we need to conform.

Bad BEAUTY HABITS

Yo, listen up guys, ladies and non-binary lovelies – you have my permission to tear this page out and stick it on your fridge. I mean, tattoo it onto your forearm. Maybe swallow the page and absorb its information into your cells.

1 **Sleeping with your make-up** – it's a silly and lazy thing to do.
2 **Slouching** – stop it.
3 **Wearing too much perfume** – *less is more*. Catching a subtle hint of scent when near someone is much more alluring than choking on their Chanel when they're feet away.
4 **Biting your nails and biting your lips** – use icky-tasting lip balms and nail glosses.
5 **Squinting** – it can lead to premature wrinkling. Get your eyes tested. (I need glasses when I'm working at a laptop or reading and, hey, glasses are feckin' adorable.)
6 **Picking at and squeezing spots** – this always makes red and purple hyperpigmentation marks stick around for much longer than they would've otherwise, and/or it leads to a worse, deeper pimple issue!

7 Attempting big hair-dye jobs at home – they rarely end well. Trust me, you'll save so much money in the long run if you see a profesh! (The number of times I've given in to these urges to do DIY jobs on myself, only to stare afterward at my frizzled hair in regret ... the memories *pain* me).

8 Peeling off your nail polish or pulling off acrylic nails – remove them properly.

9 Using tanning beds – *no no no no no*: dangerous! If you must, use fake tan.

10 Using dirty make-up brushes and sponges or gone-off make-up – wash your brushes regularly and throw out any make-up once it's out of date.

REASONS WHY I'M PROBABLY *the* WORST PERSON ALIVE *to* GIVE BEAUTY ADVICE

1 I never plan outfits for the week ahead of time and I don't fold or iron any of my clothes *ever*.

2 I can forget to clean my make-up brushes for months on end and I never throw away make-up that's past its use-by date (even though, yes, I *just* told you guys never to do this in the last section – but we all knew going into this that I'm only *almost* fully functioning!).

3 I sometimes use face masks right before big events, forever forgetting that they draw spots out to the surface.

4 I never wake up early enough to make a nourishing breakfast *and* do a good job on my make-up – one always gets sacrificed (usually the make-up job because ya girl needs a solid 10/10 breakfast and home-brewed coffee).

5 I almost always lose one half of my matching underwear sets and end up in a red bra with black knickers, even though nothing makes me feel more put together than a matching set.

6 I never remove my nail polish before it gets to the hiding-hand-in-sleeve stage.

7 I hardly ever change my bedding, figuring that because I shower every night it's somehow OK and that I'm *not* lying on top of millions of dead skin cells – just *shh*, OK?

8 I'm always out of sanitary towels every time my period comes and end up having to bunch up tissue paper in my knickers until I can get to a shop.

9 I only notice that my tights are laddered while getting ready for a big night out and I *never* keep backup pairs on hand – because I'm an idiot.

MY ALL-TiME FAVOURiTE LOTiONS and POTiONS

Moving *swiftly* on now that I've aired my filthy 'I suck at this stuff' laundry, these are the things I'm never caught without. I'm only listing products here that I've purchased over and over again, because I figure if something is good enough for me to re-fork out my hard-earned cash for then that something is worth celebrating and making other people aware of. Bitch ain't here to hog all the good stuff.

While I do always play around with products, I *need* my dependables, and I've yet to find better versions of these things.

♥ **For my skin:** Sunday Riley Good Genes All-In-One Lactic Acid Treatment, Sunday Riley Juno Hydroactive Cellular Face Oil and Vichy Aqualia Thermal Serum (these keep my combination skin soft and smooth and help my hyperpigmentation marks to fade).

♥ **For my eyes:** Kiehl's Creamy Eye Treatment with Avocado (so thick and creamy – it's my go-to eye cream for when the skin around my eyes feels tight and dry).

♥ **For when I get spots:** Lush Mask of Magnaminty or

raw manuka honey applied topically. Also any skincare containing either benzoyl peroxide or salicylic acid (all of these things help to fight existing spots, but they can't stop them from coming – that needs to happen from inside out. See my clear skin checklist on page 171).

v For moisturising my body: Roger & Gallet Gingembre Firming Sorbet Body Lotion or plain extra-virgin cold-pressed coconut oil added to my bath water (nothing makes me feel more comfortable than having smooth, hydrated skin all over my body).

v For my hair: Moroccanoil original treatment and OGX coconut milk shampoo and conditioner (my hair is naturally dry and frizzy on the ends and the roots become greasy rather quickly, so I'll only apply oil to the ends of my hair and I try not to over-wash my roots/hair, opting for dry shampoo between bi-weekly washes).

v For my hands: L'Occitane Lavender Hand Cream (I love the scent of lavender – it's super calming – and this does a great job of keeping my hands soft).

v For my lips: Rosebud Perfume Co. Smith's Rosebud Salve (it has a rosy tint which makes lips look plump and healthy).

v For my lashes: Benefit Cosmetics Roller Lash (I can't find a mascara to beat this for daytime wear).

v My favourite red lipstick: MAC Ruby Woo (a classic, loved by so many celebs – it's drying, but the colour payoff is worth it).

v My favourite nude lipstick: Charlotte Tilbury's K.I.S.S.I.N.G. lipstick in Penelope Pink (Charlotte Tilbury is a wonderful top-quality cruelty-free brand, if you're looking for a high-end make-up company that doesn't test on animals).

- ♥ **For my base:** NARS All Day Luminous Weightless Foundation (a gorgeous fragrance-free formula offering natural-looking matte coverage for oily or combination skin).
- ♥ **For my concealer:** Collection Lasting Perfection Concealer (I always buy this in number one, the lightest shade, because it's so pale and thick and blendable, perfect for under my eyes and highlighting).
- ♥ **For bronzing:** The Body Shop Honey Bronzer (I never go wrong with this when I want to look like I've had a touch of sunlight).
- ♥ **For highlighting:** BECCA Shimmering Skin Perfector Pressed Highlighter in Moonstone (I adore this powder to little pieces).
- ♥ **For my blush:** NARS Orgasm (sex cheeks, my friends).
- ♥ **For lining my eyes:** Rimmel London Exaggerate Liquid Eyeliner (it's just so foolproof and cheap!)
- ♥ **For my eyeshadow:** Urban Decay Naked 3 Eyeshadow Palette (I'm all about my pinks and coppers, as of late, plus these shades are just so wearable and dynamic, especially for us fair-skinned humans).
- ♥ **For my nails:** polishes in various shades, and nail strengtheners, by Sally Hansen (I change up the colour depending on the season, opting for lighter shades in summer and darker berry and red tones in winter).

HOW to FEEL GOOD NAKED

I know it can be terrifying to get your bits out for a new person. Or even for someone you've been with for *years* who you've forced, to this day, to put up with lights-off, under-the-covers action, just because you're not confident about how you look.

I remember the terror *well*.

Having sex with someone, *good* sex, is to experience a shared, mental nakedness, which we can only really achieve through concrete trust and mutual respect. But it's common to feel insecure getting *physically* naked when it comes to doing it, like, full-on, tits-flailing-in-open-air naked. I'm the first to admit that I find it a whole lot easier to reach a state of readiness to be vulnerable and naked with someone I trust when I'm feeling good in the skin I'm in, when I think that I look the best that I can, in any given moment, *nude*.

It's near impossible to summarise how to reach that state of 'OK, I'm good! Let's go!' so that you're not lying there in the nip with someone while your mind darts from *I look fat,* to *Is that stubble on my knee?* to *How clean is my vagina? Did I wash it long enough? What if it smells funny?*

But I'm gonna try!

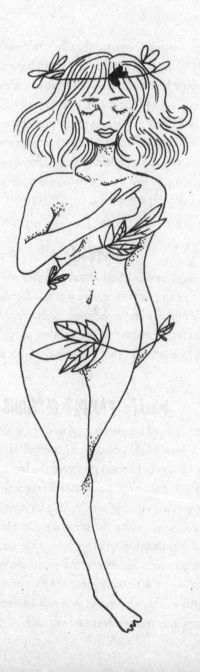

I have asymmetrical breasts. (My left tit was lovingly dubbed 'cycloptic boob' by my first boyfriend.) I also have acne scars, stretch marks, wild brown hair and an apple-shaped 'skinny fat' body type. But I'm very big on self-care and I do my absolute best to avoid allowing this shell of me to distract me entirely from *inside-me*, the me living in that shell who is an *actual person* who wants to be capable of, well, *getting screwed* and mind-fucking someone else into oblivion whilst being present to experience the visual splendour of it all!

Here's how I accomplish this.

MUSIC

I've had a lifelong love affair with music. I'll play sexy music while I set up for my weekly pamper session, every single Sunday evening! I create playlists of different genres for different moods and this really helps me escape into that far-off realm that music takes us to. When I'm there, it's easier for me to visualise and experience myself in different ways.

Weekly PAMPER SESSIONS

These pamper sessions set me up for a week of feeling proud about my body. I apply a face mask; I soak in a bath full of salts and bubbles; I shave off body hair, as I've always preferred the feeling of smooth skin on myself; I apply a thick layer of moisturiser to my whole body (in summer I might use a gradual tanning moisturiser for some sunless colour, for a change up that won't make me more likely to get skin cancer, *cough*, don't use sun beds, please, guys); I paint my nails on my fingers and toes because I love how it looks, usually matching the colour to the current season; I spritz myself with body spray or apply perfume and deodorant; I go to bed with a face dripping in skin oils and serums so that I wake up with my face glowing and feeling hydrated.

I'M KIND to MYSELF

I smile at the reflection of my natural self in the mirror – eye bags and unplucked eyebrows galore – because why not?

Squash COMPARISON THOUGHTS

I do my best to stop myself any time I compare myself to another person because it does no good at all to yearn for what someone else has or how someone else looks. If you constantly lament that you don't look like another person, you're never going to feel good naked, because you'll never just wake up as that other person! So cut that shit right now. When in doubt, look at your pets. I look at my cat Molly and how she just goes about her day being her badass adorable self, never thinking 'Why amn't I the same colour as that other kitty? Why amn't I as fluffy as that kitty? Why am I bigger, eh?' It's actually pretty funny (and terrifying) when you strip yourself back to the animal you were born as and analyse all that socialisation has done to you.

EXERCISE

When I feel motivated to, I do yoga or simple ten-minute body-weight workouts in my bedroom. Without fail, I notice a surge in body confidence when I do these things – I think mainly because I'm making a conscious decision and effort to change my mindset and to feel more confident, so then I just do.

CONFIDENCE HOMEWORK

I remind myself frequently that changing how I look, through diets or surgery or whatever else, won't make me feel any more confident. I know so many beautiful people who are cripplingly insecure and, well, at my lowest weight, I wasn't any more confident because mentally I wasn't feeling strong. I'll look through old pictures and reflect and journal and I'll talk to people to remind myself that confidence doesn't come naturally. It has to be built, little by little, every day, and maintained through self-compassion.

ACCEPTING COMPLIMENTS

Accept them with grace, and note the good ones down – particularly ones about *who you are* rather than *how you look*. Remember them. Read over them when you struggle with liking yourself enough to be naked with someone or to be nice to yourself when alone.

BREAK THE TOUCH BARRIER

Allow yourself to be touched in the places you usually try to conceal. This was so tough for me. I had a massive thing about not letting the person I was with touch my tummy where it prodded out – I'd even swipe their poor, loving hands away. But when you realise that they're not going to go running screaming through the hills of Connemara after touching you, you can let go of those ridiculous thoughts. Feeling another person's hand on that area can also make you realise your body's boundaries – it's not some expanding blimp, it's just a body, and you're not as unsightly as you think you are. In fact, you're not unsightly *at all*. And this person here trying to feel you up *knows it*.

BE WARM AND INVITING

How we look has little to do with how people FEEL about us – so how somebody views your naked body is largely related to how you *make them feel* in your company and not about those extra weights you've been lifting. If you make someone feel wonderful and accepted and happy when you spend time with them, they're going to be damn well delighted to be permitted access to your body.

POWER POSES

Practise 'power poses' and postures of confidence: stand tall, shoulders back; don't sit all hunched up into a ball; mimic the way the confident people you know move and carry themselves. This has a curious way of tricking our brains and has been shown to lead to more success for people – *even* people who fake it and just present themselves a certain way that doesn't reflect how they feel on the inside. Do this mimicking in the bedroom and I guarantee you'll reap the benefits!

BREATHE

Practise conscious breathing to feel more in touch with your body. Breathe in through the nose and out through the mouth, allow your belly to rise and fall, and hone in on that – really feel your breaths. This is a simple way to achieve serenity while also feeling more connected to your body. I do this naked all the time after a bath, while I lie down on my bed to dry off. It makes me feel all spiritual and shit! *Really!*

HYDRATE

Drink lots and lots of water! Dehydration shows up as shrivelled, lumpy and aged skin – there's nothing terrible about these things, of course, but if you want to make your skin look more supple, drink two or three litres a day. People of all ages will see the benefits of this and it'll translate into more confidence.

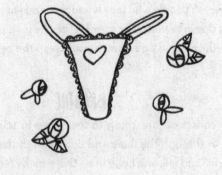

Section 4

SEX and SEXUALITY

TEN REASONS to MASTURBATE EVERY DAY

♥ It feels *amazing* and can make you feel happier by releasing feel-good hormones – some top quality *you* time.

♥ It'll help you feel more comfortable with your own body.

♥ Sex toys like vibrators are so much fun to play with! They can also keep the vagina 'in shape' by training the muscles.

♥ You'll open the doors to your deepest sexual fantasies and can (safely) mentally explore sexual scenarios you might want to try in future with another person/other people.

♥ It's a natural painkiller and can help alleviate menstrual cramps.

♥ It's been suggested that masturbating strengthens the immune system, improves cardiovascular health and even burns (a few) extra calories!

♥ Better sex – masturbating increases your libido *and* makes you better able to achieve orgasm with a partner.

♥ It's anti-stress.

♥ It helps you sleep.
♥ Multiple. Orgasms. Ladies. Practice makes perfect!

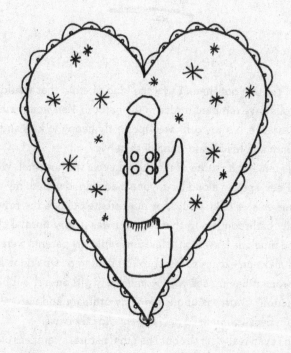

FANCYING BOYS
and GIRLS

Let's just get this out there. I was the kind of child that would make Barbie dolls have rampant orgies in the bathtub. Ken would make the odd appearance, but my girls were perfectly happy to kiss and grind without him and his plastic, penis-less pelvis.

At age ten, not an atom of me thought this was unusual. Well, no, the word 'sex' spoken aloud by *anyone* made blood rush to my cheeks and I'd never *ever* talk about it or masturbate outside the privacy of our family bathroom, so in that regard I was a very normal child. If people so much as kissed on television while my parents were in the room I'd make an excuse to leave, to run flailing out the door. But the *idea* of women having sex with women? My girl-on-girl bubble-bath Barbie action? *That* was unquestionably ordinary and natural in my little brain because, well, I'd never been told otherwise.

I didn't even really *get* sex but I had that natural awareness of sexual energy and attraction. I'd watch movies and, more often than not, end up fancying the arse off the princess; the strong businesswoman in heels; the one cute tomboyish girl in the group of teenage boys; the *pink* Power Ranger. Britney Spears circa 2000 had this magical ability to send me into a trance, and posters of Sarah Michelle Gellar from *Buffy the Vampire Slayer* wearing figure-hugging clothing adorned my bedroom walls. I'd want to hold their hands, hug them, giggle with them, *see their tits*.

From a very young age I knew that I liked girls in the same way that I liked boys, and for a blissful moment in time I got to live that reality without questioning it.

But, of course, my bliss was cut short by social norms.

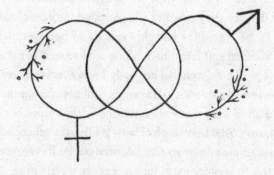

I had no idea how to identify myself for a very, *very* long time. Maybe I should start at the beginning, when I was nine ...

My first proper, all-consuming crush was a female teacher in my school. Let's call her Miss X. She wasn't even *my* teacher, and I felt sickly jealous of all the students who were lucky enough to be in her class. I'd have given anything for the chance to watch Miss X for hours each day, to be praised by her for my English essays and have her stick little gold stars into my copybooks with a warm smile, even to have her give out to me. But I'd only get to see her sporadically – her visits to our classroom for fresh chalk or books or chats with our teacher were shooting stars.

Anything and any thought involving Miss X at all made me feel fluttery and, actually, quite uncomfortable. Butterflies and panty tingles galore!

She didn't look like a model, either. She didn't wear revealing outfits. And she was at least twenty years older than me. But to me she was a goddess. She looked like a movie character that would work in a library or a bakery, possessing that elusive ability to make you feel all warm and fuzzy with a simple stare and a soft smile. Any time I heard her songlike voice or got a whiff of her divine perfume or caught a glimpse of the way she moved as she patrolled the schoolyard every other day, I'd be *putty*. She had this sparkle in her eyes, those big, wide eyes, and had soft raven hair falling wild around her shoulders. Her lower legs (the only part of her body I was ever lucky enough to see bare) were milky smooth and shapely – pillars of magnificence in heels. She'd often wear these red kitten heels that made her look so smart and quirky. And that *laugh* of hers! It filled the school corridors. Achingly beautiful and contagious, I'd listen out for it every time I had to make a trip to another room (or on random quests to the PE hall, during which I'd secretly be looking out for my dear Miss X).

One afternoon we were singing songs for choir practice in the main school hall and my queen walked through the door with some other teachers to watch us. It's as if I *felt* her presence. That thing happened, you know, like in the movie *West Side Story*, where the two main characters can only see one another and everything else around them goes blurry ... Well, it only happened on my end *ha-ha*, but, goodness, I choked up and couldn't get another note out. Her hips swayed from side to side as she walked, in one of those dark fitted skirts she'd wear, and her arms were wrapped around some folders hugged to her chest.

She was standing there then, all adorable, while kid-Melanie's heart was suddenly racing and her head was spinning and she'd become very aware of the ugly juice stain on her shirt collar and the bumps in her ponytail. Miss X made eye contact with one of the girls from her own class as I fell apart, a little red-headed girl who had solo chorus lines. She gave her an enthusiastic *go you* kind of face and I was just ... seething. *That little bitch getting all the attention!*

I'd go home after school and think of her, I'd imagine her biting her lip ... asking me to join her class and giving me good grades ... taking me to her house to bake me cookies ... undressing while I spied on her, just to catch a glimpse of her hidden treasures.

The woman basically lit my soul up like a bonfire.

I didn't quite understand the feeling at the time, or why I'd need to tightly clench my legs together sometimes when I thought of her, but, of course, I learned, *that's what it feels like when you're really into another person.*

Summer came and went, it was school time again and I was devastated to hear that Miss X had left her job. But I was young and fickle and, soon enough, a boy in class caught my eye – a boy with curly hair and big brown eyes and brown skin and, let me tell you, I was so into him I'd pretend my hand was his mouth and I'd kiss it every night in bed.

And I went on to frequently develop crushes on boys and girls; women and men; strangers and singers; teachers and movie stars. I've got a very vivid imagination, see, and I'm *very* driven by romance and sex – now, as a twenty-something, I can admit that, and I'm comfortable with that fact, but as a young teen it was this awful, dirty secret I kept locked away – something I'd only show to my *bestest* friends.

Like 'Alice'. She knew all too well my unquenchable thirst, my unusual curiosity about all things sex and love. At first we'd just play really elaborate games with our Barbie dolls, and the 'storylines' always revolved around relationships and affairs and weddings and heartbreak. We'd stick on epic movie soundtracks during sleepovers and we'd cry together just *talking* about love stories.

This girl is on my level! She gets it!

And after a couple of years of friendship I finally opened up to her about my sexy daydreams and about how sometimes I'd think about people or scenarios and put my hand in my knickers before bed. She did something then that ultimately changed my life, my focus and my expectations forever, completely stripping the last of my innocence.

She introduced me to pornography.

I was staying overnight in her house and we were snacking on the couch in the dark after a scary movie, like two typical thirteen-year-olds. Only we were having this conversation about ... well ... masturbation (I didn't know that was the word for it at the time). 'Mel, there's this really weird thing on one of the channels and I don't get it,' she half-laughed, half-whispered. 'Go on then, show me!' I said. She seemed nervous. 'OK ... but, well, just *please* don't think I'm weird for showing you – please? Like, it gives me a funny feeling down there, kinda like what you're saying ...'

She flicked to the adult section and clicked onto a channel called *something* along the lines of Triple X Babes. A 'ten-minute preview' soon began, of what, I had no idea, but the sights my eyeballs were absorbing turned my insides out.

Women kissing other women.

Topless women, licking and sucking on and biting other women's nipples.

'Why are they *doing* that? Isn't that such a weird thing to do, Mel? I mean why would anyone ever think to lick a *nipple*?' I couldn't even answer her, I was so overwhelmed with excitement and shock. I longed for that ten-minute preview to last forever. We both peered at the TV over a blanket we'd pulled up to our faces, awestruck, for the entirety. When it all finished, the techno music and alluring voices and the moaning and nipple licking, we looked at each other and, two giddy teens in the dark, *so many* repressed thoughts exploded into words.

We resolved to stay awake for the next ten-minute preview and, at the same time, we both touched ourselves, under the blanket, at opposite ends of the couch. Not until orgasm, though (I think we were too distracted by one another's presence) but, yeah, we did ... *that*. And it wasn't the last time either.

Porn captured my mind (in more ways than I liked) for many years to come. I developed a brutal addiction to it at one point in my mid-twenties, and no, I'm not disgusted at myself for that. My brain – like all our brains – evolved to respond powerfully to the kind of stimulation that was, once upon a time, very scarce, and I know that the reason I became addicted to porn is the same reason why I became addicted to sugary junk food. Not through greed – rather my very human brain just never acquired a capacity for the level of self-control needed in this modern world that's filled with shopping aisles full of delicious, artificial foods and with online galleries full of images of well-proportioned, beautiful, fertile humans banging each other and fiddling with themselves.

I became hooked on porn in the same way I became hooked on food because I was just ... generally sad. I wasn't a happy person. I didn't realise that I could become compulsive elsewhere and swap out these intense highs for much nicer things, for enriching hobbies (not necessarily knitting, but you know what I mean).

Doing that is a lot tougher than it sounds – replacing a destructive hobby with a more beneficial one. It's hard to find comparable highs when you're so incredibly into something that's easy and accessible. I actually had to *force* myself to avoid porn for six long months straight. I quit it cold turkey because it was sucking the blood from my time and relationships and well-being, like Dracula on a midnight blood bender. Unlike other addictions I've become familiar with in my time – sugar, checking Facebook – the 'slow fade out' technique didn't really work. So I banned myself. I had to! It had become my sole means to relax and zone out. But it got to a point where I was watching it up to four times a day and I physically couldn't climax *without* it – a tragedy indeed, that sort of sexual desensitisation, that numbed response to pleasure. But I found that without it in my life for that period of time, I felt more encouraged to use my imagination. I focused on creating real-life sexual experiences that turned me on just as much as, if not more than, porn did!

Porn addiction is a very real, modern problem. And it's not a sign of weakness or inherent *badness* – it's just that our brains are, for the most part, defenceless against ruthless young technologies. *They don't call us millennials for nothing.*

The taboo around masturbation in general, though (female masturbation, in particular), is almost impossible to comprehend. This natural expression of self-love was a pitiable, distracting compulsion, in my mind, for years. I associated it with intense awkwardness, partially because it involves sex organs, which were the Voldemorts of my childhood (#HarryPotterHumour). My vagina was literally 'she who must not be named' – my mammy called a vagina a *fairy*. 'Make sure you wipe your fairy, Mel. Front to back!' she'd call in when I first learned how to go to the toilet by myself.

I called my own pussy my *fairy* until a good friend told me (when I was *far* too old) that nobody called it that and that I might as well call my arsehole my goblin.

But I felt especially embarrassed about playing with myself because I mostly thought of/looked at pictures of *women* while I did it and, well, I was told, 'It's *not normal* to look at other women in that way' several times.

Yep. Seriously.

The shame blanket was first thrown on me by 'Sally', when I was fourteen. 'Sally' was a rather traditional woman, one in a long line who'd look after my siblings and me after school for a few hours while my mammy and stepfather finished up work. She had a son and he was cool (I quite fancied him, actually), and one afternoon we watched *Star Wars* together before dinner. Me being *me*, I made a passing comment about Natalie Portman's character, Padmé – a beautiful senator, dressed in gorgeously elaborate outfits. I said something along the lines of 'She's so *hot* – marry me,' and laughed. Our childminder was gathering up cups and empty packets of sweets at the time and she overheard me. '*What? She?* Melanie, don't be so weird – girls don't marry girls.' She winced, looking down at me, and I don't think I've turned such a bright shade of crimson since.

I found out that she was lying when one of my dad's friends, who'd always dated men, went to live in the US, where she dated a woman for years, and could have married her if she'd wanted to. Now she's married to a man, but I remember Dad saying she'd 'become a lesbian' – so I was only ever aware of, basically, two sexualities. Straight and gay. (It's like he never even entertained the idea that she might just like both men and women – *shocker!*)

If there are gay people and straight people and that's all, then what on earth am I?

Throughout my teens, girls in school would throw the word *lesbian* at me, and others, as an insult. *She looks like such a lesbian* when I chopped my hair off aged twelve. *Don't be such a lesbian* when I'd bring up conversations like 'Isn't it weird that women feel like they have to shave their armpits and men don't?' *That's* so *gay* when I'd opt to wear uniform pants instead of a skirt (which was mostly related to my poor body image, because, actually, I adore skirts). *She's such a dyke* was being said behind my back. And I was so confused: I'd always talk about and kiss boys, just like all the other girls in my school. What was I doing to give off this vibe? And don't even get me started on the venomous reaction in my school to the couple of girls who openly admitted to being *the L word*. In the end, all this led to the internalisation of 'gay' and 'lesbian' as negative, insulting terms. My brain soaked up the stereotypes and did everything possible to make me try to avoid displaying them. The fact of the matter was that to be *perceived* as a lesbian or a girl with 'gay traits' or a 'gay look' in my all-girl Catholic school was undesirable. It just made teenage life suck even more.

I'd discovered what *lesbian* actually meant soon after seeing the nipple-licking soft-core porn, but I never fully identified with it. I one billion per cent found myself sexually and romantically attracted to men too, so I repressed any hint of affiliation I felt with that label. This confusion, combined with the way the word was used to make fun of others, *along with* the fact that certain girls around me would kiss other girls at parties just to appeal to guys they liked (I totally blame porn for this, by the way, for the act of straight girls kissing somehow signalling to boys that these girls are more loose and easy and worth pursuing), agitated me and left me alone in a maze of self-doubt and self-hatred.

I thought there was something wrong with me. That I was a pervert.

Growing up, my world was rooted in heteronormativity. There were no openly gay couples around me. I recognised that my sexual attractions weren't limited to men at such a young age and at a time when there really wasn't much LGBTQ+ representation at all. I had no internet, there was no social media and the nineties, well, they were an odd little crossroads for gay entertainment and pop culture. To be a lesbian or anything other than a straight cis white man or woman just wasn't explored much, or at least anywhere in my eye view – anywhere in the little bubble-wrapped world I occupied.

Though I did get to witness one of the first lesbian kisses on prime-time television in my favourite TV show at the time, *Buffy the Vampire Slayer* (between Willow and Tara!) – that felt like a soul massage.

But, yeah, back then, I identified more with ET the extra-terrestrial than many of the people who were all up in my space. So for years I tried to repress the natural urges and feelings I experienced in order to fit in and feel more normal (*whatever that means*).

I was head over heels for a quiet girl in my school for two whole years, from age thirteen to fifteen, but she was straighter than a ruler. (I tried to flirt with her once by giving her the *hey, baby* eyeballs and doing all the things I'd do with boys to show interest, but she just thought there was something wrong with me and never spoke to me again. Now she's married to a man. Yeah, I stalked her on Facebook.)

Then a boy came along when I was sixteen who I fancied a lot. Like, *a lot a lot*. My best friend 'Alannah' knew him and told me we'd probably get along. I'd just been through a break-up with my first-boy-friend-who-wasn't-really-a-proper-boyfriend and I needed distracting. 'You guys like so many of the same movies and a lot of the same bands, and he's kind of your type, Mel. Go for it!' She showed me a photo of him on social media and he had the big brown eyes I've always been a fool for, but also, just seeing pictures of him sent my imagination into overdrive – *our kids would be adorable* kind of overdrive!

We started e-flirting. And after two months of chatting and teasing one another back and forth every day online, this boy that 'Alannah' had introduced me to, 'Freddie', essentially asked me on a date.

OK, we were sixteen, so it wasn't exactly a candlelit dinner – he bought me a ticket to go along to a concert with him and his friends. But that was enough for me! If anything, that was a far less intimidating way to meet for the first time than if he'd invited me to the cinema and McDonald's (where we'd have no buffers or human shields). And I was *so* excited! I spent all day every day fantasising about how it would all go down, how magical it would be.

When we met up before the gig, my insides were the fizz in a can of soda that had been shaken violently. I was incredibly nervous around him and my animal brain just kept thinking, *Does he like me the way I like him? Does he want to have sex with me? Because I really want to have sex with him* ... I craved his interest. Every little glance from him fed me the validation I was looking for. We played like children all day, pouring water on each other and poking at each other and calling each other names. You know, the usual silly things kids in lust do to flirt. We were making it known that we liked each other by treating each other differently than everyone else around us.

We kissed after the concert, around the corner from our friends, in the dark, beside a little bush. Soon after, we were boyfriend and girlfriend. We said 'I love you' six months in and then began a four-year-long rollercoaster ride. The relationship was wild and passionate and maddening and all-consuming, and there were several mini-break-ups before the final shattering.

During *one* of these break-ups, at a friend's house party among a small army of teenagers, I got (too) drunk and this one girl caught my attention. She was going out with a childhood friend of mine and I'd seen her around. I'd never found her particularly attractive before, but there was a moment that night where we danced and giggled together in a corner, and then some touchy-feely-ness happened. Both of us kept finding excuses to brush off one another, to put our hands on each other, to play with one another's hair. We held eye contact for a few seconds longer than normal, and I knew then that she was thinking exactly what I was thinking: *I wanna put my face on your face and maybe touch your boobs and see your ass in your underwear.*

Oh, the sweet sting of good flirtation. I was flying.

'Oh my god, Melanie, are you bi too?' I stared at her blankly, then smirked in my drunkenness. 'What? *Am I a boy?* Ha-ha, you're shitfaced!' 'No, no, *bi*, as in bisexual – do you fancy girls as well as boys? Like, I'm bi ...' Then my misshapen, drunken thoughts turned into colourful, powerful fireworks.

Bi – bisexual! Oh my god! I'm that – that's a thing. That explains it: I'm not a pervert, I'm not a half-lesbian, but, no, I kind of am because ... I'm bi!

All I managed to reply was, 'Um, yeah, I like girls too but I still love Freddie ...' and she replied, 'Well, my boyfriend thinks it's kinda hot if I kiss girls – he'd go mad if I kissed a boy, though!' She ran her finger along the skin over my hip at the top of my tight low-rise jeans. I trembled and bit my lip. 'You biting your lip is so sexy ... OK, well, Freddie's not here, and I'm sure there's an empty bedroom upstairs ... Wanna go up?' My legs lost all feeling and I floated along after her like a balloon up the stairs.

She was the first girl I ever kissed. All over each other, we piled into a bedroom where some guy was passed out on the bed – he didn't flinch, and to be honest, we didn't even care that he was there. We were dancing candle flames in the dark and my heart was pounding as I noted her softness and how differently she kissed. I felt somehow less embarrassed about my body with her because she too had lumps and bumps and stretch marks. Her understanding of my own insecurities through experience made her aware of how to put me at ease. And I melted into her.

We stayed there fooling around for ... a while (*shuffle*, forty fun-filled minutes) and although it took a bit of getting used to and felt downright strange and different, it also felt *right*, and I enjoyed myself immensely. Just as much as I ever had during my first time getting intimate with another person. Then, after, she said, 'I'm nervous about telling my boyfriend about this. How is this not ... you know ... cheating? It feels like I just cheated. You are wonderful but I feel terrible because we snuck off ... oh no ...'

Even though I'd finally discovered that bisexuality was a word to describe what I felt, I left in a taxi with more questions occupying my brain than had been there on the way to the party. *Is the word* bisexual *just related to sex or also to romantic feelings? Why did I like that so much if I love 'Freddie' still? Why is it OK for her to kiss girls and not guys? What constitutes cheating? How did she do that thing with her tongue? Why do I feel like I've done something really bad?*

My teenage years were filled with experiences like this. With confusion and questioning and experimenting. I was basically a tall wooden signpost with LOST painted across it in capital letters. If I've learned anything in my twenties, however, it's that more people than you'd think are attracted to the same sex or both sexes and it's completely OK. There's a whole spectrum of sexuality and gender and we all have our own journey to discovering where along this spectrum we lie or which part of it we like to dance around.

As I write this book I'm single and dating and feeling like I need 'BI' tattooed on my forehead. Everyone tells me I 'look straight' – the struggle of being a femme is real, peeps. Feminine bisexual girls have been so fetishised and struggle with invisibility as the B in LGBTQ+ – many members of the community don't recognise bisexuality as a sexuality, and feel that it's simply a stepping stone on the way to gay town. I actually created my first ever cinematic spoken-word film, named *Femme*, inspired by my experiences with this. It premiered at a festival in Canada and was really well received. Since I uploaded it to my YouTube channel, it has resonated with so many people, and I've felt less alone in my feelings.

Art is the way to the heart. (Unfortunately, art doesn't help with the fact that I live in a small Irish village and struggle to meet new *people* let alone queer, feminine girls that are my age, single, yada yada ...)

Fancying boys and girls presents me with some dilemmas. Girls rarely come on to me, and guys or lesbians that I *do* hit it off with often become concerned as soon as the bisexuality elephant enters the room. The stereotypes are overwhelmingly frustrating and it's upsetting when you really like a person but they pigeonhole you based on all the bi-phobic nonsense they've heard. *Bisexuals are way more likely to cheat* (ehm, because straight people *never* cheat, right?). *If you haven't dated a girl you're not really bi* (sexual orientation has nothing to do with sexual acts – if a straight man is single, his orientation is still 'straight'). *Bisexuals are greedy* (don't even get me started). *Bisexuals are afraid of commitment* (anyone can experience that, for a variety of reasons, such as heartbreak or where they're at in their life). *Bisexuals are just experimenting, going through a phase, and they'll pick a side one day* (OK, why would *anyone* want to pick a side if they're attracted to both sexes? Imagine having to choose between looking at sunsets and purring kittens ...). *People just say they're bisexual for attention* ... This list of stereotypes is longer than one of my receipts from an Ann Summers sale (*psst*: too long).

But they're just things I've had to wade through. You've gotta own who you are and shake off the shit that people say. Otherwise, just embrace the quicksand.

Having finally had the opportunity to taste freedom and explore all sorts of relationships – with men and women, long-term and short term, monogamous and polyamorous/open – and to play the field and go on dates, I've come to know myself so much more and I feel like I'm finally *friends* with my bisexuality. It's not a nuisance to me anymore. I know that I'm more comfortable to be the dominant, door-holding, hand-leading one with another girl, as I'm attracted to rather submissive femmes, and also that when with a man I immediately take a more submissive role, as that's what I'm used to and that's what I'm comfortable with. I know that I don't prefer either sex, that each sex and each *person* is gloriously different and special.

And for all its complications, from giving me too many love options to being something I have to continually come out of the closet about because I 'look straight', I bloody love fancying both guys *and* girls. I adore my sexuality, my being, my capacity to love and to appreciate.

But sharing this fact about myself is still sometimes a frightening thing, a challenge and a half. Let's talk about coming out.

COMING out

I'm holding out hope for a day to come when the whole concept of 'coming out' is something that astonishes the future's youth, when they read in their history books about how we olden-time folk faced this uncomfortable and scary process. I hope they laugh and rejoice in how great things are for them.

But right now, I'm actually nervous to write about this. I'm nervous because, even now, in 2017, homophobic people comment on my videos online – regularly. I log into Twitter sometimes and see tweets telling me that I'm going to burn in hell for talking about bisexuality online. And I'm completely aware that I'm privileged to be in a position to 'be out' and to have a voice on this issue, thanks to my online platform and all of the opportunities that brings. I'm here, writing these words, while so many voiceless LGBTQ+ people live as shadows of their truest selves. The weight of that is *immense*.

Deep breaths, Mel.

I think the need to 'come out' *at all* should die off as something *completely* unnecessary. Why should anyone make assumptions about another person's sexuality or gender, anyway?

Really think about it. In the same way you can't look at someone and just *know* they like Italian food, you can't look at them and guess their sexual or romantic preferences in that particular moment. I mean, *sure*, a lot of us love pizza – the law of averages and all that jazz – but realistically there'll always be *some* people at your house party that might not *want* pizza. Or they might be vegan. Or they might have an intolerance. Maybe they want rice and spring rolls from the Chinese takeaway. There's gonna be a conversation that begins like, 'So, what does everyone wanna order in?' Because we can't tell that kind of intangible information from looking at someone, so why do we put people's tastes in other humans into boxes without asking first?

Why assume that someone is straight, or bi, or gay, or anything else for that matter?

Our obsession as a society with straightforwardness (straight – geddit, geddit?!) and finite categories limits and moulds people's life experiences so much and I can't wait for it to stop. Not just in the Western world, obviously, but *globally*. And don't get me wrong – I think it's wonderful that more and more people are finding the courage to pave the way for their best chance at happiness and a life lived and shared with others as their genuine selves, be that with a self-chosen label or not – but the battle is not yet half-won. I mean, some people out there still support conversion therapy – pseudoscience aimed at 'curing' LGBTQ+ people. *Yep.* So we've got to talk about it, and continue talking about it, until those sweet cows come home to momma.

I don't recall ever choosing to be in the proverbial closet in the first place. And what I mean by that is I never lied, never told people, 'Hey, I'm Melanie and I'm straight!' It's always just been assumed by others, and I've always hated that. Every time it happens I step into that compartment in my brain where I go to violently crumple up pieces of paper to vent stress. (You can tell I'm in this weird headspace when you catch me chewing the insides of my cheeks and shaking my leg.)

Of course it's not other people's fault – we're sort of brought up to assume everyone is attracted to the opposite sex. There hasn't been much representation of anything other than the straightforward heterosexual relationship in romantic literature, in movies, in shows. And in my case, well, I *do* like men! I've *been in* heterosexual relationships. So my struggle has always been, *How do I let new people know that I like girls, too? Or do they even need to know? Maybe only girls I'm attracted to need to be able to tell. How do I be more obvious? Ugh, no, no – my sexuality doesn't define me. I gotta stop overthinking. But I wanna be able to open up and tell people I love personal stories without it being weird for them.*

Most of us like to be able to talk to our family and friends about our attractions sometimes. (Especially me – I'm totally that person who'll see a face in the crowd or hear a sexy voice on the street and stop in my tracks to gawk/drool. I audibly moan when Ryan Gosling or Mila Kunis is on the big screen. I fall in lust so hard and the other person clouds up my whole brain.) And of course, like pretty much everyone, I like to introduce people I'm dating to the important people in my life – I like to be unapologetically and authentically *me* around these people, and to do that, no conversation can feel off-limits.

I need things to be I-just-farted level comfortable in my bubble of humans.

But in all honesty, I do find sexuality to be a difficult subject to approach with certain people I care about. As a bisexual, I have to come out again and again through life to new people, or to people who don't yet know. I don't want loved ones scratching their heads because of something I've said.

Making my sexuality known was particularly hard when I was younger and a lot more shy, and especially as I went to a school run by nuns, decorated with holy crosses and Jesus paintings. My goodness, do I wish I half-lived in an online world back then ... to have had internet anonymity would've been a wonderful thing; to be able to write in forums I FANCY GIRLS TOO, just, ahh. Telling people now feels like pulling off a Band-Aid – it's easier because I can at least anticipate a variety of reactions. But it still makes my heart race and my palms sweat, that lead-up to saying the words out loud and face to face with another person.

And sometimes I just decide not to tell a person, because it might not be a topic of importance to that relationship, because it'll make my life easier when around them. My ex's elderly mother, whom I adored, likely would've choked on her afternoon cake and clutched at her rosary beads if I'd ever told her I'd kissed other women. She's a devout Catholic and, well, *yeah*.

Let's go there.

I haven't darkened the doorway of a church in years, yet I'm still infected by Catholic guilt. Aged thirteen, before I'd entirely distanced myself from organised religion (note here that I consider myself to be a spiritual person, but the institution of the church and so much of what it stands for just isn't for me), I told a priest about my 'dirty' sex thoughts and late-night porn-viewing sessions during 'confession' – something Catholics do to obtain absolution for 'sins' committed against 'God'. I *believed* I *had* to do this – that it would make me pure again. The priest went silent for about thirty seconds before absolving me, and it was one of the most itchy, awful silences of my life.

Religion stigmatises sexuality even for the non-religious like me, people who grew up in religious schools or families but who aren't all that religious themselves. For some people around the world, coming out can sometimes mean being attacked or even disowned. In America, for example (where a huge proportion of my online following are from), 40 per cent of homeless youths are LGBTQ+ – it's *heartbreaking* to know that.

I feel an ache in my chest if I stop and imagine, hard, being *part of* that statistic.

I'm incredibly lucky to have never faced worry of abandonment (my immediate family are accepting and tolerant people), but because prejudices and discrimination are still so rampant in general, it's still considered an 'act of bravery' or defiance to be here and queer and vocal about it. And while I don't feel brave or defiant, and actually feel uncomfortable when people label me as such, it definitely hasn't been a frolic through the tulips.

I started telling good friends that I liked girls as well as boys at a very young age, but only those I became so close to that we were essentially welded at the hip, like my porn-and-masturbation pal. She was a good bean – one of those friends I really trusted, one of the friends that made me feel safe.

And because I didn't identify as a lesbian and had no idea what bisexual was as a young teen, my way of telling friends was just to be pretty in-your-face-obvious about girl crushes in the same way I'd be about boy crushes (or, to them, 'normal crushes'). I'd make references and use language to communicate how I felt about other girls – 'I'd give anything to date her,' 'She can kick me out of bed any day!' – and sometimes friends would snigger and berate me for being an oddball and it would burn my confidence to ash. Other friends would shrug their shoulders and we'd carry on telling tales and singing songs and doing kid stuff (not breaking into houses or stealing sweets from the shops or anything ... definitely not ...).

This is still how I come out to new people in my personal life now, aged twenty-seven. I drop hints to test the waters before any deeper conversation or sharing of experiences can happen, rather than, say, offering it up as a *fun fact about me* during a first encounter: 'So, yeah, I'm really into science fiction movies and I'm all about vampire lore and baking and by the way I like pussy as well as penis.'

I've never really wanted to use a label to define how I feel about people, but labels *can* be helpful. I use the label bisexual, for example, when I talk about sexuality and whatnot in YouTube videos, because I want the right audience to find the content. Yeah, who am I kidding, labels are *important*. Humans identify (almost) everything through language, and labels do serve a purpose, whether people choose to adopt them or to live fluidly, label-free.

I've noticed too that there are definitely right moments and wrong moments for me to come out to new people.

- ❤ **Right moment:** in the middle of a deep one-on-one conversation with a very open-minded somebody about love and dating.
- ❤ **Wrong moment/moment when it would cause more awkwardness than I'm willing to deal with:** when surrounded by older relations who are laughing and discussing, over a few drinks, how impossible it is to be trans and gay – 'Pah, what has happened to the world?' (This actually happened – genuine quote, people!)

Here's an example of one of those right moments. After meeting 'James' (who would become my long-term boyfriend of six years) in a nightclub when I was twenty, it somehow came up that he'd also been attracted to this *other* girl from our town and had been making attempts to chat her up (before we hit it off).

Well ... she happened to be the last girl I'd kissed.

When I heard who it was, wave upon wave hit me. *We like the same girl. Does he like her more than me? Do I like her more than him? This is too weird. How awkward. She's such a good kisser. Crap, he knows that – and how hot she is.*

I just swallowed my pride and went for it. I took a deep breath, hoped for the best, giggled and said, 'Oh man, that's funny – she and I actually recently hooked up! We have the same taste in women, I guess!'

And, well, we just had a little laugh about it. The world didn't implode. He didn't glance me up and down in disgust nor did he go, 'Oh, damn, that's *hot*' – which is equally annoying because, mate, *I'm not into girls for your benefit.* I think he asked one question just to clarify things, and then my sexuality never came up as a topic of conversation again. It was just a thing that existed. Like my wrinkly elbows and the birthmark on my neck and my raging pre-menstrual syndrome. A part of me.

I'd talk to him about girls in the same way I'd talk about boys. I got to just ... *be*. I set myself free of chains I'd never agreed to wear in the first place.

We'd go to the cinema together, and if I found an actress attractive, I'd tell him, and he'd do the same. It was actually pretty fun – sometimes we'd sit on the bus and play this game of 'who on this street is hot' to see if we'd pick the same people! We were in a monogamous relationship and we trusted each other completely, never cheated on each other, but I really appreciated how comfortable he enabled me to feel in myself around him. Neither of us had to turn off our sexualities just because we were building a life together – he never projected insecurities, was never jealous, and *never* judged me.

Coming out was *much* more intimidating when it came to telling my parents and my siblings (and even other family members, as I come from a ginormous extended family). I'd love to say that it was super easy, that the people closest to you are the easiest to tell, but for me that wasn't the case. Frankly it terrified me – the thought of saying 'I'm bisexual, I'm attracted to women' out loud. To *them*. To (*very* heterosexual) people I'd spent my entire life around. People who knew me inside and out – or so they thought. And, like, I knew they wouldn't hate me or cease contact for all eternity. But I still thought in the back of my mind that *maybe* their opinions of me would change, or maybe they'd think I was going through another phase – like my 'emo' panda-eyeliner-and-chains-and-black-nail-polish phase.

I never really had 'the talk' with any of my family members. I just kind of *let it out* through my words and actions.

I think my baby brother knew first, as we're insanely close and always have been, so I felt safe saying things about girls in front of him (girls in movies and at parties), and I was comfortable telling him about girls I'd kiss or fancy. He never questioned it or grilled me or made me feel ashamed. He was entirely indifferent, actually. Which felt wonderful. It's so nice when someone you love as much as I love my brother is so accepting. I'm incredibly grateful to have had that positive experience of feeling completely accepted.

Dad knew since I was a teen (well, I'd made it abundantly clear) but I don't think he believed it for years – he played blind to my passing remarks and he'd often change the conversation. That would always feel like a little grey cloud pissing rain on my defeated real-life sadface. He didn't get it, but he didn't question it or challenge me on it, either. He came round to it more during my mid-twenties, after a couple of chats we had about girls I liked – girls I was seeing or had hooked up with. Dad and I are super open in our conversations and I really love that! I can say anything in front of him now, and it won't be awkward – I have time to thank for that. Over the many years living with him I've peeled back all the layers of myself (who else just thought of that *onion* quote from *Shrek*?!). I feel like everyone needs at least one person they can be *that* comfortable around, and I decided I wanted Dad to know me inside out. And I guess because he's from that older generation who grew up in a time when many people were still anti-LGBTQ+, it means that bit more to me that *he* accepts me.

And, well, not living with my mammy (and the fact that we weren't close for a few years after I moved in with my dad, after a rather ridiculous anxiety-fuelled argument about nothing) made it near-impossible to tell her. For *so* long. I never felt like I could grasp and hold on to the right opportunity during my short visits throughout my late teens and early twenties. And my then-boyfriend often visited her with me and, I dunno, I figured it would be inappropriate to bring up that I'm attracted to other people (women or not!) with him sitting there lovingly gazing at me. I felt no real need to talk about it.

But *now*, in my exciting and colourful singledom, my mam knows more than *anyone* about my love of women. I'm *way* more likely to share the juicy details with her and my friends! Mam is so warm and giggly and she *really* listens when people talk and open up – once our relationship strengthened as I got older, once my confidence thickened, bringing it up with her was a non-issue. I think I just blurted it out (maybe I kept talking so she couldn't interject before I'd fully explained myself, but that's just me all over – I never shut up). And even though Mam doesn't fully understand it, because it's not of *her* world, she supports me completely – and that's a blissful thing.

I'm pretty raw with my little sister, too. The age gap grew insignificant when she turned eighteen, and we became *so* much closer – now I can disclose anything to her without fear of skewing her perception of me. We often film videos together and talk about all sorts – vaginas and sex and all the rest. We've become such good friends. Not once has she looked at me funny or questioned my sexuality. Then again, she has grown up in a world where it's a lot more acceptable to talk about these things.

Coming out isn't easy for everyone. It won't always elicit the desired response, especially from our elders, who endured very different conditioning. For some, though, it is easy – like admitting to a fart. (A good gay friend of mine said this to me one day while we reminisced about telling people for the first time and I laughed *so* hard I dribbled tea all over myself – so I'm borrowing the simile and publishing it and there's nothing he can do about it!) Or better yet, coming out can actually feel like, I dunno, sharing good news because, *it is good news*!

I try to treat my sexuality like it's the best news *ever*.

Sharing it with others is me taking ownership of my feelings. It's me sharing with every new person that comes into my life that I find *more* people attractive than if I only fancied the opposite sex. And finding people attractive in general is flipping glorious. *Why not* scream that from the rooftops?

I've realised that we can help the people we love, the people who matter, to overcome a lack of knowledge about the scale of sexualities. It's unfair to expect them to just *know* stuff, or indeed to adapt and change overnight. We can reduce their discomfort by talking things out with them, pointing them toward statistics and reading material and documentaries that'll broaden their minds and increase their understanding.

But also, sometimes we might need to hold strong and avoid discussing it until we can move out and be independent, *if* signs suggest that shit could go down.

In an ideal world nobody would ever be turned away from their home, their nest, their safe space, because they love too much to stay silent. Nobody should be denied love for loving someone that another's moral compass or religion disapproves of. But people constantly go through this – and if any of those people are reading this right now, know that you're a soldier of love; you're championing the visibility of our community; you deserve respect and kindness and my compassion wants to wrap its arms *so* tight around you.

I've not walked a mile in the shoes of the lesbian, gay, bisexual, transgender and queer humans who've been ridiculed and tortured and beaten and shit on by society, but I *will* walk a thousand miles alongside them toward a brighter future where love is love is love is love is love, in solidarity.

We'll win the war.

We'll slay the fear that keeps us in cages.

And I'll love *whomever* I love (all that's safe to say at this point is that they'll have big, wide eyes, 'cause that's ma thang).

Having SEX

I don't know about you, but I bloody love sex. And for some reason it's still quite a taboo subject, this primal, animal act – I just *don't get it*. The logical side of my brain says, 'Sex is the reason we're all here in the first place – one of the few things we have in common. It really, *really* shouldn't be so difficult to talk about. IT FEELS SO GOOD!' While the *rest* of my brain cries, '*Ugh*, don't start writing about sex, Melanie – your family might read this!'

People have sex. Whoopty-fuckin'-doo. Sex sex sex sex sex sex *sex*.

I'm going to wipe aside all the sex-related shame and disgrace that's been knitted into my very existence by talking about it here, now and forevermore, by smashing the taboo that admitting to enjoying sex is bad and something to be ashamed of.

I hope to do this by talking about it like I'm talking about breathing, or eating food, or sleeping, or any of the other few things that unite our *entire species* ...

Sex and all the lovely pleasure it brings me can be summed up as absolute release from the restriction I experience in the rest of my life – a release of those things I usually keep hidden. We all have our own erotic interests, and there are countless theories suggesting where they stem from. These interests or fetishes vary from person to person and for some, like me, day to day!

The act of having consensual sex with someone else transports me to this safe, warm place full of care and trust where I can take someone on a tour of the buried, wilder sides of me.

I once thought of sex as some kind of purely athletic act that people only engaged in to procreate, and while, yes, sex makes use of our bodies and burns some extra calories, it's all about what's going on *upstairs*. Experiencing good sex and being 'good' in bed is one million per cent a skill of the mind.

Some people (myself included) figure this out pretty quickly, after first having sexual experiences that are entirely focused on the wrong things – worries about not being attractive enough, or being bad at the physical set-up of it all, at positions, at skill, worries about getting tired, or being boring – and *then* going on to have remarkable sexual experiences that are achingly fantastic, thanks to self-confidence and real attraction, to the presence of connection.

When I sleep with a person who wholeheartedly encourages my secret self while being honest about their own needs, I lose all sense of the world around me ... I'm just gone, in nirvana, having a jolly oul' time.

A lot of people complain about bad sex. I've had the good, the bad and the ugly when it comes to sex and, the thing is, no one person can be *bad at sex* – only two people (or three, or four, whatever you're into!) can be a *bad combination*. Some people just don't click in that way and might force it for the sake of it or because of a perceived lack of options. OK sex can be had between people who *technically* 'know what they're doing' when it comes to placement and motion and all the mechanics of it, but *really great sex* only happens when there's a mind connection and a surrender of self-awareness and second-guessing.

I first had sex when I was sixteen, before I met 'Freddie', with a guy who was two years older than me, and it *wasn't great*. Nothing like the fairy-tale experience I'd envisioned after watching far too many Hollywood sex scenes (the ones where the camera pans to a closed door or a billowing curtain just as things start to get all hot and steamy).

Nothing I'm proud of.

And I say that because I did it for all the wrong reasons. I didn't have any real feelings for the guy (we'd only been dating for a while, and I was mainly going on dates with him out of boredom) and for years I've been ashamed to admit that I felt pressured into having sex with him – and I don't just mean *by him*. I caved to peer pressure from my friend group. I'm not actively ashamed of this anymore – I know that I did nothing wrong and that it wasn't my fault. I didn't ask to be pressured into anything. But I *did* agree to it.

I remember, at the time, trying to convince myself that I wanted to do it. Because lots of my friends had already had sex and would brag about not being able to walk straight after a good lashing – about missing classes because they were off riding in their boyfriends' cars. I felt left out. And I wanted to do it because I thought about sex all the time. But, nevertheless, deep down, I didn't want my first time to be with *him*.

It was late on a Saturday night, and we were walking slowly together after a (crappy) date night, me and this guy – let's call him 'Greg'. We saw a dumb movie at the cinema and ate some stale-tasting popcorn. He pawed at my legs and breasts like a hungry dog throughout. I can still distinctly remember the stench of his horrible hair gel – every time I get a whiff of that same hair gel now, off anyone, I mentally curl up in a ball.

See, after the movie he dragged me into a laneway beside the cinema and pushed my head down forcefully toward his dick, urging me to give him a blowjob. This had happened previously, after a couple of other dates with him. Don't ask me why I laughed it off as him 'being excited', why I did it instead of just punching him in the balls and dumping him there and then, because I honestly couldn't tell you. I don't recognise the girl I was then – so placid and agreeable at the wrong times, so desperate to please people even when it meant displeasing herself.

I was very clearly uncomfortable, but 'Greg' didn't seem to notice, or care. Then we were caught up in a tug-of-war conversation for over an hour before IT happened, during which we walked aimlessly as he convinced me why *he* believed I should allow him to do what he wanted with me. Why I essentially 'owed' him access to my body. Being so young, I had no idea that this was so radically *wrong* in every way – that as an eighteen-year-old, he should've known better. That I should've followed my gut and gone home.

We eventually did IT, after the will-I-won't-I-dance was cut short by him taking me on a guilt trip: 'I always buy your cinema tickets. I come to see you every week even though I'm busy with exams ... You're dressed like *that*' (glancing at my low-rise jeans and belly top). 'Come on, Melanie, you can't really blame me for wanting this – please?'

We'd wandered onto a moonlit sports pitch where we then undressed, under a little shelter at the side of the pitch. (No way would either of our families have been comfortable with us being left alone in a room together in one of our houses.) I angled my head so that my hair fell into my face to mask my expression, my acne and the watery green windows to my apprehensive, sixteen-year-old soul. Elbows clashed, there was stumbling and my bra got stuck as for *some* reason I'd tried to pull it over my head instead of unhooking it.

I wasn't thinking straight because the inevitable nervous-poo-syndrome cramps had entered the scene. And that only happens when I'm literally shitting it! There wasn't a soul around and I *couldn't stop trembling* – and not only because it was cold outside that night.

My body didn't want it to happen.

I wanted to stop and reverse and rewind my footsteps till I was safe at home, in my lovely messy bedroom with my Green Day band posters and my freshly washed bedding and my annoying little sister nagging at me to read her a bedtime story.

But I went ahead with it, ignoring my instincts, to keep him happy.

Shudder.

So I could go into school on Monday and sound all impressive in front of my friends.

That first time was unpleasant in every regard, though. I wasn't aroused, so it was near-impossible to get his penis inside me, no matter what position we tried. For me it was sort of like trying to put in a tampon, because I suffer from this common thing called 'vaginismus', which makes my vaginal muscles tense up when I feel uncomfortable about inserting something, especially something artificial – hence why I'm a pad girl all the way when I get my period and why I never use tampons or 'pussy plugs' as we called them in school.

But, yeah, the sex that night just felt a bit like a mini rake poking my insides; I wasn't turned on and wet, and the whole time I awkwardly bopped on top of him I thought things like, 'Why am I not moaning in pleasure like the girls on Triple X Babes? Why is it so ... quiet? I want to stop but, *ahh*, his hands are digging into me ...' I rolled off him moments later, after he'd come into a condom, and I basked in the sheer underwhelmed-ness.

And then the worst bit. 'My ex-girlfriend was a ballerina – your body is ... a lot different to hers. It's all squishy!'

I nearly died on the spot. I dressed faster than I would've in a burning house and held back my tears until I got home and into a piping hot shower, where I washed off the night's events for a solid forty minutes.

LESSON ONE

Warming up with foreplay is fundamentally important, as is only sleeping with people who I want to sleep with.

I semi-despise the phrase 'losing your virginity'. It implies that you're losing some special, irreplaceable part of you, some ethereal thing without which you're somehow impure. Day-old bread. When really you're not *losing* anything – you're actually opening yourself up to a whole new side of life, to new experiences. It's just another 'first', your sexual awakening, a thing that you did one time (for me – a shitty bastard of a thing).

If I could give advice to any 'virgins' reading this, it would be that there is no right time to go for it, and there isn't necessarily a right person, or a right place to do it, either. Do I wish my first time had been with someone I loved dearly, in a swanky candlelit hotel room, with classical music playing and cherry-flavoured lube and the works? Sure! But there's been plenty of time for that. Think about how your first ever *meal* of life was plain old milk – you weren't stuck with that forever, *right*?

A terrible first time (at anything!) does not reflect how the future will be.

There's no age that's best to first do it at, no perfect circumstance, so try not to build it up too much in your mind and just roll with it when it happens, when you're *ready*. All that matters is that you feel comfortable and that you *want* to do it – only then will you be able to enjoy yourself! And if you make the same blunders as I did, don't worry: things can get *much* better.

Because my first time sucked so hard I actually didn't have sex again until I was in a long-term, committed relationship. I mean, my practice run was bad bad *bad*. But let me tell ya, with the right person, and a bit (a lot) of practice, it's *totally* fireworks and unicorns and glitter just like in the movies – only with a lot more sweat and fart noises from your fanny. Maybe a few bite marks and scratches. And flecks of cum in your hair (it washes out, OK, calm down!).

When you sleep with someone that loves you, who you love and trust, who you want, you really start to get why sex is so talked about and so craved by humans. It. Can. Be. *Delightful*. But *guess* what?

LESSON TWO

Orgasm isn't the end game of sex. GASP! We're led to believe that intimacy is all about screeching to climax, but sex isn't some massive fail if you don't (or can't!) come during it. It's not all about that and it can be mind-blowingly pleasurable just to explore another person's body in such an intimate way. Plenty of people can't come during sex. It's common to struggle with orgasms, *especially* if the other person doesn't really know how to please you. Here's the thing ...

LESSON THREE

Never fake it. If you're faking it regularly then STOP IT.

Scenario one

Without any build-up through kissing, without nipple play and most definitely without a map, guy stabs girl's dry-as-fuck vagina with his fingers for two entire minutes, seemingly trying to reach through to tickle her womb and somehow hoping this will get her off. Girl moans because she believes she's supposed to do that, and she doesn't want to disappoint him. She doesn't say anything or stop him during, even though it's super unpleasant, and she accepts it when he just gives up to shift focus onto his cock.

Scenario two

Guy starts to prod after lots of laughing and cuddling and kissing, and girl gently guides his hand to her clitoris. She fumbles for a second, to place two of his fingers in the right place, just how she does when she masturbates, and with a cheeky smile she kisses his neck and then gently whispers into his ear what she wants him to do – all the while providing him with valuable feedback. This turns him on so much that he becomes set on getting her off and keeps doing everything she tells him to until she decides she's ready to progress.

You don't have to be Stephen Hawking to figure out which one was better and led to a magnificent sex life. DO. NOT. FAKE. IT.

Faking an orgasm only encourages your partner to *keep doing* things that *won't* make you come. I used to fake it all the damn time, and even though, sure, I enjoyed the sex part, I was selling myself short! I was having frequent sex and *never* orgasming and I became pretty expert at faking. I knew exactly what to do – how to tense up my vagina at the right time, the sounds to make, the way to shake and writhe. I mean, if somebody makes pleasure noises every time you give them a back rub, you're gonna *keep giving them back rubs* in the same way that they originally signalled that they enjoyed. Well, the same thing applies here.

LESSON FOUR

Ask for what you want in bed. Don't be shy! Teach your partner(s) what to do and how to hit your spot – it's hot. There's *nothing* hotter! Learning to communicate your desires and having your partner know how to read your body's sensitivities is better than the freshest, fluffiest Italian baguette smeared with Nutella. *Really.*

I've had guys be like, 'Mel, please – be gentle at the tip there,' and, sure, at first I'd think, *But the last guy wanted me to be firm there?*

I read about this whole 'just communicate in bed' thing in an agony aunt column as a teen, in one of my mammy's magazines, and it changed my life. And now it's a gift from me to you!

LESSON FIVE

Everyone likes different things in bed, the same way people like different movie genres. It's all about finding someone who meshes well with you and your, eh, sexual style!

Trying on different styles can be so fun, though. It's a bit like playing dress-up or taking a car out for a spin before you buy it.

Sometimes people are lucky enough to learn what they like *with* a partner, of course – not everyone already knows what they like entering into a shared sex life. But for me it was totally the opposite because I became sexual so young. I grew so good at pleasing myself over the years through masturbation that, initially, I was simply horrified at the idea of telling someone else how to handle me – pressure, speed, all that good stuff. People can't really *guess* those things. You've gotta give some guidance if you wanna be satisfied. Unless you're having sex with the actual *character* of Sherlock, who could read you like a book in seconds.

And of course, sex isn't all about penis and vagina and baby-making and missionary position. Right now, all around the world, there are all kinds of sexualities and genders mixing together – so many unique combinations of people and fun things to try – and it's beautiful! The *variety* of it. It's not something to cringe about or something that should make you feel uncomfortable. The fact that some couples are out there right now making sweet, tender love (OK, I'm with you if the phrase 'making love' has the hairs on the back of your neck standing up). Some might be participating in *group* sex (yep – that's a thing! A very fun thing!). Singletons might be having solo fun with rose-gold clitoris stimulators or hooking up with a 'fuck buddy'. Nothing should feel off limits *if you want to do it* because no enjoyable (legal) sex act is inherently bad, and no (legal) combination of human beings in the bedroom is wrong.

If you like to be tied up and spanked? Great. Love threesomes? Marvellous. Can't fathom the idea of *anything* outside of lights-off sex with the other person on top? That's fine too! Everyone is different and has their own kinks and comfort levels, and you'll always be able to find someone who matches up with you and your needs. Even if that's having *no* sex. Abstinence is a thing; asexuality is a thing – the human race truly is a technicolour spectrum on which we all sit.

Please shake off your worries about your sex life like a wet coat you don't need to be wearing because that's all those worries are. If everything is consensual and legal and if you're looking after your emotions and *not*, for example, sleeping with someone you love who has told you they love someone else, then go you! Do yo thang! Put your bits and pieces with the bits and pieces of whoever you like!

CONSENT and SEXUAL ASSAULT

For some bizarre reason, the meaning of consent appears to, *still*, be blurred and misunderstood by a lot of people. Including the two people who interfered with me when I was seventeen.

But we'll get to that.

Sexual consent is an explicit agreement of permission for sexual behaviour between you (when you're of age, in whatever country you're in) and another person. Even married couples need consent. *Each and every time*. It's not just some wishy-washy concept that only crops up in relation to intoxicated university students at parties. It's a big bloody deal.

Consent *doesn't* have to be verbal, but verbally agreeing to various sexual activities can help both you and whomever you decide to sleep with to respect each other's sexual boundaries. Body language is really key here, though.

Because, like, I don't know about you but I don't make a habit of having conversations with sexual partners along the lines of 'Hey, so, I'd like to have sex with you right now, and I know you'd like to have sex with me, so here's a little contract I did up on the computer that we both just have to sign first to make sure that we're *completely clear* that we both want this, OK? Get a pen, will you? Sign on that dotted line

– I'll scan it and email it to myself, and then I'll consensually remove my knickers ...' I'm joking because I'm uncomfortable talking about this because it's so *seriously important*, but you know what I mean ... In most situations, sex sort of just happens between two adults who want it, and that's usually *largely* down to developed perceptiveness and being able to read the other person's body language.

Ideally we'd always verbalise that we want it in any given situation, but it's important to learn how to pick up on nonverbal cues that mean an enthusiastic 'yes, continue!' or 'no, please stop' so things can flow – if it is indeed a 'yes, do me now' kind of moment. If that lovely erotic tension is there – you know the one: eye contact; smiling; leaning in to one another; non-invasive touching, such as a soft brush of the fingers against the other person's arm ... If there's a lot of this sort of flirtation and giggly chatting, then it's clear that there's mutual interest. You can always pace things nice and slowly, and look out for *any* hint of the other person pulling away, freezing up or seeming uncomfortable.

I was just eight years old when I first heard the word 'rapist' and I genuinely thought it meant some kind of mass murder with knives as fingers, like Edward Scissorhands. The word 'rape' just sounded like it described the movements Edward made when cutting up bushes in the movie ... *Little did I know.*

Evil. Vile. Psychologically damaging. Degrading. Disempowering.

Of course us girls should be able to go wherever we want, wearing whatever we want, with ANY amount of drink on us, *without* getting attacked or taken advantage of. *Duh!* But it's important to remember that we're *not* Terminators, and there *are* dangerous people out there.

Like the two strangers, back in 2007, who ripped my tights open with a set of keys. They felt me up and then sauntered off as they heard voices approach – didn't even run – which is the part of this memory that always makes my skin *crawl.* They just stopped and walked off together, casual as anything, seemingly sure they'd get away with it.

This incident is so hard for me to write about, even now, but it's important. It's one of those hateful things that shook me, shaped me and that might help even one person reading.

It happened during a weekend night out in a town called Navan. I'd had a drunken argument with my best friend's boyfriend. I stormed out of the club alone, before the night had ended, and having promised my friends that I'd stay with them all night. My phone was almost dead and I felt like a total bitch leaving early, but I was being dramatic and standing up for my friend in the only way I knew how.

With my bag and my coat bundled up in my arms, I stumbled through the dark town toward the local McDonald's, guided only by the lampposts and the part of my subconscious that clung to direction – even in my state, I knew the McDonald's stayed open pretty late. I had no idea what time it was at this point, though, and I could hardly walk straight in my ridiculous Primark heels.

I was seething and crying with frustration, and I just wanted to scoff a double cheeseburger then jump in a taxi home.

I made it to the McDonald's laneway only to realise the place was closed, and within seconds I was forcefully grabbed from behind. I dropped everything in my arms and found myself pinned to a shop window opposite the McDonald's doorway, paralysed with fright, with a hand over my mouth that stank of cigarettes and salt and vinegar.

The silence of my surroundings choked me then. You know when you're *so* drunk that nothing appears to be solid matter anymore – everything's fluid and your surroundings flow into one another, like in a dream? So drunk that you're thinking in slow motion? I was that far gone. I felt stuck in place, but the blur of a man in front of me – well-built, bald (I think) – had both his arms in my sight.

I realised that there was another man present, holding me prisoner.

They talked to one another in a language I couldn't understand, and the guy whose hands I could see removed a set of keys from somewhere, probably his pocket. They clinked (little did I know then that the clinking of keys would strike up unease in me for *years* to come). I didn't feel my tights being torn apart and only noticed afterward, but I *did* feel a rough, fat-fingered hand suddenly inside my pants, groping at my vulva, and another grabbing at my chest. The two men kept talking and then the main fucker laughed, and I was overcome with a sense of embarrassment in the midst of my powerlessness – I remembered that I hadn't shaved my bikini line in days, so it was all stubble.

I still *can't believe* I felt aware and ashamed of my pubic grooming while being sexually assaulted.

My boyfriend 'Freddie''s face flashed into my mind too, and my stomach churned. *He'll probably never want me again.*

This monster kept poking around and laughing and saying things in another language as silent tears drenched my cheeks and, still paralysed, out of nowhere I became almost entirely disconnected from my body. It was too traumatic and I was too drunk and ... it's like I mentally checked out. I thought I was about to be raped. Maybe I would've been if the location hadn't been so obnoxiously public. I mean, that's the worst thing! It's not like I went off wandering in some barren wasteland – I was in the *middle* of town; there was a streetlamp just metres away outside the laneway.

But nowhere is completely safe.

I must have been let go soon after – I came back round halfway to the ground, hearing distant voices that seemed to be getting closer with each passing second, on the main road beside the laneway. Half a minute could have passed, or less, or more, I had no idea. I was frozen stiff like a plank of wood and my voice was stuck down my throat, like I was choking on a teabag. I glanced to my right, taking short, sharp breaths, and spotted the two guys strolling along in the other direction, back toward the shopping centre. Then I resumed control of my everything and I burst into tears. I cried so loud and so hard and I threw up on my own lap, onto my ripped tights.

That night, my dad and I sat in the back of a police car as it did laps of Navan town, and I made a statement, but nothing came of it. The two men were never found. I daren't imagine the other horrors they've inflicted. No good, upstanding pair of human beings could do something like that to a defenceless teen and walk away without a bother on them.

This attack on my person taught me the importance of being safe and prepared but it also set me back in ways I couldn't then anticipate.

People experience these things – being played with like rag dolls by bloodthirsty wretches and far worse – day in, day out. That fact *doesn't* make it OK. But when my therapist (I was referred to one by my GP, just to talk through what had happened, and I recommend this to *anyone* who has suffered any kind of assault) told me how frequently this crap happens to children and teens and women – *even* by their partners – I felt a little bit less ... tainted. You'd think being told that I was now part of some disgracefully unlucky 'club' would make me feel even worse, but it helped me to stop blaming myself for what happened. I wasn't in control of that situation, but I could at least try to ensure that I never landed in a similar one again.

Having a stranger's disgusting hands on me like that left me feeling unclean and weak. But, with support (therapy, family, friends), I focused on the fact that that was just *one* cruel, momentary blip (that could've been a whole lot worse, let's be real) and that I'd retained my power – my ability to stand back up. I couldn't/cannot allow that to keep hold of me!

And after opening up about it in therapy, while sitting on a bright-orange beanbag, I was filled with an overwhelming urge to fight it: to learn why it happens, *why* people do such things; to in some way educate and positively impact young people. *Don't be barbaric, kids.* To encourage young girls to cling tight to good people in circumstances where their bodily autonomy may be threatened by the savage nature of those in this world who've meandered way off course.

I'm doing that right now. Hey you: *be safe, be strong.*

I wish I could also demonstrate that it *doesn't* have a lasting effect but, alas, I can't. Having my space invaded in such a brutal way has affected my behaviour around strange men for the past ten years.

The experience etched itself onto my skin and is now this tattoo that I can't rid myself of. I've covered it up, I've tried ignoring it, but it's still there. It's why I've since struggled to just hook up with a total stranger, after meeting in a club, say, like many of my friends do. Sometimes I meet people when I'm out and I like them, but the memory of that night holds me back from going off and having my fun. I actually think it's the main reason I'm so wary of dating apps, too, like Tinder – apps which *many* people use for straight-up sex with strangers.

I feel so much safer getting intimate with a person who I know, or someone I share friends with, or someone who's easily identifiable and traceable – everyone I've dated since my last relationship fell apart has resided within my friend circle or been someone from my industry.

And as I reflect, I realise that hasn't just been happenstance.

I can't help but draw a comparison between myself and Bilbo here – *no*, not the character from *The Hobbit*, but one of our family cats, named after him. We rescued him from an animal shelter when he was only a couple of weeks old – far too young to be separated from his mother. He'd been found in a bush with his siblings, and even now, years later, he's terrified of new people. I mean, his constant state of hesitancy makes him *him*, and he's adorable and I love him, but it's difficult to watch him sometimes – so stiff, so unsure. When he gets anxious he tenses up and hides, and every time a new person calls round to the house, Bilbo will be lodged in behind the washing machine, shaking and crying for hours.

Well, I've become a little bit like Bilbo when it comes to meeting strange men on my own. Even for work stuff. And when strangers (guys) come on to me in a forward way, regardless of how lovely they are, my mind's eye flashes to that night in the laneway and I instantly bring up this thick barrier. I'm distrusting because of it, and the worst part is I doubt this will ever change, because I can't change what happened to me.

I've grown from what happened, I've channelled it into wanting to impact people in a positive way, but I can't alter this scarification it's left behind. I always need someone with me if I have to meet a man who I don't know, or if I'm going to be in a place surrounded by strange men – a buffer, or a mutual friend, to play shield.

The one 'stranger' I've agreed to meet, alone, in my *life*, was only a stranger in that I'd not *physically* met him previous to our first date. But we'd watched each other's YouTube videos! And although he didn't appear in any of his videos, preferring voiceover and graphics, he was traceable through social media, which helped to put my mind at ease. We spoke for a solid month (every day) *before* meeting up for a date. And while we hit it off, and he was frightfully wonderful and respectful, it didn't work out. Still, that was a *huge* step for me in overcoming my fear of putting myself out there and being physically taken advantage of again. I'm so grateful for that experience. He holds a special place in my heart for that reason.

I don't think I even told *him* that. Perhaps I should ...

And it's important to mention here the awful truth that *three out of four rapes are committed by someone known to the victim*, a statistic that paralyses me.

If you have ever been in a situation where you felt forced to have sex, where you tried to communicate with your body out of terror of speaking up; or if you've ever had someone (even a partner) interfere with you while you've slept; if you've been threatened with injury for not following through with sexual demands, then that counts as rape.

If someone confides in you that they were raped or sexually assaulted in any way, *believe them* and encourage them to press charges *as soon as possible* and to seek therapy. Only a very small percentage of rape accusations turn out to be false or fabricated, so it's always worth having confidence in anyone brave enough to come to you looking for help.

And if you're one of the *many* people who've been interfered with, in *any* way, let's get one thing straight: *it is not your fault.* Whatever you do afterward is up to you – it's your life, your body, your well-being, and only you know what's best for you. But if you *do* choose to seek assistance after an assault, there are many people out there who want to help you. If the assault came from someone within your family or your social circle, know that you have places to turn to.

You're not alone. And you *can* get through this.

The BABY
I NEVER HAD

The world of sex is like a too-full bubble bath that you want to dive into *without* flooding your bathroom floor – there's just so much to consider. Why can't it be straightforward? The first-time nerves, the practising and finding bedroom confidence, the going out of your comfort zone, the learning how to please and take pleasure, the overlapping and intensifying of feelings of love which can make new relationships or casual flings messy 'coz attachment hormones (when women have sex, oxytocin is released, 'the bonding hormone', due to the evolutionary drive to attach to someone who may be the potential parent of a possible child), the issues of consent and, of course, the constant consideration of protection against pregnancy and not-so-sexy diseases.

I've always been so careful with contraception, yet in my twenty-seven years on this earth I've somehow managed to fail at fully protecting myself on a couple of occasions.

I've come to terms with the tale I'm about to tell now, after years of being reminded of it with each period and of talking it through with loved ones, so I'm going to open up about this – and, no, *not* about the time I caught chlamydia after being cheated on because, well, that one I'm still trying to cope with, even though the disease is gone. Just. *Ahh.* I can't be dealin' – I feel like I should wrap my entire body in a condom and just be done with it. Anyway …

Aged nineteen, I got all dolled up with friends and popped my contraceptive pill, Dianette, last minute (swallowed it down with a red bull and vodka while pre-drinking in the back of a taxi). I proceeded to get far too drunk and then *very embarrassingly* threw up in the smoking area of the nightclub. Moments after cleaning myself up, I trotted out of the girls' toilets like Bambi learning to walk and ran headfirst into my first love – the one I'd dated for years. 'Freddie'.

He'd come looking for me after hearing I was out. Emotions ran high that night. 'Freddie' knew I'd started casually seeing someone else in the weeks since we'd broken up, but he still felt like I was his. And, admittedly, I wasn't over 'Freddie' either. I'd been trying my damnedest to move on, though, and in that instance, getting *under* someone else really hadn't helped (like everyone around me at the time had assured me it would). You can't deal with true heartache by diving into a herd of antelope and grabbing on to whichever one you land on!

Swimming in my intoxication, the old jokes and the familiarity between 'Freddie' and me, paired with the intensity of how he was staring at me, led me to (foolishly) agree to go home with him.

We didn't use protection. In my drunkness, I *completely* forgot that I'd puked – rendering my pill out of order.

Pills always come with warnings, in minuscule writing on the shitty little leaflets and from the doctors who prescribe them. Basically: if you get the shits or vom or take antibiotics, use extra protection because the tablet may or may not be useless. Turns out those teeny tiny letters in the leaflets are *bloody important* – the doctor should scream them at patients. They should be highlighted and bolded on pill packets in the same way *smoking kills* is plastered onto cigarette boxes.

I didn't think much of it at the time. I was too caught up in the drama that sleeping with a recent ex brings. (Why do we do these things to ourselves? Sometimes we're like those stupid bluebottles that keep banging into the same window for hours.) But weeks later, I'd noticed I hadn't gotten my period and that I felt unusually bloated.

My breasts were sore and more rounded than normal. A good friend at the time suggested that I take a pregnancy test, and when it showed up as positive I felt a numbness like nothing else I'd ever felt.

I really, *really* wasn't ready for a baby. I was still a baby myself. I had no job, I was a very single, immature teenager – my life was a table with two legs. The racing thoughts came thick and fast then: *Who'll pay for it? Will it destroy my body? Will it look like 'Freddie'? Will I have to be attached to him now forever? Dad is going to kill me ...*

But Dad didn't kill me. In fact, he was incredible – stressed, sure, but he didn't scold me or call me a slut or any of the other horrible things I'd envisioned. 'When I was younger, it was pretty common for women your age to have babies. It'll all be okay, Mel.' The more I think of it, knowing him so well now, I'm certain he was just wearing a brave face for me. I'm so glad he did that.

My mam wasn't happy about it, understandably, but it was during a time when we didn't get along anyway so I tried not to let that dampen my spirits even more. (They were already a little bit drenched, let's be real! A giant red X had been scribbled across my life map of 'babies whenever I'm settled down with a house and a husband or wife' in one forgettable, drunken fumble.)

'Freddie' said he'd be there for me, even though he was clearly shaken to the core.

I was still feeling numb, and like an idiot, but nature kind of kicked in, and I just dealt with it. Life has a way of helping us cope with the unanticipated dung droppings that fall from the sky and hit us in the face.

I was going to be a mother before I reached my twenties.

I told myself things like, 'Well, Mel, not everyone even *can* have a baby. Some women spend thousands of euros and years of their lives trying to get pregnant.' And, even though I'm most definitely *pro-choice* and I've always actively campaigned for Irish women to have the right to choose, abortion isn't something I'd necessarily consider for myself. It didn't even cross my mind back then as a viable option. My life wasn't in danger from the pregnancy and it wasn't a child of rape. I resolved that, for me, my babies would be neither planned nor unplanned, and that they'd likely just land ... whenever.

My friends and I talked about names and baby clothes shopping, and I started to get used to the idea that it was going to happen. I even remember feeling random pangs of excitement and butterflies. Dad bought me baby books and I started reading up about the pregnancy process with fascination, gazing at the diagrams of baby-filled female bodies at various stages of pregnancy. They were like crop circles to me. Strange, alien.

Then one morning, a month later, while dancing around the house tidying and listening to the soundtrack from the movie *Grease*, I felt like I was going to piss my pants. I legged it into the loo, squatted and whipped my PJ bottoms down mid-hum of 'Blue Moon' – I wiped, went to flush and glanced into the toilet (as usual – weird habit but I *know* I'm not alone in my fascination with post-excretion toilet contents) and I spotted blood. The water was red and the toilet paper was stained with flecks of what looked like a period.

I stared blankly, confused. *I thought you didn't get your period when pregnant?* I honed in then on my body, my stomach (back then I'd often have indigestion due to a terrible diet so I was always focused on that feeling). I noticed some mild pain lower down, but more toward my back. I'd figured that was just a pulled muscle or something. It was a *little* bit like period cramps but still different ...

That was the prelude to one of the worst weeks I've lived. I had a miscarriage after about eight weeks of pregnancy, and I was kept in Drogheda hospital for I can't even remember how long, as the doctors wanted to make sure everything was OK.

It broke me.

So much pain and cramping, and guilty thoughts of *I've dodged a bullet.* The week in hospital was a blur of my teeny white portable DVD player and *Sex and the City* episodes, my dad's face and my friends' faces and nurses' uniforms and blood. So much blood. Sometimes accompanied by pinkish, spongy-looking tissue. It was too much for me – I needed to escape it so I channelled as much of my mind as possible into the glamorous life of Carrie Bradshaw in New York through my DVDs.

That show, and the kindness of the people who cared enough to see me through, saved me.

We never think these things will happen to us. And when they do, we've got a remarkable ability to cope and to recover and to move on. And while I mourned the loss of that baby and of the life I'd have lived in a parallel world in which it survived, it wasn't time for me to be a mother. I'd known that deep down all along, but I was wearing my strong suit – the one I keep pressed and hung in my wardrobe for the *really* tough moments. When I eventually do have kids, I want to be as amazing for them as my own parents were for me during those early years. Well, aged nineteen and single and broke and sad and unhealthy, I wasn't going to have the best shot at emulating my wonderful parents. It was likely for the best. My life wouldn't be what it is if I'd given birth. Heck, perhaps my life would've been *better* – who knows?

See, this is why I don't dwell on it. Or on any things like this, things out of my control. The littlest action can have the most far-reaching effects, sometimes in ways we can't even fathom as mere mortals, but we've got to stay present and avoid living in the past or in a world that no longer exists or one that never existed in the first place!

The world in which that child was born and all the phantom memories I made up in my head, none of it is real. I needed to push past it all and my way is through escapism and filling my time with people who can make me laugh and make me analyse and grow from my actions (like my dad).

The experience of expecting a baby that I never had was a painful, but necessary, part of my journey.

Section 5

LOVE and HAPPINESS

THiNGS *that* MAKE ME HAPPY

I used to be chronically unhappy. And I'm not referring to when I was depressed – the rest of the time I hate to admit, I was a soggy biscuit. A wallower. An insufferable poster kid for emo. I really thought it was cool to be all miserable and *woe is me*. I didn't think to, or want to, ask anyone for help or advice either, assuming that feeling *meh* every day was entirely ordinary.

We're notoriously terrible as a species at knowing what will make us happy in the first place, and sometimes we develop a strange familiarity with dissatisfaction. For me, the deep-rooted insecurity I experienced for years labelled me, in my own mind, as *undeserving of happiness*, and that impacted many of my choices. I'd take people back after they treated me badly. I'd refuse to demand respect from friends. I'd lower my standards. I'd avoid at all costs 'working on myself' and I'd self-sabotage like a mofo by procrastinating instead of studying, by drinking too much, knowing full well I'd lose an entire day to a hangover.

Even during times when my mental health was generally *fine*, I prided myself on realism so much that I believed being 'realistic' was the same thing as focusing on the negative in life.

And I perceived happy experiences as a prelude to disappointment. I trace much of that feeling back to the early days of my mam and dad breaking up – even though that ended up being, well, brilliant! (Literally – two Christmases, double presents for every birthday, two homes, extra pocket money, a third parent!)

I took on the world's problems as my own, too – *how can I allow myself to be happy when there are people out there starving?*

A lot of people confuse happiness with *elation*, and feeling fine with *unhappiness*. To me, happiness is an overall feeling of ease and peace. It's regularly entering that state of flow – the zone – becoming fully immersed in a feeling of energised focus. It's *not* being overtly joyous and full of glee *every second of the day*, like the character Parker from *Friends* – you know, that painfully enthusiastic dude who thinks that everything is 'aglow with the light of a million fairies'? And it's not about the accumulation of stuff either. (For me, anyway. Although I'm a bit of a secret hoarder, my things don't define me. If anything, *I* define *my things* – they reflect the choices I've made; they're just objects to which I've attached experiences and memories.)

I'd argue that true happiness is more, just ... feeling OK and mostly satisfied with your lot in life.

I get stressed, I get upset, but in general I'd describe myself as happy. And I understand that a lot of people struggle with happiness nowadays. In honesty, a lot of my happiness comes from the optimism I developed thanks to my astounding support network. Remember I told you guys about how I got into all that law of attraction malarkey? Well, when I was about twenty, I decided to stop waking up and thinking about all the worst things in the world that I don't have any power over and about everything out of my control getting me down. When you're *not* suffering from poor mental health you *do* have that choice, and after several sessions with my therapist I figured out how to channel my energy into reminding myself that *I'm free, I can do things that I love doing any time I like, I have some really fantastic people in my life, I'm capable of doing things to help others, and there are many things to care about that are bigger than myself and my own happiness anyway!* Most people reading this will be able to admit that these things are true for them, too.

Maybe this list will help you to spark off your own, a list that you can read over any time you feel not-so-great – you don't need to be a billionaire superstar with perfect teeth and thousands of Facebook 'friends' to find happiness in the most basic-ass things! Here are a few things that make me happy:

1 **My cats cleaning each other's faces.** Molly is jet black and purrs so loudly and has a big, bushy tail like a fox. Her tongue always hangs from her mouth and that sight is too precious for this world. She makes up for what Bilbo lacks in affection. Bilbo is our scaredy-cat, the one who jumps at everything, but we love him for it.

2 **Seeing genuine smiles** on the faces of my family and friends.

3 **Orgasms**.

4 **Surrendering my body** to a big candlelit bath filled with pink water from a Lush bath bomb and *mountains* of bubbles.

5 **Salted, good-quality dark chocolate** washed down with a generous glass of red wine (even better if it's Châteauneuf-du-Pape).

6 **The feeling I get right before a new movie starts in the cinema** – right after the lights dim and the conversation dwindles, when the age rating pops up and when all I can hear is the crumpling of packets and all I can smell is popcorn (and the tang of cheesy Doritos that I've snuck in and am opening now because there's no *way* the cinema staff will be able to see).

7 **Singing Disney songs** through unrestrained laughter with my twenty-five-year-old brother while we clean the house. Apparently, according to Dad, we communicate through song and will finish lyrics from separate rooms of the house without realising ...

8 **A night-time stroll** in the seaside village where I live, especially when the stars are out and when a particularly emotive song pops on from my playlist. Walking alone with music is my favourite way to zone out and meditate.

9 **The face my dad makes when I catch him out in a white lie.** It's the perfect combination of mischievousness and embarrassment and it makes his eyes light up.

10 **Taking time out in the morning** before the day begins to prepare and eat a freshly made breakfast, with fresh-pressed coffee. The smell of coffee alone, from our cafetière, fills me with peace. It's weird – I hated coffee when I was younger and now it gets me out of bed with a soul smile!

11 **Helping people in need** through donations or small, well-meaning gestures, or making someone's day a little better with a compliment. I don't think anything can top the feeling that brings. I try to keep my eyes wide open, always, for opportunities to help others.

12 **'Sexual liberation parties'** with my dear friends Hannah Witton, Riyadh K and Calum McSwiggan (all of whom I met through YouTube). These are times when we all open up about sex and discuss things that we often keep bottled up. It doesn't matter where we are – once the four of us are together it's a sexual liberation party because almost every conversation comes back to the topics of sex, love, desire and experimentation! When I spend time with them, I feel like I'm Carrie Bradshaw and they're my girls at the coffee shop – my Samantha, Charlotte and Miranda.

13 **The changing seasons.** I love that, living in Ireland, each season lasts just long enough to *not* become entirely sick of it. Just as I'm craving autumn, I'll see a leaf fall from a tree; just as I'm gasping for brighter evenings and more sun, I'll notice that I no longer need to wear my housecoat!

14 **A good twist in a book.** I love it when my mind is challenged.

15 **Re-watching Bo Burnham's stand-up shows on Netflix.** Very few people can make me laugh that hard.

16 **Falling in love.** It's spectacularly different every single time and I never anticipate it so it's always an electric shock.

17 **Snuggles.** Especially with people who play with my hair or scratch my back.

18 **Ordering something brand new at a restaurant** and waiting for it to arrive at my table to either change my life or make me cry and wish I'd stuck with pasta carbonara.

19 Blaring epic soundtracks while I cook – *Game of Thrones, Gladiator, Braveheart, Hook, Harry Potter, Lord of the Rings, The Da Vinci Code* – you know the sort! I listen to them and dream up romantic scenarios that I want to experience. (In these dreams I always have butt-length hair and a white horse.)

20 Sitting on the couch with my mam and my sister and having long, deep chats about what's going on with my sister's dating life, and mine.

21 CHRISTMAS! All three of my parents worked hard to make Christmas an incredible and magical time every year when I was a child and teen ... and it's still my favourite time of the year because of those fond memories! Wine, way too many chocolates, family movies and PJs all day. Oh yes.

A TRIBUTE to my DAD

Ah, my da! Dad means so much to me that I feel like nothing I write here will convey it: no combination of words could possibly measure or capture the love I feel for him. He's up in bed right now as I type, snoring away after pottering in from a few pints down the village pub with his friends. (I moved home after a couple of break-ups, back to the safety nest, really adulting it up in here, WOO.) He's in the box room of the house, which he took instead of either of the two bigger rooms, because he wanted my brother and me to have those.

That's Dad all over.

The sounds of his breathing right now, the rise and fall of his chest, brings me tranquillity and contentment, not only because I've lived with him since I was sixteen and because I've battled distressing separation anxiety all my life (he's, like, one of my limbs. Imagine leaving the house without your leg! That's how I feel *all the time*), but because he had a heart attack recently, while I was on a trip with my YouTube friend Hannah Witton, and I first tasted the concept of a world without him in it.

That *almost killed* me.

And even though I don't think I can possibly describe how much I love him, I'm going to try.

Dad

A PICTURE OF MY DAD:

♥ His name is Paul.

♥ He's in his early fifties and he's a simple, uncomplicated man, but with more layers than an onion.

♥ He gets up for work every day, rarely complaining (even though he doesn't have the *most* riveting job in the world – he's a manager in a factory that coats hospital tools, *yawn* – oh, sorry, I fell asleep).

♥ He's also a science fiction fanatic, and he brought my little brother and me up to be obsessed with space and the possible existence of aliens and other worlds. We'd stay up until all hours with him playing computer games and watching movies and TV shows, escaping together into alternative realms of the mind.

♥ Dad's the kind of person who's impossible to stay mad at because he's just so daftly *nice*. When we fight, we'll both slam doors and snap at each other (we're so very similar), but we'll make up after about ten minutes because he's excellent at making me laugh and he'll *always* at least try to defuse tension with humour.

♥ He has one of those faces where all you see are his eyes. Sure, if I focus I see lots of laughter lines and stress lines, but he's got the warmest, kindest eyes and they distract from the bald head he's spent most of his life self-aware of – and from the non-existent fashion sense (sorry, Dad! *Ha-ha*).

♥ The man can sing like a Beatle, and when we were kids he'd belt out songs in the car on the long drives to and from my mam's house, where he'd collect us on weekends. Now that we're older, though, he gets all embarrassed and only lets rip after eight too many drinks at a party.

♥ He's annoyingly tidy and one of the only things that frustrates him in this world is mess.

♥ He's got insane general knowledge and knows so much about so many things, even though sometimes he just makes up his own facts and passes them off as real. My brother and I call these 'dad facts'.

♥ Dad loves animals and talks to our cats like they're babies, putting on a goo-goo ga-ga voice when he thinks nobody's listening.

♥ He swears like a trooper and my YouTube viewers love him for it – for his 'fuck offs' and his grumpiness and for the random, weird faces he pulls when he doesn't know what else to do with himself.

♥ When he was in his twenties, he defended some random guy against a pack of homophobes. One of them bit the bottom of his ear off and it had to be sewn back on in the hospital.

♥ He hates everyone I date and makes them jump through hoops, but I think it's pretty hilarious. He made both my long-term partners work so hard for his approval (which neither of them ever really received), and any time I fancy someone he eyeballs their pictures (or their videos if they're a fellow YouTuber), weighs them up then grumbles at me while necking a cup of coffee. 'Ah, Mel, you can do better, come on!' he'll whine.

♥ He's not afraid to be vulnerable, even though he grew up in a home where you don't talk about feelings or mental health or any of that nonsense. It makes me happy that he feels safe enough to open up and that he realises that doesn't make him any less 'a man'.

♥ I watched him jump out our kitchen window once in the middle of cooking spaghetti Bolognese to tell a bunch of teenagers on the street to fuck off after they'd kept looking in our windows and throwing things at our house. Iconic!

Now that you can picture him, let me tell you why I admire him.

Dad pushed through his divorce all the while balancing a social life with spending weekends working nights *and* seeing my brother and me. For three days every week, he basically just wouldn't sleep so he could spend time with us. He'd spend every last euro he had on us, to the point that one weekend we were demanding he take us to the cinema – so he went to take out cash from the bank machine to find that his balance was zero. He then called our uncle to borrow some money to bring us regardless. (Thankfully, he's always had a great support network with *seven* brothers and sisters, which is actually why I myself want a big family! I've seen how much they're all there for one another in times of crisis.)

He would drop anything to help my brother and me out, too, *to a fault.* He's the most giving, most compassionate person I've ever known and he's also, surprisingly, the happiest.

Dad's days are basic: wake up at 6:30 a.m., coffee and porridge, go to work, come home, have dinner and watch the news, flake on the couch with the cats, ramble down to the pub a couple of nights a week or catch an early night (alone – he hasn't remarried. Wink-wink, ladies!). On weekends, he'll go for drives with us or with his friends, and his social circle is so tight that they go on trips together every year. You might look at his life and think it's not very exciting, but my dad is *content* and has taught me that I really don't need very much at all to be happy!

Sure, he'd love to retire early, and sure, he'd love to have more money – who wouldn't? But he's happy regardless. He appreciates the little things and he doesn't sweat the small stuff, or the stuff out of his control. He gives me so much incredible advice when I'm losing my marbles (which is a monthly occurrence with my PMS). I'd honestly give or *do* anything to earn enough money so he could own his own house, and buy that massive telescope he's always dreamed of having, and put his feet up forever to enjoy some much-deserved downtime.

Everyone who knows this man is charmed by him. He's so bloody loveable and I'm so lucky to call him my dad and my best friend. I am my truest self around him. I'd be lost without him.

And, you see, that's why reflecting on my love of him gets me all emotional (*tears spatter MacBook keyboard*). The phone call from my aunt telling Melanie-that-had-just-landed-in-Stockholm that dad had suffered a major heart attack in work and that he might die in the operating room – that was total ruinous *devastation*, pain unleashed in torrents of tears and body-convulsing sobs, but that's normal, right? To love someone wholeheartedly and without limit is to attach their existence to your happiness and sense of the world, so it's only natural to fear their loss. For love to cloud up your brain every time you focus on their great qualities and virtues, their impact on who you've grown to be.

I'm one of the lucky ones. I didn't lose him. The staff at the hospital took incredible care of him, removed the blockage in his heart, inserted stents and put him on the correct medication. He's currently going through cardiac rehabilitation and learning what to eat and how much he can exercise. It has been a massive wake-up call for him to look after his health. He's not smoked a cigarette since (and the house smells a whole lot lovelier for it).

The only thing I find funny about the stories surrounding his heart attack is that, as he was walking out to the ambulance, he turned to my auntie (who works with him) and said, 'Please make sure you feed the cats for me!' *Ha-ha-ha!* Such a selfless bastard.

I'm still working on my separation anxiety. I wish I had some advice for you guys on that but, hey, we've all got our shit. When I'm away from my dad for too long I panic – it happened recently, on my friend Riyadh's floor at a party. I was surrounded by YouTubers and one of them was having a love crisis and she was upset. We were all comforting her and then for some reason we got to talking about our dads and, well, I sort of hyperventilated and I howled into some stranger's shoulder nook. I'm unhealthily attached. And I mean, reading back over all this I don't exactly blame me – he's the best! No, but really, I've just latched a whole bunch of my feelings of safety onto him through the years, for many reasons. He's always been too available and too mollycoddling of my brother and me (and he knows it) because he wasn't able to be with us every day when we were kids, after the divorce. But he's also held my hand through so many of the most difficult challenges of my life so far and he's been one of my only constants.

I'm a tragically nostalgic little bitch and, well, you can imagine how that doesn't exactly help the situation.

My dad will always be with me, in my heart, in my bones, in my brain, in my blood, but I *really* would like him to be there to walk me down the aisle and to meet his grandchildren, so right now, I'm that person who snatches the delicious, greasy bacon off his plate; who drags him out on daily walks; who shouts at him for not drinking enough water; and who praises him (*too* much) for staying off cigarettes, which he smoked for forty years!

For all these reasons, and more that I can't articulate, my dad is the best human alive and so much of him is in me – so I couldn't *not* dedicate an entire section of my first book to him. I hope this makes him do a big, gap-toothed smile! (Dad, seriously, your gap is wonderful: you don't need to fill it in, *ever!*)

FRiendSHiP

When I finished university aged twenty-four, I figured, *Hey, I'm an adult now – that's got to be the end of sucky 'friendships', right?* The days of old are behind us, surely? Now we can all gather together every week with wine and pizza to talk politics, maybe watch funny movies and go to bed after lovely, drama-less evenings!

For the most part, this turned out to be true, but a switch didn't flick one day where the crappy friends just seeped into blackness and obscurity.

There are two kinds of people in this world: people who wipe after a poo and look at the toilet paper, and liars. I'm now only concerned with befriending the dirty swines who bare their souls to me and let me see them – *all* of them. And, no, *not* their bathroom habits but their humility, their honesty and ability to joke about their bathroom habits – know what I'm saying? Life's too short to play pretend with anyone who's on a different level in the game.

Whoever coined the phrase *our friends are the family we choose for ourselves* was a right little Yoda. Our friends are an extension of the family we're born into, and no matter how messy our family life may be (maybe your dad did a runner before you were born, maybe your only sibling is an insufferable pile of fuck), it doesn't matter, because you have literally *billions* of people to choose from to surround yourself with.

But, of course, it's not quite that simple. That idea in theory is *so comforting* but in practice it can take years of painful, exhausting loneliness and 'fake friend' culling to cultivate the right circle of friends. Friends who'll provide that close support we desperately need to be fully functioning humans.

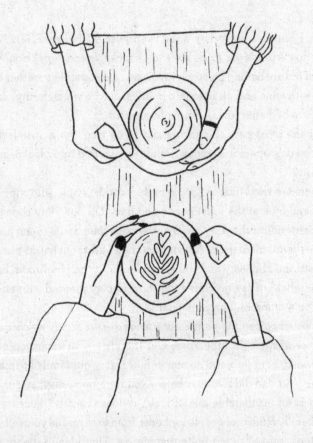

And it can take a long time to figure out how to *be* a good friend, too.

Like everything – from learning to ride a bike, to giving good head – it takes *practice*. We've got to be ruthless in ditching arseholes and finding good people, and in becoming reliable ourselves. Because we *need* to feel able to count on our friends – all of us.

Whether you realise it or not, your friends and the people you're surrounded by influence you *so hard*, in ways that are immeasurable – your online friends, too! So it makes sense that we should choose friends wisely. We're more careful about how we phrase a tweet or what we wear to a job interview than deciding on who we let into our lives these days, and that's not OK. I'd go so far as to say that we're even a product of the people who are *no longer* our friends: they're that impactful. Our peers are one of our primary agents of socialisation – along with family, school and mass media!

I believe we'd be a whole lot happier as a society if we turned to real-world, tangible friends during difficult times, rather than our bloody devices. Like, I don't know about *your* phone, but my phone can't give me a squidgy hug. My laptop can't make me a cup of tea and listen to my worries in PJs at 3 a.m. I can't clarify my mind through text conversations, because so much communication is lost without tone of voice – chat doesn't flow in the same way that it can when it's out loud, either. I'm always misunderstood through texts, and don't get me started on autocorrect.

I was one of a group of very fickle girls back in my school days. On the surface, we probably seemed like perfect friends to one another, but so many alarm bells should have been blaring – heck, maybe they were blaring and I just couldn't hear them. From competitiveness to questionable advice to never being there for each other to choosing our boyfriends over each other nine times out of ten – man, we were hos living by 'bros before hos'. I think we rubbed off each other in a bad way. We enabled each other's bad behaviour – the skipping school, the jumping on bandwagons, the making very dumb decisions like smoking hash in some strange guy's basement ...

My dad was the one to identify the sad fact that my teen friendships sucked. 'Mel, I don't like the sound of this crowd you're hanging out with. Why are you friends with them?' Of course, as my dad, his level of bias was shocking. He wasn't to know that I was a pretty crap friend, too. But he did get me thinking: *Why are we all friends? Should friendship even have a purpose?*

Our group came together due entirely to happenstance. We lived in the same area and we didn't fit into any other established groups in school. I'm sure a lot of you reading this who are my age or older experienced the same thing – pre-social media, there were just far less friend options! Some people would win the draw, and others would end up stuck with knob heads.

Take 'Becca', for example. 'Becca' was a long-term school 'friend' of mine and one of those girls who thrived on putting me in my place. One time, this cute guy I'd fancied for *ages* finally gave me his number, while we were halfway home from school, and she ended up dragging my sheer delight out by its hair onto the street to be run over by a truck (she scoffed at me in front of a group of girls by our lockers in school and made fun of the guy by birthing a rumour about how he couldn't get erections – everyone laughed and stopped being excited for me). And so, I was taken down a peg. (FYI – we later got to hand-job stage. He could indeed get perfectly healthy erections.)

This sort of behaviour from her was standard. 'Becca' would rat me out for cheating on tests (I hate admitting this because I've got a degree in teaching, but I used to scrawl answers all over my pencil case and then angle it a certain way under my desk so I could glance down and see) – sure, I was in the wrong but *who rats*? She'd tell other people secrets I'd confided in her too, all the time. Secrets like how I'd noticed an off-colour discharge in my underwear – people stuck notes in my locker for days that read, 'It's thrush, you're welcome' and 'Hey, gloopy gee, you might want to get that looked at, ha-ha.' Girls giggled at me as I walked by them in the halls and proceeded to whisper frantically while 'Becca' shushed them, and I'd catch her evil little grin and raised eyebrow. It was *awful*. On several occasions, she told me she'd meet me at a certain time and place, and then just didn't show up, leaving me alone and embarrassed – in town after school, at the bus stop, outside the cinema even. She went out of her way to flirt with almost *anyone* I found attractive (apart from 'floppy dick' guy) and she had *no* qualms about lying to my face.

This, dear reader, was an incidental friend. A person I was friends with for *no* good reason – we shared zero ambitions and very few interests, and the girl even seemed excited by my disappointments. I could never be silly around her, and she really didn't seem to want to share and grow with me.

What's the point of 'friendships' like that?

Getting rid of 'Becca', and all the other Beccas I've had in my life, went down a little bit like the end of *Lord of the Rings: The Return of the King*. I'm Frodo, she's the one ring and we've made it from the Shire to Mordor, at long last. I'm stood inside Mount Doom, at the brink of a chasm, with one of my true friends, Sam. I'm about to cast the ring ('Becca') into the fire to destroy the friendship for good. Sam's there all like, 'Eh, what are you waiting for? Just let it go!' But I just ... can't. She's got her hooks in deep. I turn my back on my plans to destroy the friendship – I mean, *ring*. I'm so wrapped around her finger that I wrap *her* around *my* finger (LOTR fans, you guys know wassup when the ring goes on the finger!) and *everything* ends in disaster ...

Long story short, it was nearly impossible to cut her out. Because *I cared* about her. Accepting that she didn't care about me was the hard part. Our relationship was one-sided in her favour. She sucked all the friendship perks out of me – she'd lean on me, ask me to help her out with school projects, seek my advice, share my damn lunch (*Joey doesn't share food*) – but she gave me next to nothing in return.

We eventually drifted apart naturally, as we both made new friends after school, but I wish I'd just cut the damn cord sooner. I could've given all that time to people who deserved it!

When I think those thoughts I need to stop myself, though – terrible friendships teach us how to spot bad eggs. I needed the 'Beccas' to learn how to distinguish them from non-Beccas. Now I know the traits I should avoid in the people I accept into my circle of trust and my life has been so much easier and more fun since I stopped routinely accepting friendship from unfriendables!

I've met some of my current close friends through the internet – through YouTube, through going to events arranged through social media – and I've had to be a bit bold in putting myself out there. I've also maintained some of my older friendships, largely through social media messaging. I think this has been easy for me because social media and creating stuff for YouTube is not only my job, it's my hobby, my passion. If *you* want to find people who you'll have things in common with, simply make a point of looking up different events and gatherings taking place in relation to *your* passion. That might mean going to workout classes or cosplay conventions. It may involve learning how to paint with a group of new people at a local community centre, or attending music festivals, or auditioning to take part in or help out with a local play – there are *so many ways* to meet people on your level. Heck, I've even made friends through online gaming!

However, I need to work *really hard* to keep the real-life friendships going. As it turns out, adults are hella busy. There are jobs, spouses, partners, kids even (my god, we're now the same age as the characters in *Friends*. I never thought this day would come!).

I know I'm incredibly lucky to have found my tribe. I kept believing that I would and, sure, many of my friends aren't friends with each other, but that doesn't matter. I've got a few mini groups going on and a handful of those superhuman friends who feel like proper soulmates. With these people I've formed unbreakable bonds.

They're the kind of friends I won't see in person for months on end, but as soon as we meet up and hang out it's like only a day has passed. The kind who'll sit in comfortable silence with me as we work away on our laptops – that, for me, is the true test of friendship! Well, that and who's there to hug me when I succeed – not only when I fail.

Superficial friendships that *aren't* deep and meaningful are OK, I guess, but as filler, to provide diverse influence and mixed viewpoints. These guys keep things interesting when you go online and fill in gaps in your time when you may be bored feckless. And here I'm talking about the kind of relationships you have with the majority of your Facebook friends – the ones who you'll like posts and photos by and sporadically exchange brief catch-up messages with. *But* ... that should never be it. You shouldn't settle for having *only* virtual friendships. Great if they're fulfilling some of your needs, of course, but I believe we all need the kind of friends who'll be there for us, in the flesh, through thick and thin, no matter what.

Don't give up if you haven't found them yet.

Knowing I can call up a friend and they'll make room for me in their day or rearrange plans, knowing I can call people on Skype whenever and they'll answer – and vice versa: *being* a good and trusted friend, helping out my pals when they're in a bind and feeling their love and gratitude – this two-way street is a *huge* part of my happiness and why I'm in such a good mood all the time. I'm often asked why I'm always so happy and, well, it's hard *not* to be when you've put yourself out there only to have rounded up *actual power rangers*, who you have contact with on tap and who you can be a power ranger for right back. I've found friends who are irreplaceable – the kind who'll make jokes about the mess I've gotten myself into or act as mirrors to show me the truths I can't see; friends who'll keep my chin up when I'm crying on the floor over being cheated on; and friends who'll help me out with stuff, because I'm a tiny speckle and I can't do all that much by my lonesome.

When others are good to me I'll always return the favour. Because friendship is about give and take. *Love needs reciprocity.*

The four key types of friendables, to me, are (and even better if someone is all four joined into one):

1 **Accomplices.** Us humans are teeny, fragile creatures and it's a big, bad world out there ... without people to work and collaborate with, people to network and join forces with, ain't nothing great getting done any time soon! We all need friends who'll band together with us to make shit happen. For you, that might be someone to help you build a bookcase; for me that might be someone to hold my camera while I jump around in front of it doing ridiculous faces and poses for a video! Every magnificent thing we've done as a species has been the result of a mass coming together. It only makes sense that we get along with the people who'll help us to build a better world!

2 **Brain soothers.** *Why am I so pissed off today? What is this uncomfortable feeling in my gut about the decision I just made to shift careers? Do I like him or am I just lonely?* Our minds are so overstuffed and overactive that plenty of issues lie confused inside them. It can be difficult to focus on thoughts long enough to figure them out. Brain-soother friends are sort of like free therapy – they ask probing questions and help us get to know ourselves better; they reassure us and offer insights about themselves which help us to judge *ourselves* more compassionately.

3 **Mischief makers.** Passing as fully functioning humans takes a lot of effort! It's important to have friends we don't need to wear our mature adult costume around, people we can get OTT giddy with, do impressions with, share dirty jokes with and take the piss out of life with – these people drink up our shame like it were the elixir of life! It's so therapeutic just to act silly with someone else.

4 **Tough-love givers.** The kind of friends who'll call you out on your shit, who'll warmly point out that you're being a pushover, or that you're acting like an asshole, or that you smell because you haven't washed in days because you're moping around after a break-up.

On that last point, sometimes our *best* friends are the ones who'll really go head to head with us – not in a dramatic *I want to have a fight right now and you'll do* kind of way but in an *OK, bitch, I really care about you, so listen the fuck up or you're going to keep making a holy show of yourself and you're better than this* kind of way. One of my good YouTube friends, Kassie, gave me some of the most valuable friendsperiences I've ever had, while we briefly lived together in LA. We had these long conversations while bobbing around in the pool outside at night, under the stars, where she'd challenge me to stand up for myself. She's such a straight talker and I really needed a bit of tough love – which only works when it's coming from an obvious place of love, I think.

Gang, we need to learn how to tell our cunts from holes in the ground here – each and every one of us needs to wrap ourselves in a colourful flag of varied, caring friends!

The biggest piece of advice on friendship that I can offer up in this little book, this token of my lessons learned, is that we all need to be more *demanding* when it comes to our friendships – we need to take less bullcrap from the friends we have; we need to be fearless in our honesty with those we care about, helping them to be better people; we need to be more selective in the friends that we keep; and to do these things we need to be self-aware and introspective enough to know how to spot when we're being used or treated unfairly – or even if *we're* unfriendables ourselves. To attract amazing friends into our lives, we need to *be* amazing friends to begin with.

WHY my MOTHER is my GREATEST TEACHER

I was a stubborn, reckless, unsophisticated teenager who once upon a time thought I knew everything and relished in painting a picture of my mammy as a wicked Disney villain. When my parents divorced, as so many parents do nowadays, I blamed her, because my dad was suddenly gone and because he was the one to leave the family home. I sided with him, even though I didn't *need* to choose a side, and I shut her out – her and her tender, fierce, protective love, for years and years.

That was *pre-evolved me* being a dumb idiot.

The incredible woman taught me some of the most valuable life lessons there are to learn. It's true in my experience that testing relationships are the most important you'll ever have because they make you stronger as a person, and the bond that endures is powerfully strong ever after.

As a young one I grabbed onto every chance to argue with my ma, and to push her away. I think I found comfort in having somebody to (unfairly) blame for my issues, because if I couldn't blame her, things weren't as black and white, and ain't nobody got time for grey areas!

Fighting with our parents is completely inevitable. When we're kids, our parents are the most important people in our lives and we hunger for their approval. But you literally can't spend *that* much time around anyone and never face any points of contention.

Only as an adult did I really come to understand my parents for the people they are and not the divine masters of life that I viewed them as growing up. They fart and pick their noses, too. They're also trying to figure out what the hell life is all about, *whilst feeling responsible for other humans that they created.*

When my mother was *my* age she had two kids, a husband, a house, a perm (*he-he*, sorry, Mam, I had to - the pictures are just too funny) and *two* jobs (she was both a home maker and business woman). If I were thrust into that position right now I genuinely think I'd drown in stress.

Growing up, I couldn't appreciate the sacrifices she made for me or how great a mother she truly was. Talking to her now over wine, and laughing about old times, I can really *see* her. She's just a woman, like any other woman, but *because* she was the woman who birthed me and raised me and fed me and disciplined me and taught me right from wrong for most of my life, my premature brain decided that she always *had to* hold it together, no matter what, and that she should be somehow perfectly robotic in her every word and action.

I could never accept the *(almost)* in the *fully functioning human* label when it came to my mother. But now I do. And I adore her.

TEN THiNGS our RELATiONSHiP TAUGHT ME

1 **Communication is a two-way street.** Through our arguments (most of which happened when I was a teenager), I learned to listen, not argue, and mam did the same. Together we learned *how* to reach a new level of understanding in a relationship (which is *super* hard when you're stubborn as fuck, like I am, but I swear it's possible - just TALK. Talk it all out and do your best).

2 **Calmness is key.** Shouting and yelling accomplishes nothing and makes things worse. As soon as one person raises their voice, the other is invited into verbal combat. I realised how important it is to cool down and take some quiet time out for myself, in any conflict. I now do many things to calm myself when I get upset or angry – I meditate, I practise yoga (well, when I'm not being lazy), I listen to soothing music online. Now, my mam and I are two of the most chill people you'll ever meet when we're together!

3 **Respect is everything.** I realised that, regardless of how annoyed I'd get at my mam over silly things, I *always* respected her because she respected me. She had consistent house rules, she always said what she meant and did what she said she'd do (apart from that time she promised to take us to Disneyland but then said we could get a dog instead and neither of those things ever happened; I'm holding you to a Disney trip, Mam!) and she always empathised too and never dismissed my feelings even though when I was a teenager – because I was a *ball* of emotion – I felt like she did. I was just choosing to be blind to her actual behaviours.

4 **Negotiation.** And *no*, not failed negotiation like that 'how about a dog instead of Disneyland?' scenario – our fights taught me about real, hardcore emotional negotiation. When making up after arguing we'd both try to be practical and considerate in agreeing to better ways of future interaction.

5 **Understanding another person's perspective.** Learning how to step outside of my own head and into hers, to best understand her stresses and her feelings of being overwhelmed, has probably been one of the most valuable life skills that she's imparted to me – because she demonstrated this herself. She'd come up to me after I'd had a bad day, and she'd try to imagine my difficult situation, offering comfort and reassurance. It was a wonderful feeling, to know she cared that much. So I practised doing that myself with her.

6 **Reinforcing positive behaviour by example.** Mam would focus on doing things and talking about things that would illicit positive responses so I started to associate her with a positive feeling, and that sort of set us off into a happier loop!

7 Not to take things for granted. It's easy to fight with family because their love is unconditional. It's so easy to lose sight of all the things we have to appreciate about those close relationships – especially with parents who are so devoted to us, spending so much of their time and money and energy on us for a *huge* chunk of their lives ... making sacrifices to keep us happy, to keep bread on the table. I now try to remember all the little things she does or has done for me, as well as the big, and those things add up to this infinite ball of love that's difficult to see past.

8 Sometimes, mother does know best. Often I've fought against her only to wind up realising that I should have taken her advice or listened to her wisdom. There's always some kind of logic to her rhetoric. And I mean, our parents don't get all up our arses to be annoying – they only ever want us to be safe and happy. Her advice always came from a place of care. Her not allowing me to go to the junior disco in that impossibly short skirt was her not wanting me to be taken advantage of or assaulted. Ugh, how dare I have screamed at her over that! A little understanding, past-Melanie, eh?

9 Youth is not age. Through our fights I've realised that just because someone looks older (well, my mammy is pretty ageless, let's be honest – seriously, I beg the universe for those wondrous genes) doesn't mean they're not still young in spirit. When I talk to my mammy now, sometimes it feels like I'm talking to myself. She's more wise, of course, but she's affected by the same things in the same way and she's not some two-thousand-year-old wizard named Murloaf – she's still that cool, lively girl from Dublin in the leather jacket, just with more mileage.

10 We define relationships for ourselves. My mammy and I don't have the same relationship that my dad and I have, or that some of my friends have with their mothers, in that we don't talk every single day or even see each other every month. But that doesn't make it any less or any more significant. The time we do spend together is always so special. Love transcends dimensions of time and space and it doesn't have to fit into a particular shape to make sense – it comes in many forms. (At the same time, if you *do* have an unhealthy relationship with a parent and those bonds weren't everlasting for you, that's OK too. Define your relationships for yourself, and find support/healthy relationships elsewhere.)

Romantic
LOVE

I tend to mark intense feelings and emotions with mental sticky tabs and highlighters, so I retain the ability to flick back and think about them even years later. *Especially* the bittersweet times, the times I wanted to hold on to but that slipped my grip. The times I walked that tightrope of romantic relationships between seas of pleasure and pain. I'm a bit of a masochist when it comes to matters of the heart – but at least that means I can haul memories from brain to page with ease!

I'm aware of the issue at hand. Trust me – I'm working on moving forward, big time, and on avoiding medicating myself with new relationships, and on building an all-round better life as a single spud!

See, one of my best friends recently and aptly described me as 'a highly romantic and nostalgic individual who never loves in halves, and who *almost*-loves in wholes'. What I *believe* he meant was that when I'm in love, or even mid fall, I go all *we're going to get married and make babies*, leaving me bare and unshielded in a coliseum full of gladiators looking to chop my damn head off.

Love is experienced differently by everyone – it's different between pairs of humans. It can even be different between two people at different times – some begin as friends and go on to be lovers, some love and break up but rekindle years later. Some people fall in love faster than

others, or suffer the immense sting of unrequited love, or even spend years with the same person and *never* fall 'in love' with them.

In hindsight, I've said 'I love you' without meaning it – I did mean it in the moment, but I *didn't* mean 'I love you in the long-term, soul-changing, life-sharing kind of way'.

Being in love/infatuated for me is that nauseatingly magical phase *right* at the beginning that lasts a few months, bleeds me dry and either goes out with a flicker or sparks a bonfire. I feel on edge, I'm out of sorts, and I can't get the other person off my mind. My brain is infected with them; their face and their voice and their every mannerism. But really *loving* someone romantically, I've experienced as being the most *me* that I can possibly be around another person. All those bits I hide from other people, the secrets I keep from the rest of my family and friends – this person I love gets *all* of that and more.

This past Valentine's Day, I tweeted (excuse the internet grammar): *I've really loved two people but was never 'in love' with one of 'em. I've been 'in love' four times, 'in like' eight times & a million crushes!*

When I have a crush, I wanna put my face onto another face. When I'm 'in like', I'm going to be all up in that Instagram, and flirting; ya girl's gonna be texting a lot and thinking about the person often – maybe even picturing scenarios in which we roll up to parties together, and what we would look like as an item, and how we'd relate to one another two hours in, when everything has gotten boring and all we have left for entertainment is each other ...

But let me tell you about one of my 'loves', and one of my 'in loves', to demonstrate how differently I experience love each time and how the amount of time I spend with a person has no strong correlation to the intensity of feeling. The contours around the relationships developed very differently in each situation, leading me to compartmentalise them under separate *love* headings – perhaps because, for me, it's often a case of *compatibility and long-term potential* versus *chemistry and passion*. (I know couples who feel both of these in their relationships, so I do hold out hope! But, alas, *I've* not yet experienced that fairy tale.)

Each one of these loves was as important to me as the other. They were both big chapters in the book of my life and this is as close to writing that book as I'll ever come so I've got to pay tribute.

And if you offered me twenty Ferraris, a home reminiscent of Disney World, Zooey Deschanel's wardrobe, a wedding to Tom Hardy, along with fifty cats, ten massive white wolf-type dogs *and* someone to look after them all, I still wouldn't go back and change a second of either of these relationships, or swap one for the other, or give up a second's worth of memory.

Eep. Here goes.

The 'LOVE' I was never 'iN LOVE' WiTH, WHO TURNED OUT to BE the GREAT LOVE of my LiFE SO FAR

I met this love when I was twenty years old. Mentally, I was crawling out of the hell of depression, while doing everything I could to distract myself from my teen ex, 'Freddie', who I was *still* madly 'in love' with, even after four years (it just wasn't working out – we rubbed each other up the wrong way). I did want to move on, but I wasn't expecting to meet anyone new anytime soon.

I've found, though, that people always come along when you least expect them to ...

I'm super tipsy in a nightclub, wearing a twenty euro dress from a charity shop, some unblended green eyeshadow and a particularly dodgy haircut. I'm flirting with this guy 'Rory', who I've had an ongoing flirtation with for years but whom I'd *never* date – he's just one of *those* acquaintances: we're not that interested in each other at all, but the flirtation is nice all the same. It feels like dipping my feet into the shallow, swaying tide, firmly planted miles away from the flesh-eating sharks.

Then walks by the last girl I kissed, 'Lucy', looking like a young Leah Remini ... My heart stops, and my skin tingles with the excitement of possibility. Nervously I fix my hair, hoping she'll spin around, see me, run over and sit on my lap. I turn back to 'Rory' and he's all perked up, looking like a kid who's just run down the stairs and is about to glimpse what Santa has left under the tree – he winks at me, knowing that 'Lucy' and I have recently been making out, and I'm instantly bitterly annoyed: another typical pervy fucker with a kink for girl-on-girl action. *I'm never going to be taken seriously as a bisexual. I need another drink. Where are my friends gone?*

I excuse myself and get up to get a drink. I'm still hoping that 'Lucy' will notice me, and in my tipsiness I smell chewing gum – just waft upon waft of spearmint. I glance around, looking to see who I can nab a piece from, and then this smiley face and these toffee-coloured eyes that I recognise responds to my 'Who has gum? Gum!' with 'Here – have a whole packet!'

This guy, 'James', who's related to a work friend of mine, whips out, like, five full packets of gum from his corduroy pocket. 'I see you came prepared!' We explode into laughter, locking eyes, because we've semi-met before so it's comfortable, and because none of our other friends are around as we wait at the bar to be served. I kick off a conversation about how he's cut his hair (the last time I saw him, it was down to his ass!) and, well, the rest is history.

We kissed that night. I don't really remember it at all. It was dark and fumble-y. Disgracefully intoxicated, we sat in a heap of laughter in someone's porch until sunrise.

I stayed in his house and met his family just three days later. We became boyfriend and girlfriend one week after that night in the club. We said 'I love you' (and both meant it) after two weeks. Within six months, we were practically living together in my dad's place. Two years in, we got a ginger kitten and we called her Lyra. And we spent years thereafter blissfully happy.

I won't go into the ins and outs of the (several) overnight break-ups and the five-month split that came even *before* we got our first apartment together (which served as a Band-Aid too weak for the many unfixable problems it was intended to cover, and which fell apart in *spectacular* fashion), but I will say this man saved my life, in more ways than one.

We were good friends, the best of friends, more than anything else – at least in my eyes; friends who loved each other romantically and, yes, were definitely that touchy-feely, overly affectionate couple at every party. He steered me onto the right path, encouraging me to branch out of my friendships, to go back to uni and even to start YouTube.

He was one of the wonders of the world, but I still maintain that I was never 'in love' or infatuated with him.

And I wonder about this a lot. Was this because it was so easy-breezy? Because I was never consumed by thoughts of him when we were apart? Because there was little drama? This love was *so* significant. I still haven't figured out why I never felt 'in love'. I mean, he was a *really good guy* who loved me wholeheartedly and unconditionally and he never had me yo-yoing or questioning where I stood. No matter the reason, ultimately it didn't last for me, in *my* head, because I didn't have those ... fuzzies. I *wanted* to have them – I tried to force them so I could mirror him, early on, so I could go along with this lovely feeling that was cradling my shattered self-image, but the fuzzies never came.

Sometimes I'd think I was feeling them – during really romantic moments, like when he'd surprise me with a handmade book of memories and photos and letters, or when he'd mind me while I vomited into a bag by the bedside and tell me I was beautiful even though I looked like death's daughter – but it was never one of those stomach-flip, all-consuming, can't-live-without-the-other-person kind of loves for me.

We were too fundamentally different, I think. Age gap, different world views – these things can add up over time.

Sometimes I wish it lasted, me and him. In the parallel world where love *was* enough for me, I'm married with kids right now, watching lots of horror movies and playing computer games and cooking pasta sauces and all that other relationship treasure.

But, as always, I followed my heart over my head. I abandoned the promise of emotional security from him in search of something that feels ... *right*.

I haven't found this yet. But in singledom, I've found myself, and I'm very happy about that.

MY LAST 'IN LOVE'

I had a great conversation with some YouTube friends recently at a convention, on a balcony, as the lulling, electronic throb of music from a party we'd all ditched decorated the background of the sombre atmosphere. That conversation was about the crippling agony that is *almost relationships*.

I realised, through opening up to my friends and having them open up to me so *candidly* (it was one of those really *perfect* conversations where everyone is just vibing off what everyone else is saying), that most of us have at least one of these people in our arsenal of exes or 'exes' (people whom you weren't officially or exclusively dating, whom you didn't experience an actual breakup with but, rather, a fake-up) – the one that got away.

The one that felt like a taxi we'd booked and that we stood outside in the rain waiting on that just ... never showed up.

Each of us recounted that deep, relentless ache that's only felt when thinking about the person who wasn't ever truly yours but who you wanted, with all of your being. This person who *seemed* perfect and was placed so high up there on that pedestal of bullshit by you, but who you still walked away from (or were left by) because one of you needed something more concrete – something you were incapable of giving one another, for whatever reason – or because of something else entirely.

And your heart urges you to stay, to just wait it out like a beggar, ravenous for crumbs. But your head takes over, whispering, *It's best to leave now, or muck it up on purpose, before things get messy, before you get far more burned than you will if you stand here like a bloody lemon in front of the flamethrowers ...*

As my long-term, *great* love turned to embers, I found myself sat next to someone I'd never met before, one summer in a hotel lobby. We were worlds away from home, two strangers in the night, and yet within about five minutes I knew I was 'in love' with him.

I didn't just think he was cute, or nice, or friendly, or funny. All those things – yes – but this was like drinking petrol. I just died and floated off to some other place entirely. The chemistry was so electric, it felt like all the atoms inside me were throwing shapes at a rave. My cheeks and ears started to burn, as they do when I'm embarrassed, and my eyes glazed over – my hands felt numb, too, and I had no idea what I was saying to him. We talked about the movie *Hook* for some reason. That, I remember!

My favourite thing about him was his voice and his use of language – I remember that, too. How words sounded coming out of his lovely mouth. And how he'd randomly hold my gaze, eyebrows raised, breathless as I was. *He's not my type ... He's way too young ...* but the logical side of my brain had checked out, and the non-logical side was drunk on the fuzzies.

The fucking fuzzies, fuck off, I thought. *This is too soon. Bad timing. Please, not now, not when I'm finally free and single and ready to mingle ... not him.* But we bonded over film, and past experiences, and dreams of grandeur, and I just fell. I fell off the cliff, into the 'in love', with nobody to catch me, as it was to be short-lived.

Fast forward through some weeks, or months (who even *knows* when you're in the thick of dating a new person), of travelling to see him and hotels and dinner dates and West End shows and cosy evenings in with his friends, eating brownies, of exchanging closeted skeletons, of his words promising 'we'll be together, this feels so right' – words I desperately wanted to believe, words I found myself mentally fighting against because I needed *non*-monogamy after a decade of monogamy. And then everything was just ... sucked up into a vacuum.

Via a Skype call. One of the 'we need to talk' variety.

I mean, I still don't know exactly what happened or where 'it' went. IT was entirely unresolved, for me, because me being *me* (replace 'me' with 'a twat') acted like everything was fine and dandy. 'I'm fine! Honestly – I wasn't expecting this to go anywhere, anyway.' *There's no use in causing drama, Mel. You'll get over this in no time. It's fine – he wasn't all that, anyway. But he said ... no, never mind. You probably projected half of it – it was all in your mind, only you felt all that ... He's moved on already anyway, and she's great, and you were nothing – a mere blip ... You want him more now because you can't have him ...*

I wasn't fine, though. Far from it. I obsessively checked his social media and reread old messages. I cried down the phone to my friends on a bi-weekly basis. I was a mess.

I'd been ripped out of the 'in love', the infatuation phase, and that's possibly one of the most heart-crushing feelings of all – to lose something that never really was.

This kind of almost-relationship relationship is becoming as common as cancer in the digital age, and as a generation, we've had no time to figure out why or how to cope, so we bash ourselves for 'screwing up'. It's like being blindfolded in a room with spiked walls.

I mean, we're taught from a young age that an intense connection like that *needs* a label to count as something real. There's an assumption in society that if love is real, it must by definition be somehow eternal! The desire for a lifelong love story was planted in me growing up, but I'm learning that a short-term love isn't 'a failure'. A relationship can be meaningful and important yet be limited in duration – it might last a few days, or weeks, or months, or a couple of years.

Again with the therapy, *ha-ha*, but a couple of therapy sessions really helped. *So much.* I needed to seek it out again after this guy, because months and months went by and I wasn't feeling any better – or any more back to myself. I was grieving the loss of my great love *and* the loss of this temporary, flash-in-the-pan 'in love', as they both happened so close together. (And not to mention, I'd also gone and jumped into an 'in like', to try to rebound after both of these situations, all the way across the world to LA – holy mother of meatballs, I'm a chandelier-swinging Lost Boy from Neverland ...)

I came away from my therapist with several realisations.

Continuing to feel devoted to an unrequited love for a long time is simply a way for our brains to ensure that we won't end up in the happy relationship that we crave – where we'll have to suffer the *realities* of love. Because lasting love isn't all swanky hotels and daydreaming – it takes mind power. Fixating on an ex and talking it over, and over, and *over* with our friends allows us to be publicly committed to 'love' while, actually, we're sheltered from its demands in private. We're wrapping ourselves in bubble wrap.

In therapy, I brushed upon my fear of real love – that perhaps a fear of self-revelation was the reason I left my one great love, because we'd gotten *uncomfortably* close. Maybe I was reluctant to show him certain parts of myself, after all.

I decided that keeping the spotlight on this 'in love' ex was only going to hold me back for as long as I allowed it to.

So I cut ties.

I'll still be friendly and say hello, if I see him. I still respect him and I care, deep down, but I've unfollowed his social media, snipping a *him*-shaped paper man out of the page that is my life.

The way to un-fixate on a person isn't to tell yourself the lie that you never liked them or that they're a waste of space – it's to analyse what the attraction was actually based on. I've come to see that the qualities I so admired in him – and, well, in all my exes – these *do* exist in other people, new, fresh, shiny people who don't come with the same baggage and problems and clashing issues and points of contention.

We can love someone else.

I *will* love someone else (and hopefully fall 'in love' at the beginning, too).

It's been fantastically liberating to accept that what I want and need in a partner does exist out there – I know this through meeting so many gorgeously exquisite human beings over the past couple of years. (I know I'm very lucky to be surrounded by so many amazing YouTubers and creative types, but I feel like anyone can open themselves up to new people by simply taking up a new hobby!)

This experience with the 'in love' taught me that true love isn't about pining for a person with whom things don't work out.

In saying that, something I'm ever so grateful for is the past year or so, in relation to my love life. In this time I've had my first real chance to experience casual dating and I've even brushed up against polyamory, after *ten years solid* in two separate long-term, monogamous relationships.

I don't think polyamory is really for me (although I feel the capacity to fancy and care deeply for several people at the same time), and I say that having gone on the group dates and holidays, having tried and failed to keep multiple close relationships on the go at one time (if you think it's hard having a boyfriend, try having a boyfriend, and a girlfriend, and her girlfriend, and another boyfriend, and another boyfriend, and a sort of almost girlfriend), but there's this one couple I've had a hell of a lot of fun with ... *(Insert devil ears emoji here.)*

WORTH IT.

I'm grateful for everyone I've met and for every awkward date, every amazing date, every horrific and brief relationship (OK, there was only one of those), simply because I've learned a lot more about *who I am, what I like, what I want* (to be the big spoon, daily back rubs, lots of laughter, separate friend groups, dominance and submission, 'thinking of you' texts, space, even more space, public displays of affection, pet names) *and what I don't want* (arrogance, to spend every waking minute together, to have my privacy invaded and my phone looked through, vanilla sex, beards, lies, cheating, uncertainty, jealousy, controlling behaviour).

And, goodness, *flirting*. Flirting is so much fun. I'd always perceived it to be some terrible thing – a manipulative promise of sexual interest – because the confusion of being flirted with *without* any follow-up always left me feeling vulnerable and thinking things like, *So this other person was interested in me but then something changed ... I did something to make them think I'm hideous! I'm unlikable.*

Then I learned what it means to be a *good* flirt, and that flirtation knows no bounds – age gaps, rings on fingers, socioeconomic differences, general incompatibility – anyone can flirt, and when done right it can have an amazingly positive impact on a person's day – week – month, even!

Ya see, good flirting exploits a truth about sex that so many of us are blind to, the truth that what's often most enjoyable about sexual interactions *isn't* the physical process of intercourse (or foreplay, even!) – it's actually the basic idea of acceptance that underpins all that other stuff: the notion that another human being could like us enough to accept us in our most raw, animal state. *That's* the bit right there that really gets us going and yanks us up to cloud nine! That's what turns our self-esteem up to eleven and makes us feel confident and energetic and content.

Flirting *doesn't* have to be a prelude to actual sex – it can just be an end in itself, a process occurring between strangers or friends, something we do while ordering coffee even, to simply inspire another person to believe in their own desirability (and maybe have them return the favour by flirting back).

Helping other people to feel erotically appealing is a wonderful skill and when you master it, with the right person, well, you can bag yourself a partner. Someone with whom you can explore the depths of the great sea of love and acceptance.

I'm biting my lip in anticipation for the fuzzies to come at me again, because I know how good it feels ...

Through dating, I've explored my sexuality and I've found that I communicate better with women than with men, so I'm totally open to settling down with a wife and making a family, though I'm finding that it's harder to meet women here in Ireland. But I'm becoming more OK with myself and that's all that matters!

It's funny – I always thought being single equalled a terrifying existence of constant seeking-out-of-another-to-fill-a-gaping-void-within. Turns out, nope! Connecting with new people is so nice and so enriching, regardless of the presence or lack of fuzzies.

And something I'm finally open to admitting publicly, after some deep chats with some great friends, is that I struggle with, well, *loneliness*, being single. I wouldn't say I'm *lonely* full stop – I've got a fulfilling, full life and lots of friends, I love my job, all that jazz, but I definitely miss the intimacy that comes with a relationship. The kind that my platonic friends can't really provide, magnificent as they are.

Rather than continuing to sit around *waiting* for the right person to show up, I've decided (having watched a recent YouTube video by my dear friend Hannah about setting up an online dating profile) that I'm going to be a *bit* more proactive about finding the right person for me, for this stage of my life! Aside from the fact that some of the ghastly dating websites out there don't even allow you to enter 'looking for both men AND women', they're bizarrely helpful for us childer of the digital age. *Nothing like Tinder, of course, 'cause, yuck, I can't just swipe on pictures – how do people know if they'll be attracted to someone purely based on a picture and one or two lines of a bio?* I mean the kind of sites that actually make you fill in a crap ton of information about yourself.

There are so many probing questions when you sign up, I have a whale of a time filling them out! I face some dark truths about myself too, every single time. You know you've got a way to go when you're shocked by your own answer to *How tidy or untidy is your room, on a scale of 1 to 10?* (I wouldn't be surprised if a dead body resurfaced in and among my stacks of unwashed Ted Baker dresses worn at YouTube events!)

So that's where I'm at now, people. Putting myself out there, going to events, meeting and mingling, accepting the odd date request from a stranger (which is still the most impossibly difficult thing in the world for me), and I just know in my heart that I'm in for a tasty, tasty treat. Because that's how I've programmed my brain to think, at all times – especially when I'm feeling so lonely that, at night, I shape my spare pillows like a person under the duvet beside me ...

Silver linings, baby.

My next great love will be an awfully big adventure.

Things I've LEARNED/ AM LEARNING from DATING AND RELATIONSHIPS

1 Bagging an exceptionally happy relationship is all about that pace, 'bout that pace (only fools rush in, and I *need* to stop being a fool and moving too quickly – slow and steady, gang, no rush. If they're right for you, they're not going to go anywhere soon anyway, right?)

2 Real love means making a deliberate effort to see beyond the surface of another person in search of the real them, inside – it's about fostering generosity toward our partners' less appealing sides. Movies would have you thinking it's all about finding 'the one', this mythical, perfect creature who shits Maltesers, but, alas, movies are fantasy.

3 Betrayal *really hurts*. It pierces our ego, it smushes (temporarily) our ability to trust, and it often means the end of something beautiful (something we're not quite ready to part ways with).

4 There's no use being afraid of opening your heart just because it has been bruised, no matter how bad a beating it has taken. That's the same as thinking, 'I had a bad meal – I'll never eat again! Farewell food!' because every person and every situation is so intricately different.

5 Time heals all wounds of the heart.

6 We need to take risks sometimes. Memory-making in love and lust *always* comes with some risk. It's literally like being on a diving board sometimes – if you dive in without arm bands, you'll figure out how to swim once you hit the water or you'll drown (but only metaphorically, of course)! Drowning is where growth happens anyway, so don't sweat it: go make some mistakes, they're important.

7 It's surprisingly easy to repeat the same mistakes over and over and to continue falling for emotionally unavailable, manipulative narcissists (I'm working on it, I swear) – if you constantly find yourself in destructive and toxic relationships, *talk to a therapist to at least figure out why*.

8 Lust and infatuation can be hella confusing but are *not* to be confused with real love. If everything seems to revolve around sex, and there's zero talk of the future, take some deep breaths and figure out if it's real emotion and attachment driving you, or if it's your pointy nipples and your throbbing clitoris (or pulsating penis – I don't know who's reading this, do I?)

9 You've got to know your worth and value and be able to communicate your standards, whatever they may be. Don't want to sleep together until you're super close? Then *don't*. You don't fancy tolerating flakiness and excuses on the regular, after your last head-melting relationship? Then put your foot down and demand more. We teach people

how to treat us through the treatment we accept.

10 Non-platonic intimacy is one of the greatest gifts of life. Really. Brushing your teeth with someone you love, giggling, post-sex, before spooning all night ... just, *ah*, there are no words. That's the stuff of dreams right there.

11 Good relationships are built on grand marble pillars of rationality, compromise, trust, respect and the ability to laugh when the other person farts.

A FEW WORDS on 'GHOSTING' in MODERN DATING

Let's be real. It's difficult to *fully function* in modern dating because the landscape of dating has changed, but *people* haven't changed. So we're sort of fighting against the tide *as one*, as a species longing for companionship and looking to make/bring up babies with one another.

It's hard to be decent, upfront and honest in a world full of perceived choice (not the same thing as *real* choice, mind you! We just *think* there's an abundance of options simply because we have access to *seeing* how many more people exist, via technology).

Times are tough in love and lust because we basically have 24/7 access to one another – Facebook *tells* us that someone has 'seen' and ignored our message. We can check up on what our love interests are up to on social media. And technology provides platforms for *the bad eggs* that are all too prevalent in modern dating culture – the breadcrumbers among us (y'know, those people who drop 'breadcrumbs' to string you along, flirtatious and non-committal texts here and there to lure you in *without* expending much effort at all – keeping you hooked) and, perhaps worse still, *the ghosters*: the people who suddenly cut off all contact with a person they're dating or talking to romantically, without providing said person with a heads-up or closure.

Ghosting is, essentially, dumping someone without actually dumping them.

I've realised that, sometimes, *I myself can be one of these bad eggs.* I hate admitting that, but it's true. I've ghosted people without realising – people I clearly wasn't all that invested in (people who called me out on this behaviour of vanishing in phantom-like fashion after an OKish date). I've also been ghosted by people I really liked, so I know how soul-crushingly *awful* it can feel.

I was confronted just last week by a perfectly lovely guy who I'd ghosted and who was hurting and confused. This served as a massive wake-up call because *I* was literally feeling hurt and confused because *someone else* was in the middle of ghosting *me*. The fact that I myself hate the feeling of being ignored, *but still* sometimes see ignoring others as the only viable course of action in dating situations that I want to step out of, is kinda blowing my mind just a little bit. It's made me get all reflective and analytical of myself and of modern dating at large.

I believe there's a massive lack of empathy in our modern world, bred through looking at people via a screen – it seems many of us feel that we're almost entitled to treat others poorly. And ghosting someone is, objectively, a really shitty way to treat another human being, regardless of how easy it is to do, regardless of 'I'm busy' or 'I don't like confrontation'.

Apparently 80 per cent of us kids-of-the-age-of-technology commonly ghost or experience ghosting early on in new relationships – mostly long before any kind of 'talk' has happened to establish what's going on between you and this other person.

Being ghosted stings and gets you down, yet often we do it to other people without stopping to give a *toss* about how they might feel when they realise we haven't communicated our true intentions and have just stopped replying to them, as though they never existed as part of our lives.

In my defence, I'm often duped by my own assumptions – 'They know this is casual ... right? They have to know.' I always just *think* that the other person is on the same page as me. But *na-ah*. Assuming anything is a bad dating habit.

The reason ghosting hurts so bad, firstly, I think ('cause, y'know, I studied a bit of psychology at uni) is tied to attachment theory in humans. The basis of attachment is trust and security, and often when we meet someone we like a *lot* (for reasons we don't understand – there's just a click on our end, at least) we gotta remember *we don't really know these people that well yet* and our attraction isn't based on all that much. Doing this will stop us investing too much *before* they've invested in us. Because when we do start going down that rabbit hole of liking a new person, a sudden ending to the 'thing' we have with them leaves us feeling vulnerable and filled with self-doubt.

That's just human nature.

You're not weird or weak or needy and you don't need to feel bad for having emotions.

When you've been ghosted, zone out of your own head a bit and realise that *maybe* the relationship (or fling, or first date) *wasn't* fantastically magical rainbows and unicorns, that maybe you're really just bothered by the *lack of clarity* in the situation.

There are some very solid reasons to explain why we ghost one another. I know it sounds terrible, because it *is* terrible, because humans suck sometimes and that's that – but it's much easier to vanish on someone and avoid confrontation. Confrontation in this instance is defined, not by conflict, but by being *upfront* and letting the person know, 'I'm just not there.'

I don't know about you, but I'm the worst person in the world at vocalising something that might hurt another person's feelings – I hate upsetting people – so sometimes if I go on a date with someone who's very lovely, but I'm not getting the desired level of fuzzies about him or her, I'll opt for a *slow fade out*. I really dislike that about myself, because when I'm on the receiving end of that behaviour I feel on edge and my mind is screaming, *Why couldn't they have said, 'Not for me, we won't be hanging out again – just, by the way'?*

I think too that, because the pool of humans on dating apps *seems* huge, the thought *maybe there's something better out there* rings in our heads a lot. And that's a really gross and sad reality of modern society. Looking at studies and current divorce rates, a lot of people seem less likely to settle and to work through things than they would've been if they'd been born a hundred years ago, *even when they do have something special with another person*, which I feel is causing us to lose out on the intimacy we crave and which perhaps contributes to widespread modern feelings of anxiety, depression, sadness and loneliness.

When I really do like someone, nothing will stand in the way of it. There's never a need for an excuse when you've met someone you *really* want to get to know more – they immediately become a priority. So, when you think about it, if someone else isn't feeling you in the same way that you're feeling them, it's *definitely a good thing* that it ends sooner rather than later – through ghosting or otherwise – because your time is being freed up to find something real.

People are *allowed* to be just-not-that-into-me, in the same way I'm just-not-that-into 99 per cent of my romantic options. We're all picky shitebags and we can't be annoyed at people for not liking us when there are *plenty* of people we don't like back.

'... and then I never heard from him/her again' is one of the most common endings to great date stories for millennials, and you know what? I think we should all stop bloody ghosting each other and have mature, adult conversations. I really, really want to stop and I'd encourage you to avoid it, too. It's emblematic of how we communicate in the digital age, but we have the power to change that. And when this crap *does* happen to us, we should see it as a chance to grow and improve for the next person or the next situation we find ourselves in.

A GRATEFUL
Farewell

Well, writing this 300-pages-plus pile of words has been a ride and a half!

I'm finishing my first book on a train from Skerries to Dublin city. I'd want future me to remember that. I've just scoffed a raspberry-flavoured marshmallow bar coated in dark chocolate, and I'm smiling, and the sun is out, and it's a perfect morning to be closing the lid on this project – a project that's had me distracted from all of my problems for the past year and a half. What on *earth* do I do NOW? Finally write my epic fantasy trilogy, maybe? Sleep for more than five hours in a night? Either one of those two things, probably.

Professionally, I'm in a very positive place (but I have an accountant now and I'm trying to remember to keep my receipts 'cause self-employment is just a little bit bollocks). Life is a watercolour wash of creating videos and attending YouTube conventions and embarking on exciting new ambassador roles (I just found out *Game of Thrones* want me to be an official ambassador for the show – *how is this real life*?!). My younger sister has joined me on YouTube with her own YouTube channel, and we're making videos together regularly – my viewers seem to be really enjoying our dynamic together on camera, which I love. Our last collab hit a quarter of a million views after a week! So that's fun. And exciting. I love filming with my friends, but having my family involved in what I do means so much to me.

Domestically, I'm still living with my dad and my cats by the sea, and I'm super happy about that. I spend about a week a month in London – on jobs and visiting friends – and it's perfect. I'm hoping to get a joint mortgage with my dad over the next couple of years, because he'd struggle to get one himself at his age with Ireland's current housing crisis, and at least that way we'd both be on the property ladder. Plus I enjoy living with him, and my separation anxiety will be delighted about having him around plenty! So will my future children, I'm sure. He's a grand old bastard.

Romantically, well … shit. I'm falling in love as this book goes to print, with someone I've been acquainted with for over a decade. Only time will tell, of course. But I feel like all the waiting and dating has been worth it. I've got a lot to offer the right person and I *just might* have them within reach now. Stay tuned.

In terms of what's waiting for me in the future, I don't like to think too far ahead. I just like to attract more of the things that I love into my life – health, fun, friends, family, trips, love, art. That's what I see in my mind. And whatever I put my mind to work-wise, I know I'll succeed because I'm fierce and *I don't give up.*

If you've taken anything away from this book, I hope it's simply that you should think for yourself, and love yourself, and be positive and kind.

I want to gratefully acknowledge the following people, who were absolute pillars of support during my writing process:

♥ **Hannah Witton**, my dear friend and champion. I owe you so much, because seeing you get your head down and publish your book *Doing It* inspired me to push through the mental block I experienced after deleting my very first draft when the big move to LA went disastrously wrong. Thank you, thank you, thank you for being so motivational, and such a hard worker, and such a bright and shining talent!

▼ **Riyadh Khalaf**, my closest Irish pal, for encouraging me to chase my dreams and for setting an amazing example by chasing and catching your own.

▼ **Calum McSwiggan** for making me cry laughing and for killing my stress *every day* during the writing and editing process of this book. I'm so happy to have you in my life, and I love being able to talk to you about writing and storytelling. I love you dearly and you got me through some bad brain days.

▼ **Emma Cross**, my sister from another mister, you're a rock in my life and you've always made me feel like I'm capable of anything I put my mind to. Can you believe this!? It's a BOOK! Remember during uni when we'd lose our minds over the idea of writing a thesis!? Haha.

▼ **Charlie 'Belle' Shaw**, thank you for contributing your beautiful artwork. This book is so much more beautiful and inviting thanks to you! You were a dream to work with.

▼ **David Anderson**, my manager, my mate, thank you for putting up with me and my stressed-out head for months on end as I tried to balance writing a book with the million other incredible jobs you bring to me!

▼ **Ciara Doorley** and the rest of the Hachette Ireland team. Thank you for the careful and attentive work on this book. Ye were a magnificent bunch to work with! Warm hugs forever for this opportunity.

▼ My supportive sister, **Jessica** – I love you.

▼ My brother **Andrew**, one of my best friends, thank you for always believing in me and for listening to me read my writing out to you ever since we were little kids. You are kind even when my work is crap, and sometimes all any artist needs to keep on going is kindness.

♥ My aunties **Trisha, Anne and Tina**, thank you all for always pushing me to write a book and get published. Thank you for watering me like a plant with your words of wisdom over the years!

♥ **The internet**, for challenging me and enabling me to reach millions of people around the world, without whom none of these words would exist. So much of this book was inspired by questions I receive online from viewers. And, goodness, viewers, thank you for waiting so long and for buying this and for being there for me in so many ways across virtual platforms *every single day*.

♥ **My three parents – dad, mam and stepdad.** If I'm being honest, I reckon about 80 per cent of my drive to get this book done came from the desire to make you three proud. Your love is my reason. Thank you for giving me life and for supporting me through it.

♥ **Nana**, who is here no more, I'll never forget you, and all those times we hobbled around to the library together, and how magical and wise and strong you were. I'm sad and even a little bit angry that you're not here to read this. Watching you run through four books a week impregnated me with the dream to one day create a book that would be by your bedside. But you're on every page of this book, because you're part of me, forever and always.

Farewell, dear reader – get out there and live. And *maybe* dip back into this book any time you need a Melly boost!

Love, Melanie X

HELPFUL INFORMATION

—

I've listed some organisations in Ireland, the UK and the US who provide support and/or information on topics I've talked about in my book. There are lots of fantastic organisations out there but unfortunately I can't list them all – hopefully the below will be of help, and offer you some valuable information no matter where you are.

MENTAL HEALTH

Aware (Ireland)
Offers information and support to those affected by depression, bipolar and related disorders.
Phone: 1800 80 48 48
Email: supportmail@aware.ie
www.aware.ie

Jigsaw (Ireland)
Provides vital support to young people with their mental health by working closely with communities across Ireland.
Email: info@jigsaw.ie
www.jigsaw.ie

Mental Health.gov (USA)
Provides one-stop access to U.S. government mental health and mental health problems information.
www.mentalhealth.gov

Mind (UK)
Provides advice and support to empower anyone experiencing a mental health problem.
Phone: 0300 123 3393/ Text: 86463
Email: info@mind.org.uk
www.mind.org.uk

Samaritans (Ireland, UK & USA)
Offers a safe place for people to talk any time they like, in their own way – about whatever's getting to them.
Phone: 116 123 (UK & Ireland); 1-800-273-TALK or local area branch (USA)
Email: jo@samaritans.org (UK & Ireland)
www.samaritans.org (UK & Ireland)/www.samaritansusa.org (USA)

SpunOut.ie (Ireland)
Ireland's youth information website – provides access to relevant, reliable and non-judgemental information on a range of different topics, such as education and health.
Phone: 01-675-3554 / Text: 087-773-0000
Email: info@spunout.ie
www.spunout.ie

EATING DISORDERS

Bodwhys – The Eating Disorders Association of Ireland

The national voluntary organisation supporting people affected by eating disorders.

Phone: 01-283 4963

Email: alex@bodywhys.ie

www.bodywhys.ie

BEAT (UK)

Offers information and support to anyone affected by eating disorders.

Phone: 0808 801 0677, or 0808 801 0711 (if under 18)

Email: help@b-eat.co.uk, or fyp@b-eat.co.uk (if under 18)

www.b-eat.co.uk

NEDA (USA)

Supports individuals and families affected by eating disorders, and serves as a catalyst for prevention, cures and access to quality care.

Phone: 1-800-931-2237

www.nationaleatingdisorders.org

LGBTQ

BeLonG To (Ireland)

The national organisation for Lesbian, Gay, Bisexual and Transgender young people, aged between 12 and 23.

Phone: 01 670 6223

www.belongto.org

Gay Switchboard (Ireland)
Offers confidential support and information to LGBT+ people, their parents, family, friends or anyone with concerns relating to sexuality, gender identity, sexual and mental health.
Phone: 01-872 1055
Email: ask@ghn.ie
www.gayswitchboard.ie

Switchboard (UK)
Provides a one-stop listening service for LGBT+ people on the phone, by email and through Instant Messaging.
Phone: 0300 330 0630
Email: chris@switchboard.lbgt
www.switchboard.lgbt

The Trevor Project (USA)
The leading national organisation providing crisis intervention and suicide prevention services to lesbian, gay, bisexual, transgender and questioning young people ages 13-24. Also provides answers to frequently asked questions and resource information.
Phone: 866-488-7386/ Text Trevor to 1-202-304-1200
www.thetrevorproject.org

PREGNANCY & SEXUAL HEALTH

Brook (UK)
Promotes the health, particularly sexual health, of young people and those most vulnerable to sexual ill health, through providing information, education and outreach, counselling, confidential clinical and medical services, professional advice and training
www.brook.org.uk

British Pregnancy Advisory Service (UK)
Provides advice and support on contraception, abortion and sexual health.
Phone: 03457 30 40 30
Email: info@bpas.org
www.bpas.org

FPA (UK)
Offers information and support on sexual health, sex and relationships.
www.fpa.org.uk

Planned Parenthood (USA)
Provides reproductive health care, sexual education and information
www.plannedparenthood.org

Positive Options (Ireland)
A website designed to help people find counselling services that will support them in dealing with a crisis pregnancy.
Freetext LIST to 50444
www.positiveoptions.ie

SEXUAL ASSAULT

RAINN (USA)
Operates the National Sexual Assault Hotline in the US, and carries out programs to prevent sexual violence, help survivors and ensure that perpetrators are brought to justice.
Phone: 800-656-HOPE
www.rainn.org

Rape Crisis Network (Ireland)

A specialist information and resource centre on rape and all forms of sexual violence. The representative, umbrella body for Irish Rape Crisis Centres who provide free advice, counselling and support for survivors of sexual abuse.

Phone: 1890 77 88 88 (Helpline)

www.rcni.ie/www.rapecrisishelp.ie

Rape Crisis (UK)

Promotes the needs and rights of women and girls who have experienced sexual violence, to improve services to them and to work towards the elimination of sexual violence. The national umbrella body for the network of member Rape Crisis Centres across England and Wales.

Phone: 0808-802-9999 (Helpline)

www.rapecrisis.org.uk